Techniques of
Family Therapy

Techniques of Family Therapy

David S. Freeman

New York   •   Jason Aronson   •   London

ISBN: 0-87668-431-2

Library of Congress Catalog Number: 80-69669

Manufactured in United States of America

With love
to my wife Virginia

CONTENTS

PREFACE

Techniques of Family Therapy is intended to be a guide for the practitioner, whether student, beginner, or experienced therapist. The text is organized to facilitate the reader's moving from deductive thinking to inductive practice. The model that is presented is one I have been practicing and experimenting with for over twelve years. In today's field of family therapy there are a number of models and a wide variety of therapeutic strategies being used to treat families. Most individuals familiar with the field of family therapy have been exposed to the structural approach, the problem-solving approach, the behavioral approach and the Bowen systems approach. There already exist a number of texts that deal specifically with these approaches, as well as a number of survey books that compare and contrast them.

In this text I avoided contrasting the various approaches and comparing my model of family practice with other practitioners' models. Rather, *Techniques of Family Therapy* presents a point of view on how to work with families. I have used a systems approach to organize my thinking about family behavior and to develop consistent therapeutic strategies which flow naturally from this perspective. The text attempts to identify and explain the theoretical underpinnings of a systems perspective.

Organizationally, the book moves from a general theoretical discussion of the field of family therapy to a specific discussion of the importance of using systems theory to organize ideas about practice with families. Chapter 1, "What is Family Therapy?" provides an introduction to the text. This chapter contains a discussion of the major misconceptions and misunderstandings currently surrounding practice with families. The chapter also discusses the importance of goal formation and the use of a theoretical framework to organize ideas about practice.

Chapters 2 through 4 are essentially theoretical. These three chapters move from a high level of theorizing about family behavior (chapter 2), to analyzing the family as an emotional system (chapter 3), to conceptualizing the major systems that affect family practice, i.e., the practitioner's own personal family and the professional family (chapter 4).

Chapters 5 through 7 are clinical chapters organized around the phases of family therapy. Chapter 5 discusses how to begin treatment with a family and includes a transcript of a typical initial session. Chapter 6 deals with the middle phase of family work and discusses a number of techniques which may be used to help a family move from a reactive stance to a proactive one. Chapter 7 deals with the terminating phase of family work.

Chapter 8, the final chapter, contains a discussion of several therapeutic dilemmas and issues which influence family practice. Finally, there is an appendix to the text consisting of two additional transcripts of beginning and middle interviews; these provide in-depth illustrations of these phases of therapy.

I hope the reader will find this text useful in developing a family therapy orientation. The text represents the result of my struggles to be clear about what I do when I practice. This book has been a difficult one to write but is a satisfying one to have completed. If it were not for the families who have struggled with me there would be no text. The families have been my teachers. I have come to respect the great diversity of family life through my intimate contacts with the families I have worked with. I hope the reader will agree that working with people produces only learning and change, never finality and knowing.

Techniques of
Family Therapy

1

WHAT IS FAMILY THERAPY?

COMMON MISCONCEPTIONS
ABOUT FAMILY THERAPY

Over the past twenty-five years, family therapy has grown enormously in importance. However, as a workable model of practice, it is still not well known. Many mental health practitioners view family therapy as yet another model of practice, one comparable to casework and group work.

A lively controversy continues over whether family therapy constitutes a new way of viewing behavior that in turn necessitates a significantly different approach to treatment. Many non–family practitioners believe that family therapy is a model of practice that can be used only with certain people. By contrast, family therapists view family systems theory as providing the theoretical underpinnings for understanding family behavior and, consequently, all family members. From this understanding flows a different set of strategies for practice. Basically, how we define problems also defines how we solve them. The definition is as important as the strategy for resolution. Defining problems in systems terms automatically reframes one's thinking regarding their resolution.

If one believes that behavioral problems rest within and are supported by social systems, then one must be able to understand how social systems contribute to behavioral problems. However, if one believes the individual alone is responsible for his behavioral difficulties, then one would view social systems more as a backdrop and would expect the basic change to occur solely within the individual. A family systems approach suggests that

3

problems rest within social systems such as the family; therefore individuals within the family become part of that problem, and if change is to occur it must do so within the social systems in which the individual operates.

What follows are some major misconceptions frequently encountered among mental health practitioners unfamiliar with family systems theory, or having only a rudimentary understanding of it.

Misconception one: the family therapist is the expert in resolving family problems

This misconception is popular because the traditional role of the therapist has been that of the expert who gathers information, diagnoses the problem, and provides the solutions. In this traditional model the therapist is viewed as the knowledgeable one who will figure things out based on the information the client or patient provides him. Many family members enter family sessions with this expectation, especially if they have had prior therapy.

I have discovered in my teaching and consulting with mental health professionals that many therapists and students also place these high expectations on themselves. It would appear that much of the anxiety that professionals have about their work lies in their accepting responsibility for solving problems that probably are insoluble as they are presented.

In a family systems approach, the experts are the family members. The goal of the therapist is to help the family develop its own way of discovering how it wants to move from point A to point B. One of the therapist's jobs is to encourage the family to assume the expert role. The expectation of the family early in therapy that the therapist will have the answers presents one of the first challenges to the therapist. Consequently, there may be an initial struggle between the therapist and the family to decide who is going to do what. If the therapist takes responsibility for the solution of problems, then he must take responsibility also for the outcome. If the therapeutic endeavor works, it is because he is a bright therapist; if it fails, it is because he is inadequate. In either case, the family does not assume responsibility for resolving their problems.

One of the more powerful experiences a family has in therapy is the discovery that they have their own very effective ways and ideas about resolving their dilemmas. The therapist's initial task, then, is to encourage the family to find their own solutions. Typically, when families enter therapy it is because they have been ineffective in trying to resolve their problems. Often their definition of who has the problems is exacerbating the situation and preventing them from finding better solutions. Therefore, one of the first tasks in family therapy is to redefine the problems. To accomplish this task, the therapist must help the family understand how their problems are affecting the entire family. This process helps the family members gain a broader, more sophisticated definition of themselves as a system. As this occurs, a new set of ideas will emerge within the family about how they want to resolve their dilemmas. As the therapist focuses on the family's ideas the members begin to see themselves as experts in dealing with their problems.

Misconception two: significant change occurs in the therapy hour

The usual frequency of family therapy sessions is once a week. The idea that significant change occurs during this hour is unrealistic, as lasting change will occur only if the family is motivated to experiment with new ways of relating. The therapeutic hour can provide this impetus. The therapist, through his own inquisitiveness about how certain patterns develop within the family, helps them experience something new during the session. However, the emphasis must be on encouraging the family to continue the process outside therapy. In each session, the therapist might well ask the family what new matters they have been working on. Gradually, the family recognizes that the major work is accomplished through their own efforts outside the session.

Since a family systems therapist takes the position that change occurs in the environing social systems, that is, within families, schools and communities, he acts as a consultant during the therapeutic hour. His role is to help the family discover their internal resources and ways in which they can position themselves differently, within both the family and the community.

By the time a family enlists the aid of a therapist, their problems are usually long-standing and firmly entrenched. Often family members will fantasize that the therapist will agree with them that it is a particular family member who has the problem. Frequently, family therapy begins with the family telling the therapist that a certain member has to change. One of the family therapist's initial tasks is to help the family understand that change has to occur within the family, not simply within a particular member. For the family to experience and act upon this new perception, they have to begin to behave differently, not only within the session but, more importantly, outside it.

In order for significant change to occur, the therapist must concentrate on helping the family recognize the sorts of things they can begin to do differently with each other between sessions. As their views and assumptions about each other change, so will their behavior toward one another. Therefore, each session will emphasize whatever new methods for interacting the family has been experimenting with, and deemphasize the family's need to "understand" any one family member whom they have seen as the cause of the problem.

Misconception three: a major goal of family therapy is helping family members develop insight into their problems

This misconception is related to the preceding one. The therapist who takes the position that understanding the problem will bring about a solution will emphasize the gaining of insight. In contrast, the systems therapist focuses on how family members relate to each other and what they expect in the relationship. He believes that the solution comes about as basic behavioral patterns change, whether or not this is accompanied by insight. Not until people begin to behave differently will they begin to experience anything new about each other. There are in fact times when understanding problems contributes to a lack of motivation to experiment with doing something differently.

Misconception four: family therapy begins with the first session

It is commonly thought that therapy begins at the time of the first interview. However, family systems therapy actually starts with the referral or initial request for service. One of the most important preparatory maneuvers of the family therapist is to ensure that the first session will bring people together in a way that will help the family perceive the situation in a new light. If the therapist begins by focusing on the identified problems or by accepting the family's ideas about who should be present, this may preclude his ever being able to offer the family a new perspective.

One of the most important decisions the family therapist makes is who to invite to the first session. This selection in itself helps the family begin to experience its difficulties differently. By inviting several family members to the first session, the therapist sets up a situation in which he can help them learn how to turn to each other for help and understanding in dealing with their problem, instead of turning to the therapist as the only expert.

Misconception five: the major role of the family therapist is to help family members express all their concerns

Central to this misconception is the idea that each family member should talk about everything that bothers him or her. In fact, one of the concerns that many family members have when they come into family therapy is that the therapist will in some way force them to talk about subjects which make them uncomfortable. It is critical for family members in family therapy to be able to hear things about and from each other that they have not been able to hear before. This is not accomplished by the therapist's encouraging one's most private thoughts out into the open; rather it is achieved by the therapist's maintaining an atmosphere that allows family members to hear each other differently. Often there are so many distractions in the family home that it is difficult for family members to even listen to each other. The therapist, by controlling the atmosphere of the session, can create a neutral zone in which family members can begin to hear new things about each other. What they hear are not necessarily secrets, but rather ideas, goals, hopes, and expectations that have not been expressed before. Or, if they have been expressed, they have been misunderstood because of the charged atmosphere of the home.

Another aspect of this misconception is that it is most important to be able to communicate about the here and now. For many family members, however, the past is a much safer subject than the present. A family therapist should be skilled in being able to move back and forth through all three time dimensions: past, present, and future. I have found that many family members can express their feelings more freely about the present by discussing what they wish they had done differently in the past. The skilled practitioner is able to make good use of the past and recognizes that people's hopes and ambitions for the future affect the way they deal with each other in the present.

Misconception six: all members of the family have to change equally if family improvement is to occur

The ideal in family therapy is a change in each member and a group effort to solve the family problem, thereby effecting a significant improvement in the entire system. Of course, such an occurrence is rare. However, it is not necessary for all members of a system to change at once. If one or more family members begin to respond differently, while maintaining communication and contact with the rest of the family, a very powerful dynamic for change throughout the family is catalyzed. Hence one major task of family therapy is to identify the more powerful members within the family and to assist those members to respond differently. The others will respond in kind as change occurs at the top of the power structure.

These major misconceptions were discussed to illustrate that there are several areas of confusion about family systems work. For non–family therapists, the family is often seen as a backdrop to the problem. When the family is invited to a session by the therapist, it is mainly for the purpose of gathering information about the problem. The family therapist takes the opposite approach; he engages the entire family in a systems change. The family is not only the provider of information but the very mechanism through which change can occur.

GOAL-SETTING PROCESS IN FAMILY THERAPY

In any type of therapeutic endeavor it is important to have specific goals or aims. Therapists are placing increasing emphasis on clearly defined therapeutic goals, an emphasis reflected in numerous recently published books (e.g., Reid and Epstein 1972, Barten 1971). A number of these discuss methods for setting contracts with clients and, more specifically, methods for stating contract outcomes.

When using psychoanalytic or psychiatric models in working with individuals, a statement of goals is not usually difficult to produce. In this type of case, it is usually the client who specifies the areas in which goal setting is desirable. However, goal setting is more difficult when the therapeutic work involves a social system such as the family. It is more difficult because family or community goals must be considered along with individual goals.

In work with families there are at least four levels of goal setting. Each individual within the family has certain personal goals and hopes, and the family unit definitely has certain group expectations regarding what it wants to experience. The third goal-setting level is the community at large. Often dealings at school or work, for example, can be improved through the accomplishment of definite goals set at the family level. Therapist goals and expectations comprise the fourth level. Keeping these different levels in mind, one can see how complicated goal setting can be.

To facilitate goal setting at both micro and macro levels in family work, it is important for the therapist to communicate his interest in helping the family as a whole, as well as each individual member, to achieve their goals. One of the more important principles to keep in mind is that the family is the major system that simultaneously works for individual autonomy or development, as well as for group or family solidarity. The two major developmental goals the family group has are: (1) helping its individuals to be competent and somewhat independent, while at the same time (2) maintaining links and commitments to the family as a whole. On the surface this seems like a contradiction. However, one of the major successes of family living is to learn about how to be part of a group and at the same time be separate from that group.

Many families have difficulty achieving this balance. Either they emphasize family solidarity to such an extent that individual members have to relinquish their autonomy, or they emphasize individual autonomy to such an extent that there remains no family commitment whatsoever. Very often, the difficulty in balancing between these two poles, individual autonomy and family solidarity, underlies the problems that families in therapy experience. In the early phase of family work, the therapist has to help the family articulate their goals.

It will become increasingly obvious as we proceed that symptom relief is one of the major goals a family wishes to achieve in the therapy situation. Symptom relief is the elimination or alleviation of the problem being experienced with one of the family members.

It is very unusual for a family to enter therapy with the understanding that family change or some change in the structure of the family is desirable. The usual complaint, for example, is that Johnny is acting up and the family is having trouble controlling him, or that Dad is drinking and it's very disruptive to the family. In any case, the family usually puts forth one of its members as the problem and states that the primary goal is to make that problem go away. The job of the family therapist is to help the family develop additional goals in order to expand their perception of the problem to a group-interactional level. To accomplish additional goal setting, the therapist must first help the family get a better composite view of their stated problems. This is achieved by asking each member to elaborate upon how he or she sees the problem. This process quickly illustrates how differently family members perceive the problem. It also provides an opportunity for each member to give voice to related difficulties, thereby bringing additional goals into focus. The following case examples illustrate how family goals can be broadened:

The W family entered therapy because they were experiencing severe difficulties with their oldest son, age 11. The family consisted of a father, age 45, a mother, age 40, and two boys, ages 11 and 6. This was the W's second experience with therapy. Their first therapeutic experience had been with a child psychiatrist who the W's had hoped could alleviate severe behavioral problems in their eldest son, who at the time of that contact was 7.

During the initial family therapy interview, the father was quick to define the problem to the family. He continued to see his oldest son as the problem, saying he was stubborn and refused to do anything the family wanted to do. He was also concerned that the boy was not "masculine" enough and felt that most of the activities with which he was involved were "feminine." The mother agreed entirely with the father. They were both convinced that the 11-year-old was the problem and said that they had no difficulty with their 6-year-old.

When family members were asked to talk about their other relationships, it became clear that the father, a senior executive in an aeronautics company, was seldom home. When he did come home, Mrs. W told him about all the problems that she had with her son, and he then proceeded to deal with his boy on the basis of what his wife said. There seemed to be very little involvement with the husband and wife in their own relationship. Mrs. W was very involved with her boys and also had strong ties with her own parents. She divided her time between taking care of her children; meeting her husband's needs when he came home; and taking care of her aging parents. Mr. W seemed to have very little time for the family and he wanted the little time he did put aside to be free of conflict.

The children, on the other hand, did not really know their father. The 11-year-old boy complained that he did not know what his father did at work, that he seldom saw him, and that he felt he was always angry at him. This concern was an eye-opener to the father, who did not realize that his son wanted to know him better. Although he was aware that he was spending little time at home, he thought that he was available to his whole family when he was there. Mrs. W was quick to say that in the past eleven years they had not been out alone and she felt that they were growing apart.

By the third session this family had begun to redefine their problems and goals. Rather than talking solely about their concerns about their 11-year-old boy, they were discussing how they wanted the family to be structured to allow family activities and time for Mr. and Mrs. W.

The Q family provides another example of how complicated setting goals can be in working with families. Mrs. Q called for an appointment because she was concerned about her 18-year-old son's behavior. She explained that he was acting irresponsibly; could not be depended upon or left alone in the home; and at times frightened other members of the family. She went on to explain that she had taken total responsibility for her sons since her husband was seldom at home and did not seem to care much what was going on in the family. She said that there were two other children in the family who were much younger than her son and presented no difficulties whatsoever. In fact her concern was that her oldest boy's behavior would have disastrous effects on the two younger, good children.

The mother of this family was adamant in her belief that her husband would not come to any of the sessions and it would not be helpful to have her younger children involved. She thought that her 18-year-old son should be seen, and if necessary, she would come along too. I explained to her, that if therapy were to begin, it would have to begin with the whole family unit because it was important to get all the family members' ideas about what was going on, including her husband's since he had a vital influence on the family. Under duress, the mother consented to having the whole family come to the first session. The family consisted of the father, age 45, the mother, age 43, two sons, ages 18 and 14, and one daughter, age 12. The husband and wife had been married for nineteen years, neither had been divorced, and there had been no separations during the course of their marriage.

The first session began with my asking each member of the family to explain why he or she was there. The father saw the problem as his wife's overinvolvement with the children and underinvolvement with him. The mother saw the problem as irresponsible and bizarre behavior on the part of the oldest boy. The oldest boy saw the problem as lack of communication and consistency between the parents. The two younger children were unaware that there was a serious problem in the family. It became quite clear to the family that they saw the problem in different ways and that they were all being affected by the problem differently.

One of the more interesting features of the first session was the way the mother changed her perception of her husband. When first asked what her reaction was to having her husband there, she responded that she didn't think he would be involved or concerned. The husband responded by saying he was surprised at her reaction. He went on to say that he didn't show more concern because of his wife's involvement with the children and his belief that she didn't want him to be more involved.

These two examples illustrate how each member of the family has a different goal based on individual understanding of what is happening in the family. If a therapist were to set goals with any one member of the family—or, for that matter, any two—these goals would be different from those of the excluded members. Goal setting should be a process which involves all members of the family and should respect the fact that each member of the family might have some goal which is different from the other members' goals. These goals must be considered along with those set for the family as a unit.

The other issue in goal setting concerns short-term and long-term goals. As I will continue to emphasize, the therapist should be setting goals for each session as well as goals for the overall process. For example, one of the major goals in the initial session is for the family to experience a safe environment where no one feels solely responsible for what is going on within the family. However, the therapist also develops goals for the total therapeutic endeavor. These goals encompass some significant behavioral pattern change within the family. Nevertheless, if the therapist does not accomplish the first short-term goal of providing a nonthreatening environment in which family members feel emotionally and physically safe, the achievement of long-term goals will be limited. Generally, the major long-term goals in family therapy involve helping families to: (1) improve communication; (2) feel accepted as individuals; (3) release the problem-bearer from this role; (4) develop more flexible assumption of leadership by any family member as circumstances require; (5) improve empathy and understanding; (6) improve ability to deal with and accept differences; (7) improve individual and family problem-solving abilities; (8) decrease the need to use scapegoats; (9) develop an intraobservational capacity of its own internal functioning; (10) improve autonomy and individuation; and (11) develop a balance between individual autonomy and family solidarity.

Goal setting in family therapy then, is connected with the stage of work of the therapy itself and the developmental stage of the family. Goal setting is dependent upon such factors as whether a family has teenage children, young children, or young adult offspring, etc. Goal setting is also dependent upon the family's perception of their difficulties.

It is important for the reader to keep in mind that the family problem is the entry point for the therapist. Without a family problem, the therapist would not be invited into the family. The problem that the family presents should always be taken seriously and should always be dealt with in the first several sessions. But how the family problem is dealt with or what emphasis the therapist puts on the problem will determine just what types of goals and expectations the family develops. How the therapist defines the problems is based on his theoretical framework for understanding family behavior. The next section will deal with the role of theory in family practice.

THE ROLE OF THEORY IN FAMILY SYSTEMS PRACTICE

The practice of therapy should be guided by clear conceptual thinking. The clinician must have a theoretical framework to guide and orient his practice. This theoretical foundation does not diminish the intuitive or artistic aspects of practice, but rather brings perspective to the behavior families exhibit. Many therapists shy away from seeing families because they become confused and anxious about how families behave in front of them. A strong theoretical base helps dispel this confusion.

When working with families, practitioners need to have a well-developed set of concepts that help explain systems behavior. This set of concepts serves as a cognitive map of group behavior, helping therapists to understand it. With this cognitive map, practitioners are less likely to see chaos in multidimensional family behavior, and more likely to develop hunches or diagnostic impressions about what is going on. In turn, these diagnostic impressions serve as guides for structuring therapeutic strategies. We must have a broad conceptual map which helps us perceive the widest range of behaviors. Systems concepts provide a broad understanding about behaviors and help us categorize behaviors in meaningful ways. Other concepts can be limiting, serving as blinders which pigeonhole our perceptions.

In family work, theoretical grounding is necessary for at least three system levels. It is necessary to have an appreciation of how individuals function and how they influence family behavior. Psychoanalytic theory, humanistic theory and learning theory help promote our understanding of how the individual copes in the world. Theoretically we have to account for how the family influences the individual as well as how the individual influences the family. Our theoretical orientation should be sufficiently sophisticated to account for both types of influence. From this orientation comes the recognition that from the moment of birth a child is temperamentally different from all other members of his family. Thomas, Chess, and Birch (1968, p. 4) define temperament as "the behavioral style of the individual child—the how rather than the what (abilities and content) or why (motivations) of behavior. Temperament is a phenomenologic term used to describe the characteristic tempo, rhythmicity, adaptability, energy expenditure, mood, and focus of attention of a child, independently of the content of any specific behavior." We should be able to take temperamental differences into account to understand how an individual's uniqueness influences family behavior. Personal characteristics such as temperament, physical appearance, and intellectual capacity, as well as the timing of the birth of any child in the developmental life of the family, are all important variables affecting the family. This book will not attempt to cover all the psychiatric and behavioral theories concerning individual behavior but it is important for a family therapist to be familiar with them. A family therapist focuses on the whole system but should at no time lose sight of the individual.

In addition to understanding the impact of the individual on the family, and vice versa, we also require a set of theoretical concepts to explain the family as a system. The family, especially the adults of the family, exerts a strong influence on how the child sees the world. We know that the child's set of values comes from the family, particularly during the first seven years of his life. Peer group and school experiences then help to temper, broaden or restrict some of those values. The family's ability to accept the child as a unique individual naturally influences the child's feelings about himself.

The third level of theoretical knowledge concerns the community. One may conceptualize the family as standing between individual needs on the one hand and environmental and community expectations on the other. The family can be seen and used as a resource in helping its members achieve their individual needs while at the same time satisfying and responding effectively to the expectations of the community. Family therapists should have a clear understanding of the community resources available to families. At times it is necessary for them to be able to influence what is happening in the community, quite often the school community. For example, families often request therapy because one of their children is having difficulty in school. The family might state that it was not their idea to come in for help but that the school recommended therapy. The family may complain that the school is not supportive of their child or expects their child to perform in a way they feel is unrealistic. In these situations, the families experience the school as hostile and judgmental rather than as a resource. In evaluating the family, the therapist might discover that the family has been doing a good job with its members but that their way of educating their children is in conflict with the expectations of the school system. Quite often this is the case with native (Indian) families whose value system and ways of communicating are quite different from those of the non-native community. The schools usually try to help the native children become more like non-native children. The therapist who has a good understanding of how community expectations add to familial problems will work with the school

system to help it become more sensitive to the needs of the
family. A different approach might result in a therapist agreeing
with the school system that the family, i.e., the problem child in
the family, is the one that needs the help.

The important idea here is that the therapist should have a
working knowledge of how the systems the family depends on in
the community influence how it conducts its life. These systems
can serve as resources to the family, making the family's job much
easier, or they can serve as barriers, adding to the family's
difficulties.

Figure 1 illustrates the three systems levels of therapist knowledge. The first and the smallest unit represents intrapsychic
knowledge about the individual. The second represents family
theory. The third unit represents community organization theory.

If the therapist has a good knowledge of these three theoretical
areas, he can move between and within any one of these systems
levels to produce change. There are times when the individual
needs direct work, especially when the family is not available to
him. There are also times when it is appropriate for the therapist
to work with the family as a unit to produce intrafamilial change.
And finally, there are times when the intervention or consultation
should take place in the community.

At each of these levels it is important for the therapist to
employ a set of theoretical assumptions to guide his interventions.
The most important assumptions (Freeman 1977, p. 57–65) which
guide family practice are as follows:

**Assumption one: the family as a whole is greater than the sum
of its parts**

This assumption suggests that what a family produces as a group
cannot be understood by knowing family members separately.
Many practitioners have found that when a member is seen
outside of the family context, he appears quite different. Behavior

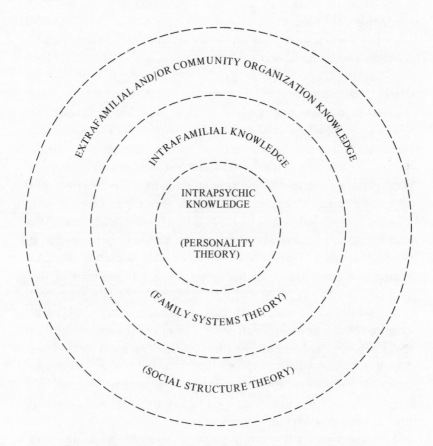

Figure 1: Three Theoretical Levels of the Family Therapist's Knowledge

depends upon environment. When all family members are seen together, their behaviors are influenced by the emotional processes going on at the time in the group. However, when one member is taken out of the group, even the most bizarrely functioning member, his behavior and performance become significantly different.

During a recent consultation, a practitioner presented a family in which the husband was said to be causing the difficulty. The practitioner accepted the wife's description of his behavior as bizarre and unpredictable. The thought of having the husband involved in therapy frightened the wife. Both the wife and the children described the husband/father's behavior as psychotic and unanimously agreed that he would not be amenable to family therapy. When the therapist finished her presentation, another participant at the consultation session said she knew this man and was totally surprised to hear this report about his behavior. She had always regarded him as being functional and appropriate. The practitioner who presented this case had relied on secondhand information about the absent member and was not able to determine its accuracy. On the other hand, the member of the group who had seen the husband/father outside the family context held a totally different perception of this individual. Who was accurate? In this context, both were. Bringing the family together would provide firsthand information on how the members behave as a unit. Although this assumption is widely recognized and accepted, many practitioners continue to be certain that the description they have received of a family member is accurate in spite of their not having seen him or her.

It is important for the family therapist to meet the family. Old myths and stereotyped ideas about individual functioning can be thrown into question when the whole family gets together. When one or more family members is absent it becomes more difficult to question ideas family members have about those who are not present.

Assumption two: if you change one part of the family system you change the whole family

This assumption stresses that change in one part of a system affects the rest of the system. For instance, if one member of the family refuses to play old games, that is, maintain old patterns of behavior, but remains in contact with the family, the family has to adjust to this change. Unfortunately that person often distances from the family and has little or no interaction with them. Hence a void is created. This void has to be filled, but the chances are that it will be filled by someone else playing the distanced member's role, especially if that role is important to the family. The scapegoat process illustrates this point: if one member of the family is scapegoated to maintain emotional calm or distance among family members, it is likely that another member of the family will become the scapegoat when the first person refuses to maintain that position.

Practitioners who have worked in psychiatric hospitals are familiar with the scapegoat process. When a member of the family is hospitalized it is usually because his behavior has become too disruptive to the family. Within a short time most hospitalized individuals appear much less disturbed. Emotional distance from one's family or community can change disturbed behavior quickly. However, soon after the person is returned to his family and community, the old behavior returns. The revolving door syndrome existing in many of our psychiatric hospitals is in part a result of this process. Unless the family changes with the individual, they will tend to put pressure on him to resume his old behavior to maintain the old balance. However, if the family can be involved and learn how the new behavior is in the best interests of the whole family, they will learn how to accommodate this behavior and appreciate the benefits of doing so.

Case example. The N family requested family work because of concern over the behavior of the second eldest daughter, Judy.

The family, and various members, had been in and out of treatment for over ten years, primarily because of problems with their eldest son, Sam. The two younger children, ages fifteen and twelve, were seen as asymptomatic. At one level the family recognized that theirs was a family problem, but they presented the problems as being primarily in Judy. Shortly before the family sought help, Judy had been hospitalized for one month because of her uncommunicative behavior and refusal to take care of her basic needs. Soon after the hospitalization her behavior improved and she became more spontaneous, alive, and concerned about herself. When she was discharged and returned home, the old behaviors recurred. At this point the family asked for help as a unit. Rather than focusing on Judy's behavior, I asked members of the family to define what they wanted to work on for themselves, and how the family as a unit could accommodate these areas. When the focus of attention was taken off Judy and placed on the rest of the family, Judy's behavior changed rapidly. As she improved, unresolved problems between the parents became a central issue. After several sessions the family recognized that attention had been focused on Judy so that the parents could avoid looking at the marital relationship.

This case vignette illustrates how change in one part of the family, i.e., the parent system, resulted in change occurring throughout the family. As the N family went through the process of family therapy and began experiencing more satisfaction and less anxiety, they had more energy available to work on other areas.

Assumption three: family systems become more complex and organized over time

This assumption stresses that familes are complicated systems which grow and develop over time. With the increase of information, resources and additional members, the family has to adjust, grow and adapt. The family must be perceived as an open system experiencing dynamic tension which constantly helps it to expand both its functions and its structure. General systems theory has emphasized that a universal characteristic of living systems is a tendency toward complexity. "Biological wholes achieve higher stages of organization in contrast to physical wholes, in which organization appears to result from the union of pre-existing elements" (Gray, Duhl, and Rizzo 1969, p. 14).

If one were to apply this assumption to practice, it would be wise to take the position that one never really knows for sure how a particular family functions and what its structure will be at all times. Each family changes from moment to moment. Each day brings new information, energy and dilemmas to the family. How the family deals with these variables will have a direct effect on its overall functioning. The family as a whole continually has to negotiate between its internal needs, wants, and resources and demands. The active negotiation between the internal and external components of a family will determine its course of action. Each time the whole gets together, a slightly different course of action is triggered. Because of this, it becomes very difficult to predict from one moment to the next how a particular family will react to a given stimulus. Therefore, a preferred therapeutic method is to question and requestion a family regarding its decisions to take one course of action over another.

As the family learns more about itself, its options, and how it has changed over time, so does the practitioner. One can view therapy as an ongoing learning process between the family and the practitioner. The better the questions the practitioner asks the family, the more opportunity the family will have to learn about itself. By contrast, the more statements the practitioner makes to explain the family's functioning to them, the greater the likelihood that the family will learn less about itself and rely more on the practitioner for explanations. The goal is to help the family realize that it is changing all the time and that change itself is natural. However, particular family changes and their consequences compose the information the family can provide for the therapist. The therapeutic position is to become a researcher for the family to help it learn more about itself.

Assumption four: the family is open, changing, goal directive and adaptive

This assumption implies that the family has resources within itself to deal with both internal needs and external stresses. One of the goals for work with a family is to identify the resources within the family so that the family can actively help itself. This goal directly relates to the third assumption. Instead of seeing the family as a reactive system that fends off change, it is viewed as a proactive system which has the potential for coming up with its own answers and strategies to meet its needs. The bulk of family literature tends to depict families as closed systems with few resources of their own to deal with the problems at hand. This view has some accuracy for those families who are experiencing extreme stress and anxiety. However, most families are not in this category and with appropriate intervention they can discover internal resources for responding to their difficulties. This type of intervention highlights the family's positive growth potential, and identifies the resources it has used in the past to survive. It can safely be assumed that a family who has experienced life together for a period of time has learned something about how to manage its affairs. This assumption changes the therapist's role in relation to the family. Rather than getting the family to talk about problems, things that haven't worked, and disappointments in life, the therapist might ask questions about what has worked, what things have gone well, and what they see as their strengths and resources.

Case example. The D family sought help for Mrs. D, who had been committed to a psychiatric hospital because of violent behavior directed toward her husband. This was her first hospitalization but the family felt that the problem had been growing over time and that her behavior was now uncontrollable. At the time of hospitalization, Mrs. D was 45, Mr. D was 47, and the two children Deborah and Sally were 19 and 18 respectively. The first family session involved the nuclear family and Mrs. D's mother and younger brother. Mrs. D described how unreasonable and inaccessible her husband was to her and the rest of the family. She explained her violent behavior as stemming from her feelings of desperation about trying to get her husband more involved with the family. Mr. D denied that he had not been involved and accessible to the family. Rather he felt that his wife was driving him away. The children tried to stay uninvolved, but as the session continued, they started to show distress about what was happening to the family. One began crying and the other asked to be excused. As treatment progressed, it became clear that members of the extended family, particularly Mrs. D's mother, were very much involved in the operation of the nuclear family. During one session Mrs. D's mother was asked to explain how she managed her family when her daughter was growing up. She said she had experienced difficulties with her husband who had a serious drinking problem and who was seldom available to the family. When Mrs. D's mother was asked how she perceived what was happening to her daughter's family, she said that she didn't want to meddle because she was only the grandmother. At that point I said that grandmothers are very important people since they are the only ones (other than grandfathers) who have so much knowledge about all that has happened in the past. She responded by smiling broadly and began to share many of her ideas about how she managed her family and the role she saw herself playing in her daughter's family. This action opened up communication between the mother and daughter, reduced the tensions between Mr. and Mrs. D, and provided a valuable resource person to diffuse the emotional intensity within the family. Rather than searching for the problems involved in family units, an attempt was made to highlight the strengths and to discover what did work for the family.

Families try to get the job of living done in the best way they know how. Some things have worked well and some things have worked badly. If one supposes that families are adaptive and goal directed, then one can also begin to ask questions about how it has managed so far and what other resources can be called into action from the family gestalt. This position is similar to social network therapy, in which the therapist involves many members of a family gestalt as a way of revitalizing a family system (Speck and Attneave 1973).

Assumption five: individual dysfunction is a reflection of an active emotional system

When an individual member within the family experiences difficulty, either physical or psychological, the family system has to respond to it in some way. This response will set up certain family behavioral patterns which could influence behavior after the original problem is gone. A family member who is seen as a problem is being compared to those who are seen as healthy. Dysfunctional behavior can be seen to serve a certain role within a family. In order for that behavior to be carried out, reciprocal processes must occur. One family told me that the mother was the mediator in the family. All family members agreed that unless she mediated, there would be nothing but fighting. The mother stated that she didn't want to continue playing this role since it caused her great stress and discomfort. The family didn't recognize the reciprocal needs this role served: the mother took responsibility and control; the other family members gave up responsibility for their behavior.

Whether the problem is physical or psychological, the practitioner must take a holistic view of the family, rather than zeroing in on the identified problem.

For example, in a family with a diabetic member, the need to control the diabetes could have a powerful effect on the total structuring of the family. If the diabetic is a child, issues arise around who will give the child his medicine, who will be responsible for the diet, who will make the medical appointments, and who will become the most concerned and anxious about keeping the diabetes under control. If one parent in the family is responsible for maintaining the diabetic child, then one can imagine how a special relationship would develop between this parent and the child to the possible exclusion of other family members. If the diabetes were suddenly no longer a problem, what would happen to that special relationship between parent and child and where would other family members fit into the overall relationship network? Whenever a family member has a problem there is a possibility that other members will set up a structure that causes two or more individuals to be overinvolved with each other to the exclusion of other family members. When this happens the immediate concern of the family may not be the major underlying problem. The important issue is how the problem has affected the relationship network within the family. A parallel issue concerns how the relationship would change if the problem no longer existed.

Each one of these theoretical assumptions has a strong influence on how the therapist practices. They help the practitioner decide whom to see, when to see them, and how to proceed in the therapeutic hour. They are guides which help the practitioner understand the family behavior he witnesses. Without these theoretical assumptions, the practitioner may rely only on his own feelings about the family interactions. These feelings are an unreliable guide since the practitioner's feelings about the family are likely to be quite different from the family's feelings about itself.

In summary, it is important for the practitioner to utilize a theoretical framework which gives meaning to behaviors which might otherwise appear as discrete or bizarre. A theoretical framework helps the practitioner formulate questions and strategies for intervening in a family system in a logical, consistent manner.

The next chapter presents a general systems theoretical framework for understanding systems behavior.

2

GENERAL SYSTEMS THEORY AND FAMILY THERAPY

THE IMPORTANCE OF SYSTEMS THINKING

There are many theories about human behavior. Probably the largest group of theories concerns individual development and intrapsychic functioning. There is also a body of theory that deals with group behavior. Recently, a number of theoretical attempts to explain community behavior have been made. As I have pointed out in the previous chapter, in order to do family practice, it is necessary to have a conceptual framework that brings together theories, concepts, and assumptions about how individuals, families and communities operate. No one theory in itself can accomplish this task. Thus, the family therapist needs a framework that helps him to interconnect ideas about how different system levels function individually as well as how they influence each other.

One of the primary advantages of general systems theory is that it provides a theoretical framework that is both broad enough and precise enough to bring together specific behavioral theories to conceptualize reality as a unified whole.

Hearn (1950) has attempted to clarify the use of general systems as applied to clinical work. He suggests that a general systems approach can be used productively to organize knowledge and help guide practice at all levels of intervention, i.e., individual, family, group, and community.

General systems theory has been defined as

the development of new forms of scientific conceptualizations, models and laws able to deal with organismic processes fundamen-

tal to the life of sciences . . . . many see the usefulness of general
systems theory in terms of its bridging function . . . . in this way it
offers potential for lessening the gap between the biological and
the mental, the social and the cultural, the specialist and the
generalist, and between theory and practice. [Gray, Duhl, and
Rizzo 1969, pp. xviii–xx]

Lanthrope (1964) argues convincingly for utilizing systems
theory as a foundation for theory building in clinical practice:

The systems approach revolves around the dual notion that reality
occurs in systems and that, correspondingly, the way of addressing
the problem must somehow be in accord with the view of reality.
The systems approach in a professional context, therefore, constitutes an avenue of thought combining cognitive generalizations
about the nature of systems as found in reality, and methodological
ideas to guide both study of a system and efforts to intervene in, to
design, or redesign the system. [p. 8]

A major contribution of a general systems perspective is that it
offers a way of formulating ideas about systems behavior, without
requiring that the ideas be wedded to a particular behavioral
theory base. General systems concepts tend to be theoretically
neutral in describing isomorphic principles of systems behavior.
"General systems theory does not invalidate previous scientific
work, but places it into a new framework, a new way of viewing
the world" (Gray, Duhl, and Rizzo 1969, p. 25). Systems concepts
can be applied to any system level to describe and formulate
principles of system behavior.

In family practice it is extremely important to be able to
understand the individual in the context of his family system, and
to understand the family in the context of the community. It is
also important to understand how each subsystem interconnects
and influences each larger system, and vice versa. The clinician
must be able to move back and forth between system levels and
choose the level that can produce the most change. The old
controversy as to who has the problem or who needs to change

first (the individual, the family, or the community) is not relevant under systems theory. Systems theory suggests that all systems and subsystems are interconnected and influence each other simultaneously. The job of the clinician is to identify the more powerful subsystems and suprasystems influencing the particular system being investigated or worked with. The major proposition of systems work is that when a powerful sub- or suprasystem changes, and stays in contact with the primary system, it forces change throughout. How does one go about organizing and understanding how systems behave?

First, we need a clear definition of what a system is and then a detailed discussion of the major concepts used to describe the structural, functional, and developmental aspects of system behavior.

SYSTEMS CONCEPTS FOR FAMILY PRACTICE

The following section defines a complex system. The major systems concepts are operationally defined to provide a theoretical framework for knowledge which should be helpful in family practice. In addition, some of the major practice principles that naturally flow from a systems perspective are presented.

According to Buckley (1967, p. 58), a complex adaptive system has openness, information-linkage of the parts to the environment, feedback loops, and goal direction. These provide the basic conceptual components that underlie the general features characteristically referred to as self-regulating, self-directing, and self-organizing.

All living systems have structural, functional, and developmental properties. When analyzing systems, it is important to identify which part of this universal triad is being examined at any given time. This analysis is difficult because of the lack of criteria for deciding which properties within the system represent its structure, function, or development. An additional difficulty is that at any given time, a structural property can become functional or developmental and vice versa. Miller discusses this inherent difficulty and suggests that a circular relationship exists between systems structure, function (process), and history (development): "Structure changes momentarily with functioning, but when such changes are so great that it is essentially irreversible, an historical process has occurred, giving rise to a new structure". Systems structure is defined as a "static arrangement of a systems part at a moment in three dimensional space"; function in a system is closely related to the concept of process and stands for "patterned events which tend to occur and reoccur with a certain amount of regularity" (Miller 1969, p. 85). Development is characterized as a system's natural impetus toward progressive differentiation of the parts from the whole over time. It must be recognized that this triad represents a tightly interwoven whole, and at any given time "history produces structure, and structure determines function" (Gerald 1968, p. 244).

Allport (1968) provides the most concise definition of a complex system: "a complex of elements in mutual interaction" (p. 344). The major systems concepts which expand on this definition are: boundary, matter-energy, feedback, steady-state, progressive differentiation, and equifinality. All these concepts can be used to explain how families function in space and time. Each one of these concepts has potential for influencing how one chooses to practice with a family and can be used as a way of organizing information and the types of questions we ask families.

Boundary

Living systems have a bounded region which serves to separate, to some degree, the "complex of elements in mutual interaction" from other elements within the environment. This bounded region is known as a *system boundary*. It serves as the structural frame of a system that helps keep objects together in some sort of cohesive organization, making the system a distinguishable entity from other entities within the environment. A system must have boundary structure, boundary maintaining functions, and boundary developing processes.

The existence of a boundary is usually determined by the following phenomena: "greater energy is required for transmission across a boundary than for transmission in the suprasystem immediately outside a boundary or within the system immediately inside it" (Miller 1955, p. 526). In actuality there is seldom just one bounded region separating a system from its environment. For any given complex system, numerous boundaries exist, each serving in different ways to maintain the system. Each component within the system has its own boundary. As the system becomes more differentiated and organized these component boundaries become more structurally autonomous, while at the same time, some direct link with the main system boundary is maintained, usually through a feedback loop.

The boundary concept is helpful in assessing family functioning. Systems theorists point out that multiple, ever expanding boundaries always exist. Every system in the universe has larger systems (suprasystems) and small systems (subsystems) surrounding it. This point of view is similar to a perception of the world as series of concentric circles, with the largest circle being the universe and the smallest circle being the tiniest microorganism known to man. The boundary concept is useful because it provides a conceptual tool for analyzing one particular system at a time. Without this focus one would become immobilized by the enormous complexity involved in viewing a number of systems simultaneously. Once a system's boundary is identified, it is possible to treat some systems in the environment as suprasystems in relation to the system under study and to view other systems as producers of internal effects on the focal system (subsystems).

In order to treat the family, one has to know what is being treated. The therapist needs to be able to identify the intrafamilial boundary of the family. The structural components of the family reveal the multiple subsystems which comprise its boundary. The question of who is involved in this family must be answered. Just knowing about the people who are living under the same roof does not necessarily tell us about the most important components of the family. Family members can live hundreds of miles away and still exert a powerful influence on family functioning. Letters, telephone calls, and visits by extended family members precipitate family crisis or alleviate problems in the nuclear family.

A family's boundary is determined by the practitioner's study of the interaction and degree of interdependence between significant others. A family boundary assessment includes knowledge about those people who have a greater degree of interdependence and interaction with each other than they do with other persons in the environment. All the significant people and their structural positions in the family's boundary must be taken into account to comprehend the ongoing interactional processes which are occurring in the family. The analysis of a family's boundary includes: (1) the hierarchical order of the members, which is represented by the division of labor and role distribution of the family members; (2) norms, values, and rule patterns which set guidelines for behavior within the family and between the family and its environment; and (3) the processing of information between family members and the environment.

Another practice principle which flows from the boundary concept is the task of identifying the structural, functional, and developmental components which comprise the family system. These components include subsystems and suprasystems structure, roles, norms, and rule patterns, feedback and information exchange processes, and structural-functional changes over time, due to developmental growth. This last component makes boundary identification difficult. Boundaries change over time and our analysis must keep up with these changes.

A third principle of family assessment suggested by the boundary concept is that a practitioner's task is to identify the degree of openness the family can allow in its exchanging of energy and information between and within its boundary levels. By their very nature, boundaries are open. This openness is partially responsible for the family growth and development. The more closed the family is to new information and resources, the less likely it is to have the energy and knowledge required to meet its expanding needs. Assessment of the degree of family openness should reveal the family's potential to grow and its competence for meeting its internal needs and external demands. The assessment process should include gathering information about (1) family boundary flexibility; (2) the family's filtering devices for screening out and censoring certain information; (3) the process of assigning certain members the task of bringing in, interpreting, decoding, and transmitting new information; and (4) the family's means of maintaining itself as a cohesive unit with a recognizable boundary which differentiates it from other social systems.

The boundary concept has implications for developing principles of intervention with family systems. For example, when an individual begins to have a significant impact on the interaction processes of the family, the family comes to depend on this individual for its own functioning. He has then entered and become part of the family's boundary. Families who request help from the therapist attempt to incorporate him into the family system. They ask the therapist for advice, try to get him to take sides, position him as the authority, and use his knowledge and skill in an attempt to modify or maintain a level of family functioning. Once the therapist accepts the family in treatment and begins to form a relationship with the members, he is, in essence, a part of that family's boundary.

A principle for intervention which flows from the boundary concept suggests that the therapist use his position within the family to help modify ongoing interactional processes toward opening boundaries to permit new information and resources to enter. The therapist's position inside the boundary can help accomplish this goal. For example, when a family has assigned one member to be its interpreter, decoder, and transmitter of all necessary information and this member attempts to inhibit family growth and differentiation because of his own anxiety over losing family unity and support, the therapist needs to open up these channels by using himself as a vehicle for providing new data. At the same time he must support those members who are frightened by the change. In this way the family is exposed to new inputs of information. With the therapist's support and encouragement, the family members can begin to test these inputs, possibly discovering within themselves a greater degree of social competence and mastery. These changes can create shifts in intrafamilial relationships which in turn could result in an alteration of the family's role structure and lead to increased flexibility within its members.

Feedback

Exchanging of energy within and between system boundaries is usually described as the feedback process. Mutual interaction between system members requires exchange of information. The more complex the system, the more sophisticated the feedback process must be to ensure a high degree of organization and cohesiveness. The feedback process also helps maintain the system in some sort of balance between its internal needs and external reality. New information must be processed, interpreted, and decoded to allow the members within the system to make the appropriate decisions in response to external pressures.

Feedback is defined as those processes which are responsible for receiving, interpreting, and transmitting information within the system boundary and its environment. The feedback process directs the system in its travels through the environment. It has mechanisms for correction of errors; making sense out of environmental stimuli; processing, interpreting and stimulating information; and procedures for bringing in new input (energy) and discarding unnecessary or harmful matter-energy outputs. In essence, the effectiveness of matter-energy dispersion, within and between systems, is a result of the developmental sophistication of the system's feedback processes. The feedback mechanism represents one of the major functional properties of a complex system.

Action and reaction within a family system are stimulated by its feedback processes. The regulatory processes of a system are dependent upon the operation of this mechanism.

Ruesch (1959, pp. 46–48) suggests that in order for a therapist to assess the feedback processes within a family system, he must define and identify: (1) the field or systems boundary in which the feedback processes are occurring; (2) the workers, methods, position, and point of entry into the system; (3) who is communicating; (4) to whom the message is addressed; (5) the contents of the message; (6) the interpretation of the content by all the members directly involved in the feedback channels; (7) the codification system and medium of communication used; (8) methods of metacommunication; and (9) the various feedback devices and how they influence action undertaken upon receipt of the message.

When using the feedback concept as a guide for operationalizing principles of intervention, a therapist's task is to identify the patterns of communication crucial to a family's dysfunctional behavior and then work with the family on improving its communication. When dysfunctional family patterns have existed over the years, families find it extremely difficult to adapt to change, primarily because they cut themselves off from new information sources. These families have had to rely on feedback loops which have contained so few new messages for so long that no one within the family pays much attention to incoming messages. Thus, new messages are heard with old ears, and consequently interpreted and translated as old messages. This type of intrafamilial communication pattern results in a serious limitation in the family unit's ability to learn about itself and its environmental suprasystems. This lack of information cuts the family off from new inputs for growth, development, and boundary openness.

The practice principle of intervention which emerges out of the feedback process is as follows: the task of a practitioner intervening into a dysfunctional family's system is to gain an understanding of the processes and patterns of communication and to intervene in them, thus opening up new channels and processes of communication. The task is accomplished by the practitioner providing a new model of clear communication to all members of the family. The practitioner should direct attention to the following areas: (1) how family members communicate with each other; (2) the differences between each family member's understanding of the given message; (3) how one's feelings distort the meaning of the message; and (4) new methods of communication for each family member and the family as a whole. Once the practitioner begins to help family members hear and speak to each other differently, more factual knowledge and fewer distortions should become incorporated into the family system. The outcome should be better decision making and a more economical use of energy to accomplish individual and group goals.

Matter-energy

Complex systems "are made up of *matter* and *energy* organized by information." Matter is anything that has mass and occupies space. Energy is defined in physics as the ability to do work (Miller 1969, p. 51). Traditionally, energy was defined as "the property of a system which diminishes, when the system does work on any other system by an amount equal to the work done" (*American College Dictionary*). Matter is considered alive when it is doing something, moving, or exchanging material (energy) with its environment (Schrodinger 1968, p. 144). The significant linkage between matter-energy and information is made by Buckley:

> Information is not a substance or concrete entity but rather a relationship between sets or ensembles of structural variety . . . the implication of this shift from energy flow to information flow as a basis for the interrelations of components in higher level systems are of central importance in distinguishing the nature and behavioral capacities of the latter, as against lower-level systems. Thus, a minute amount of structural energy or matter from one component of a higher system is able to trigger selectively a larger amount of activity or behavior in other components in the system, at the same time overcoming limitations of temporal and spatial proximity as well as the availability of energy. [Buckley 1967, p. 48]

The major matter components of complex social systems are people. People's positions within a system constitute a systems structural net representing the arrangement of matter within a systems boundary. Action, or the interactional process, is considered movement in space-time which occurs between or within people (matter-components). Interaction is defined as "any event by which one party tangibly influences the overt actions or the state of mind of another" (Sorokin 1947, p. 4). The interactional process, through feedback loops (information flow), represents a mechanism by which the exchange of energy passes between matter components (people) to accomplish work, thereby moving a system into action to accomplish its goals.

The usefulness of the matter-energy concept lies in its organizing potential. It helps to explain what constitutes a family system and how it is organized to form a complex whole. Individual members within the family constitute family systems matter and the family's feedback network constitutes the energy source which motivates the members into action. A family system is an organized complex whole. This complex whole cannot be understood without knowledge of the positional arrangement of component parts (family members) and the energy linkages between and within these parts (feedback loops). Matter within a system is triggered into movement or action when something is communicated to it. Members within families interact, make decisions, and learn about themselves and the world through receiving, interpreting, and transmitting messages. The verbal and nonverbal information an individual receives from his environment is the energy source which, converted into appropriate knowledge, helps him make decisions about who he is and what he should do.

Traditionally, helping professionals have asked what is the most appropriate system in which to intervene: the individual, the family, or environment? The matter-energy construct implies that intervention should be directed at the processes which occur between people or systems.

To a great extent, growth and development occur through the exchange of energy or information from system to system. When development does not occur as expected, it can be conjectured that appropriate energy (information) is not reaching the necessary matter components (family members) of the system. Intervention should then be directed toward those points where natural matter-energy exchanges are blocked. This blockage can occur when boundaries are too rigidly or loosely constructed or when various members of the family sabotage the input of new information out of fear of upsetting the family balance. Practice principles can be developed to deal with this situation. For example, the practitioner's role might be: (1) to provide new energy sources of information to the family; (2) to provide sufficient support to deal with the resistance of those members fearful of change; (3) to help family members realign themselves with the healthier, more open members of the family; and (4) to provide sufficient structure within the system to reduce stress so the family can tolerate being more open in inputs of energy. These inputs can in turn be used by the system to help it respond more freely to meeting the demands of its matter-energy exchanges.

Steady state

The definition of systems in this chapter emphasizes openness, exchange of energy, and continuous change. The process within a system that works to ensure that the degree of change is tolerable is known as *steady state*.

> Every living organism is essentially an open system. It maintains itself in a continuous in-flow and out-flow, building up and breaking down of components, never being, so long as it is alive, in a state of chemical and thermodynamic equilibrium but maintained in a so-called steady state which is distinct fom the latter. [Bertalanffy 1956, p. 3]

Steady state implies that systems do not automatically strive for tension reduction or complete balance, but are in a constant state of change, development and restructuring. The balance within a system is tenuous; it allows the system to expand and develop. Steady state is used "to express not only the structure-maintaining feature, but also the structure-elaborating feature of the inherently unstable system (Buckley 1967, p. 15).

In a general systems framework, steady state represents both the processes that work toward maintaining a stable balance (homeostasis) and those striving for growth and development (morphogenesis). To restrict our systems analysis to one or the other of these kinds of processes would permit only a partial explanation of a system's structure, function, and developmental behavior. A steady state is a combination of many internal processes operating simultaneously, some restricting the other's stimulating growth and development. To stay vital, a system must maintain its uniqueness, or systems boundary. This means that the internal forces working toward growth, change, and development have to thrive. The balance between equilibrium and morphogenesis should be weighted in favor of the morphogenic processes. The steady state balance of a system supports the overall tendency of the system to change and develop over time rather than maintain conformity, stability, or tension reduction (Buckley 1967, p. 29).

The steady state concept has been utilized in the systems literature to describe the complexity of living systems' regulatory processes, which are inherently unstable and in continuous flux.

A family system is never in a state of total equilibrium. Each member of the family has its own dynamic equilibrium level. The family as a group is composed of these different levels of equilibrium. When individual equilibrium states come together in some unitary whole (the family group), a homeostatic balance is achieved. However, this homeostatic balance is neither static or stable, but forever changing, to accommodate the changing equilibrium needs and demands made by the various components of the family, (the individual family members). This fluid condition can be described as the familys' steady state activity.

Rapoport suggests that one of the consequences of a system's attempts to achieve an acceptable homeostatic range is the development of a division of labor. This division of labor may develop within individual systems as well as between systems. When the division of labor occurs, it is usually followed by an increase in general homeostatic control by a system over its subsystems. One of the possible consequences of a system's increased homeostatic control is regressive behavior in individual subsystems. As a subsystem is further incorporated into an inclusive unit, its functions are taken care of by others through the division of labor process: "You may find that the regression of a former individual adaptation is made possible by a greater homeostatic control by the group (Rapoport 1959, p. 245). This idea helps explain why the adequacy of one family member may be maintained and supported by the inadequacy of another. Overadequate/underadequate reciprocity in relationship structures can be understood by looking at how a system maintains its steady state balance. This is explained in more detail in chapter 3.

The practice principle emerging from the steady state concept is that the practitioner should strive to understand how family systems maintain themselves in some sort of workable balance. This understanding would be based on a conceptualization of the interdependent equilibrium relationships between family members. Family systems have several equilibrium points, some stable, some unstable. Taken together, these points represent a mulitplicity of equilibria, with each component responding to its own needs, goals, and expectations and the collective demand made upon it by the family whole. It is important for the practitioner to be able to diagnose the differential cluster of equilibrium points. Different family members either resist change, thrive on change, or act as mediators to bring about a more stable homeostatic level. Once these different levels of equilibrium adjustment are identified, the intervener can determine which members need: (1) support; (2) encouragement to ventilate; (3) confrontation; or (4) help with the development of new feedback channels to increase the input of information.

The practitioner can use the steady state concept to improve his analysis of the regulatory processes of family systems. Once these processes are better understood, the therapist can develop treatment strategies which can be used in the selection of precise treatment techniques. These techniques will be geared toward helping the whole system to change, rather than sacrificing one or more members' adjustment in order to maintain homeostatic balance. When we can accomplish this, the family's need for scapegoating, double-bind communication, and vicious circle behavior will be likely to decrease.

Progressive differentiation

A universal characteristic of living systems is their tendency toward increasing complexity. Progressive differentiation occurs over time as a system negotiates with its environment via its input-output energy exchange processes. As a result of these negotiations, the system has to expand its structural and functional relationships, both internally and externally. Division of labor, feedback mechanisms, and the quality and quantity of components within the system expand as the process of progressive differentiation continues. The result is that a system evolves from a primitive state of unorganized and amorphous wholes that are only slightly differentiated to a state of progressive differentiation with recognizable boundaries and a hierarchical order (Gray, Duhl, and Rizzo 1969, p. 14).

Progressive differentiation is the major theoretical concept used to explain the developmental sequences characteristic of complex systems. All systems concepts have developmental features which contribute to our understanding a system's continual movement and change. Progressive differentiation is the explanatory concept which details the process by which a system moves from a state of undifferentiated wholeness to one of highly differentiated parts, linked through feedback loops.

A developmental perspective is useful for practice because it conceptually combines the past with the present to explain the past development of a family system in relation to its current state. This knowledge is important for treatment because it provides an understanding of the family's position in its developmental continuum and an indication of where it should be. Once this is understood, treatment goals can be set on the basis of the present developmental level of the family.

Many writers (Feldman and Scherz 1967, Scherz 1971, Pollak 1969) have discussed how a family's growth is determined by its ability to handle the crises which occur at various developmental points or stages. The progressive differentiation concept alerts practitioners to the importance of evaluating the family in relation to its pattern of responses to points of developmental crisis such as: marriage; birth of the first child; the child's development of autonomy through walking, going to school, adolescence; launching of children to their own nuclear families; retirement; and death. These are all points of normal developmental progression. Each point or stage requires that a number of tasks be performed by each member of the family and the family as a whole, to meet successfully the challenges and demands of the crisis without undue regression on the part of any member. The practitioner who uses the developmental framework to assess a family's functioning can determine a family's (1) adaptability, (2) range of homeostatic balance over time, (3) feedback and communication processes at various points in the family life cycle, (4) vulnerability in relation to particular developmental tasks, and (5) strengths and weaknesses over time.

Once the family has been evaluated according to a time perspective, some predictions may be made about potential points of stress which may occur in the future. Intervention can then be geared both to helping the family to deal effectively with current developmental needs and to prepare for future crises. When a family becomes aware of the natural processes of change and does not experience a change as a serious attack on its stability and security, its chance of being able to cope with the developmental crisis in a growth-producing way is enhanced. Using this framework as a guide, the practitioner's task is to help the family learn enough about its own developmental stages so that its members can anticipate developmental changes and accept them as part of life. If a family can develop this attitude, less energy will be used to fend off change and more energy will be available for mastering developmental life tasks.

Equifinality

The final concept in the operational definition of a complex system is equifinality. Equifinality is a particular property of open systems. It is closely related to progressive differentiation in that a system's development or growth is not dependent on initial conditions, as in closed physical systems, but may be reached from different initial conditions in different ways.

> If . . . the system is open, it can be shown that the final state will not depend on the initial concentration. It will be determined entirely by the properties of the system itself, that is, by the constants of proportionality which are independent of the conditions imposed on the system. Such a system will appear to exhibit "equifinality" or metaphorically speaking, to have a goal of its own. [Rapoport 1958, p. xviii]

The equifinal process illustrates a system's goal-seeking tendency. Growth, development and purposeful behavior are products of the interactional properties of the system itself. The structural, functional, and developmental elements within a system come together continuously as a system attempts to deal with its internal needs and external pressures. The existential condition largely determines the course of action a system takes. This action cannot be understood by examining only the initial conditions that brought the system into being. The ongoing interactional and transactional processes within and between a system's boundary, its feedback processes, matter-energy components, level of steady state, and developmental history must all be examined before an action taken by a system can be understood.

The importance of understanding the equifinal process is that it directs our attention to the ongoing, dynamic, interactional processes in the system. To comprehend family behavior, it is necessary to understand the existential moment of the family: how do the members currently interact and deal with issues? One must also remember family systems represent the past, present and future in any given moment in time. All three dimensions need to be reflected in our diagnostic assessment and selection of treatment strategies. It is important to keep in mind that when a family begins therapy, it brings along its past experiences, its hopes and its current patterns of behavior.

The following chapter uses the basic general systems framework to describe the family as an emotional system. The concepts presented there will further refine our understanding of how families behave.

3

THE FAMILY AS AN EMOTIONAL SYSTEM

STRUCTURE, FUNCTION, AND DEVELOPMENT
OF THE FAMILY

Structure

The family emotional system can be viewed systematically as a structural, functional, and developmental unit. Structurally the nuclear family has four basic subsystems: the individual subsystem; the husband-wife subsystem; the sibling subsystem; and the parent-child subsystem. Each subsystem has its own boundaries and set of needs and expectations. A family in emotional balance is able to satisfy the individual needs of each subsystem. In addition, the family has to interact with its suprasystems, i.e., emotionally significant others (friends), neighbors and community people. Figure 2 will illustrate how the various intrafamilial and extrafamilial systems interact and interface with each other.

Family therapists who work with the nuclear family should know how to assess its structural makeup. A family usually begins when two people decide to marry (although there are many variations on this theme). Each partner brings into the relationship expectations and assumptions about how the relationship and the family should be organized. Initially, two people are attracted to one another because each feels somewhat comfortable and fulfilled in the relationship. Gradually, the couple develops a lifestyle and communication style which allows them to continue to be emotionally and socially comfortable with each other. Prior to having children, the couple has time to identify their personal

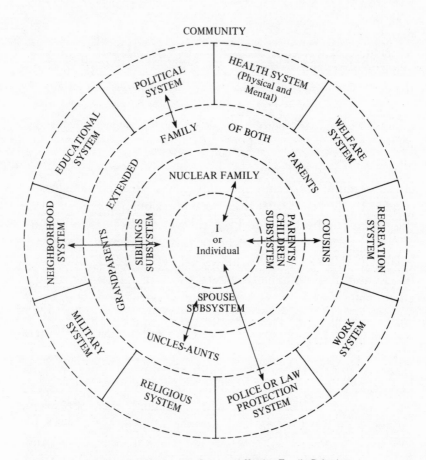

Figure 2: Interconnecting Systems Affecting Family Behavior

needs, their relationship needs, and the needs of the external suprasystems.

When a couple brings a new member, i.e., a child, into the family unit, their relationship, communication, and lifestyle patterns have to change. They have moved from being a dyadic unit to a triadic unit. Communication is now between three people. In addition, the child brings into the family his own temperamental style, particular modes of relating and personal needs. The flexibility of the spouse relationship helps determine the couple's ability to accommodate the child's manner of relating.

If the child's temperamental style and manner of relating is compatible with his parents, an adequate adjustment is usually made. However, if there is a significant difference between the child's propensities and the couple's expectations for him or her, discomfort occurs and problems will develop within the parent-child relationship. This is especially likely to occur if the couple is uncomfortable in their own relationship and have difficulty dealing with this discomfort. Often the couple will transfer their relationship difficulties to the child in an attempt to use the child to stabilize the discomfort in their own relationship.

The parents must decide how much time and energy they wish to reserve for their own relationship as well as how much time they are going to devote to their parent-child responsibilities. When the therapist is assessing the development of the parent-child subsystem his framework should be multidimensional, i.e., it should focus on the father-to-child relationship, the mother-to-child relationship and parents-to-children relationships. These subsystems have to be balanced so that members in one are not excluded from being able to relate to members in another. An example of an imbalance occurs when the parents become overconcerned and involved in their spouse relationship and feel they don't have time to meet the child's demands, which are perceived mainly as an interference. Another common example occurs when one parent becomes so involved in parenting that the other parent is effectively eliminated from involvement with the child as well as the spouse. The only way this excluded parent can relate to the overinvolved parent is around parenting issues; generally in this situation very little time and effort is put into husband-wife issues.

If the family has more than one child, a new subsystem will be created, namely, the sibling subsystem. The siblings develop a relationship with each other which is unique from all the other relationship systems in the family.

Sometimes parents feel excluded from the sibling relationships when their children have conflict with each other or form very close relationships. However, a family that is in balance accepts the sibling subsystem and allows it to develop. The balanced family can use the sibling subsystem as a resource in the workings of the family. In contrast, serious sibling disharmony often results when parents interfere with the sibling relationship. When parents have difficulty allowing the siblings to work out their own conflict by giving preferential treatment to one sibling over another, or when they do not respect the birth order positions and try to make younger siblings responsible for older siblings, disharmony results.

This imbalance was present in a family I worked with in which there were four children, three girls, ages 20, 18, and 14, and one boy, age 15. The parents requested help because of their concerns about the behavior of the 18-year-old, Susan. They felt that she was difficult to handle and generally a disruption to the whole family. During the first several sessions with this family the parents revealed that they made the only boy in the family senior to the oldest girls. Mainly because of this, the two oldest girls, Judy, 20, and Susan, 18, vehemently disliked their 15-year-old brother. The parents also encouraged the brother to protect his younger sister, Joy, who was 14. In the third session, both Susan and Judy said that whenever they tried to work out a conflict with their younger sister, their younger brother jumped in and tried to protect her, acting as if he were in control of the family. When the girls complained, the parents sided with their son. This caused both older girls, especially Sue, who was more dramatic and temperamental, to create a disturbance in rebellion. Both parents wanted to decrease the conflict and dissatisfaction between their children, but did not realize how their actions had fueled the conflict. As the parents learned how to stay out of intersibling disputes, the children began to organize a way of dealing with each other that reduced much of the conflict in the family.

A common dynamic which is found in families where there is serious conflict among the children is that parents will often see one child(ren) as functional and another as dysfunctional. When families seek treatment for the dysfunctional child, it is especially important for the therapist to assess the family's intrafamilial structure. He must understand the methods by which each of the subsystems develop relationships within their own subsystems as well as across subsystems. When these dynamics are understood, the imbalance can be more precisely perceived. It is helpful if the therapist can meet all family members in order to understand the interactional levels of the subsystems. To understand the problems of one sibling, the therapist must understand the pressures exerted by the other siblings as well as by the parents. If the therapist aligns himself with the parents in trying to deal with a problematic child without taking into consideration the sibling impact and involvement, chances are great that the siblings will defeat the therapist's and parent's efforts.

Implicit in this discussion of the importance of understanding how a family organizes structurally, is the notion of roles, norms and values. Structurally, all families have to organize themselves in terms of a role network in order to get the job of living done. Role network is influenced by the family's value system and norms. Perlman has been explicit in discussing role theory in relation to family behavior and views family structure as a network of role relationships. She defines a role as

> a person's organized pattern of actions and attitudes, fashioned by the position and function he is carrying in relation to one or more other persons. It is a cluster of reciprocal behaviors in which certain obligations and expectations of oneself and others are held to be inherent. [Perlman 1961, pp. 11–12]

The assignment of roles depends upon how the family organizes itself in its various subsystem relationships. For example, the oldest son in the family is given a quite different set of role expectations from that provided to the youngest daughter or youngest son in the family. The father's expectations usually differ from the mother's. In family work, a therapist has to understand how a given family has assigned various roles.

Role assignment is almost always connected with a set of values or beliefs about how things ought to or should be done. This value or belief system comes primarily from the parents' own experiences in their families. We all come out of families believing that relationships should be organized and that responsibilities should be carried out in particular ways. This set of "oughts" and "shoulds" has a strong influence on parents' expectations for their children and each other.

There are two types of role assignment. Family members have ascribed roles which are assigned automatically according to age and sex of the individual, that is, mother, father, son, daughter. There are also acquired roles which are assigned according to social status or personal characteristics, i.e., leader, follower, scapegoat. The combination of the ascribed and assigned roles within a family comprises the complex role network and represents the basic arrangement of the parts within the whole.

Everyone in a family operates within a role network. Each person plays a number of roles simultaneously. This role playing may act as a constraint upon the individual or add to his growth and development as a personality. There are three levels of roles represented in the family system: (1) individual roles which are performed by family members; (2) subsystem roles, carried out by various units within the family, i.e., sibling subsystem, parent subsystem; and (3) family roles which are performed by the family as a unit for their environment, i.e., the social control of its members.

A family develops norms concerning how it should behave as a whole and how individual members within it should behave.

These norms emerge out of the marital pair's own experience in their respective families of origin and through a process of incorporation and internalization of cultural values.

When two people marry or form a family, an ongoing process of socialization is set into motion which produces a meshing of both partners' values and norms. This ongoing process develops patterns of attitudes, feelings, and expectations which define acceptable behaviors. These patterns can be considered family norms. They serve to govern the behavior of individual members and the family system as a whole. Norms function to bind the family in a common culture, specifying right and wrong behavior and serving as a mechanism of social control.

The value system which operates within a family strongly influences the selection of norms, rules, role assignments and behaviors. Values are defined as

> the system of ideas, attitudes and beliefs which consciously and unconsciously bind together the members of the family. . . . values provide definitions of the time dimension, contain concepts concerning the responsibility and worth of individual members of the family, point to certain commonly held life goals, impose a framework within which the pursuit of—and risks connected with—pleasure impluses take place, and involve a system of sanction. [Parad and Kaplan 1966, p. 58]

Several levels of values influence family structure, namely, societal values, family values, and individual values. Society attempts to dictate what a family ought to do, what structure it ought to adhere to, and how it ought to behave. The family as a unit holds certain values as a result of its cultural identification and the meshing of value differences of its own members. Individual members, through their own experiences, develop personal value systems which govern their choices of preferred behavior.

The family's subsystems, suprasystems, roles, norms and values are all concepts which help to define family structure. These concepts help the therapist develop a systems portrait for each family in treatment. A systems portrait gives the therapist insight into how the family has chosen to behave functionally.

Function

The functional workings of a family are closely interconnected with the family's structural development. The way the family chooses to organize its life will influence how it chooses to relate within its intrafamilial system and to its extrafamilial systems.

There are two aspects of family function: (1) the actual functional responsibilities delegated to the family by its environment, and (2) the behavioral phenomena or processes that occur within the family which move it into action. The major functions assigned to the family by society are as follows: the meeting of survival needs; the protection, care, education and rearing of children; the creation of a physical, emotional, social, and economic setting which nurtures the development of individual family members; the nurturing of affectionate bonds within the family which will help each member become a contributing member of the family and community; and the responsibility for the social control of its individual members (Feldman and Sherz 1967, pp. 5–6).

Over the last hundred years, the function of the family has changed dramatically in our society. At one time the family's major function was an economic one, with the family preparing its members for economic survival. With the advance of the industrial revolution, technology, and various social welfare institutions, the family has moved away from a predominantly economic function toward a more affectional or emotional function. Today, the major responsibility of the family is to prepare its members for coping with society emotionally and socially, rather than economically.

One of the ways children learn how to relate to the outside world is by experiencing relationships within the family. The modeling that goes on within the family constitutes the most powerful experience children have in learning how to deal with society as a whole. It is generally recognized now that the child's peer group and school influence also play a powerful role in helping to socialize the child. However, the child continues to use his family as a frame of reference for understanding what goes on outside the family unit. Intrafamilial behavioral patterns influence, and in many cases reinforce, what the child experiences outside the family.

Development

The individual developmental stage of each family member and the developmental stage of the family as a unit are both part of the systems perspective of the family therapist. Ideally, the individual's developmental stage and the family's developmental stage will be mutually supportive. Unfortunately, in many cases this does not happen. For example, consider the 15-year-old girl who is having a child. We know the late adolescent years are a time when individuals want to experiment and test out reality as a way of discovering who they are. However, the adolescent who is responsible for taking care of another human being has to put personal desires aside while meeting the dependency needs of the child. Adolescence is a time of ambivalence. The individual moves back and forth between wanting to be cared for and wanting to be independent. It is a major reactive period in an individual's life. For the adolescent who has to meet the responsibilities of a caretaker, a developmental conflict is created.

The family as a unit experiences significant developmental stages, beginning with the creation of the spouse subsystem and then working toward the development of a family with the birth of the first and subsequent children. In the early years of the family, development is related to the caretaking, nurturing, and dependency responsibilities. When the children begin school the "letting go" stage begins. As the process of letting go and the gradual emancipation of the children continues the parents begin to reassess their individual goals and desires. By the time the children are leaving home, the parents are coming to terms with being a couple again rather than caretakers. Ideally, this process should be gradual and the family as a unit should always be preparing itself for different needs and expectations as the children grow older. However, many parents delay preparing for changes and during the first fifteen years or so of family life devote themselves primarily to caretaking responsibility and neglect noncaretaking roles.

THE FAMILY AS AN EMOTIONAL SYSTEM

This section deals with the functioning of the family as an emotional system. The concepts defined in this section illustrate the behavioral phenomena or processes that occur within the family.

Loyalty

Loyalty is the emotional commitment a person has to another or a group. Almost from birth the child develops a commitment to his own family. That commitment is reinforced by being given the family name and becoming part of a family history that goes back many generations. The child becomes identified with that history through his relationship with his parents, siblings, and extended family. The child's commitment to his family is also reinforced by his realization that there are certain things he is able to do within his family that he cannot do outside his family. Family stories communicate to the child that there is a rich history connected with his particular family which he doesn't share with any other family. However, the most significant reinforcer of family loyalty for the child is his relationships within the family. His family members become the most familiar, the most comfortable, and usually the most accepting, even if there is conflict or disharmony in the family. There are many examples of children who are abused in the family but would still rather be at home than anywhere else. One's commitment to the family is probably the strongest early bond that the individual experiences. Loyalty contributes to the strength of family bonding. Such bonding does not usually exist in the individual's relationships with people outside the family.

When loyalty becomes too controlling it effectively excludes the individual from freely and spontaneously experiencing other individuals in his environment. If the loyalty bond is too loose or inoperative, the individual does not feel significantly connected with a group of people he can call his own. How a family deals with loyalty issues will have a strong impact on how easily an individual will be able to move within and outside of his own family system.

In therapy, loyalty is the most crucial issue the family must confront. The therapist has to help the family members recognize that talking about individual needs and wants does not mean they are being disloyal to family commitment and unity. The balance between individual needs and family needs is a major loyalty issue.

Alliances

The family, from the moment it is created, develops various types of alliances such as dyadic alliances, triadic alliances, intrafamilial alliances, and extrafamilial alliances. In the earlier discussion of the structure of the family, the three major subsystems, spouse, sibling and parent-child, were discussed. Each one of those systems results in the development of an alliance. The husband-wife have an alliance with each other apart from their relationships with their children. The siblings have an alliance which makes their relationships with each other different from their relationships with either parent.

Functionally, alliances can serve as useful mechanisms within the family. An alliance allows one to talk to another about a concern or idea which couldn't easily be shared with others. An alliance makes one feel he belongs and is accepted by another. On the other hand, alliances can be functionally maladaptive.

Maladaptive alliances are collusions, coalitions, or triangulations. These maladaptive alliances cause certain family members to join forces against other family members as a way of dealing with discomfort in relationships.

These maladaptive alliances were often formed in the Q family which had great difficulty with communication and were involved in frequent, nonproductive fights. Conflict between any two members eventually involved a number of family members but nothing ever seemed to get resolved.

A typical situation occurred one night when Mr. Q came home from work and saw that his wife was upset. He immediately assumed that his 17-year-old son was responsible for his wife's mood. Rather than asking his wife what was troubling her, he accused his son. In turn, the son became upset and began to fight with his father. The mother joined the fray and was upset that her husband was fighting with their son within minutes of coming home from work. However, when the father clarified he was fighting for her sake, his wife sided with him against the son. When the fight subsided, the mother and son made peace with each other and the father removed himself from the scene. The mother, however, continued to be visibly upset. After a while the second child in the family, who was upset by the family turmoil, attacked her brother for upsetting their parents. This led to a fight between the sister and brother which resulted in the girl beginning to cry, at which point the father again attacked the boy about upsetting another family member. The mother again tried to intervene and around and around they went. In this family two-party alliances against a third prevented any new learning from occurring within the dyadic relationship.

Fantasies, distortions, and secrets

Family members learn about each other almost from the moment of birth. They learn what each person likes and dislikes, what sorts of issues to avoid, when it is permissible to talk about certain topics, and so on. Many family members feel that because they have lived with each other so long they know each other best. However, I have found that many times the people we know the least well are the people we have lived with the longest. Because the family is an emotional functional system, most of our experiences with family members occur around emotional events. The more emotional or conflictual a family, the more likelihood there is for distortions and fantasies to develop. Consequently, many family members grow up with fantasies about other family members and distortions in how they view the family and each other. These fantasies and distortions often serve to confuse and alienate family members from each other. Family members may feel misunderstood and exasperated because other family members are not able to understand what they are going through.

It is preferable that fantasies and distortions be kept to a minimum within the family. The best way to achieve this is for family members to check out their assumptions about each other by being able to state clearly what they are experiencing at a given time.

Secrets, like fantasies and distortions, serve to mystify certain events and people within the family. Whenever there is a secret there is also a conspiracy. The conspirators are the secret keepers, who try to keep the secret from others. Functionally, the power is in keeping the secret not in the secret itself. As long as several people are in conspiracy to keep the secret, it prevents other family members from being able to speak freely about what is happening in the family. Many people who sense that there is a secret in the family develop fears about what exposure of that secret would do to the family. In therapy, family members may try to confide secrets to the therapist. If the therapist becomes party to the secret keeping he lessens his ability to relate to all members of the family spontaneously.

Legends

Each family member develops a legend about himself, his ego ideal, and self-image. An individual's legend is often connected with the history of his birth. For instance, the name a child is given may be connected with an expectation that he will become like this person. The role assignment a child is given in the family also molds self-image. This role is often connected with birth order, or perhaps with a crisis the parents experienced while the child was young. The child who is somehow identified with a family crisis may be expected to behave in a certain way connected with the crisis.

The following example provides an illustration of how legends and expectations interact. A couple gave birth to their first son at the same time that the husband's grandfather died. The grandfather was a powerful, influential member of the family and his name was given to the firstborn son. Both the extended family and the nuclear family expected that this boy would have some of the characteristics of his powerful great-grandfather. As the boy grew up, he did not live up to the expectations of his name, and increasing disappointment was expressed. Until the family entered therapy, the boy didn't know why he was supposed to live up to these expectations. The parents began to talk about the pressure that the extended family put on them to make sure that the firstborn son developed certain attributes. Their attempts to pass along this pressure to the son failed to produce the desired characteristics. The legend that a person inherits can serve as an impetus to motivate him but can also serve as the burden that forever discourages the person from attempting new tasks. In this family, the latter was the case.

Unpaid dues and ghosts

Many people develop the notion that they owe family and extended family certain debts. Many feel that eventually they will be able to pay off these debts. However, if a member of the extended family dies before the debt is paid, "unfinished business" develops. Many adults feel that if given the chance to "do it over," they would make amends or become more charitable in a relationship with an extended family member. When that extended family member dies before amends are made, the individual feels guilty and the death becomes even more traumatic. In some cases the adults try to pay off the unpaid dues through their own children. When parents try to make their relationships with their children different from the ones they had with their parents in order to make retribution, they are actually allowing their guilt to carry over to a new generation.

We all carry in our own minds a picture of how we experienced our parents. Many times we want to ensure that our relationships with our children are as good, better, or different. We maintain mental images of our experiences in other relationships, especially family relationships. These images or ghosts influence how we perceive and relate to our own families. These ghosts have a strong influence on how we see and deal with our current relationships. Many children do not understand why parents take certain stances on issues unless the parents are able to articulate to the children the basis for their thinking. Consequently, children may personalize their parents' reactions without recognizing that these reactions are a reflection of events the parents have experienced in their past. The way in which such ghosts influence how a family organizes itself can be a revealing phenomenon. Knowledge in this area can help children develop a perspective about their parents that is quite different from their usual personalization of their parents' reaction to them.

Communication

All that has transpired in a family, the legends, secrets, distortions, roles, goals, and values, are dealt with through the family's pattern of communication. Communication can be seen as the lifeline of the family. Anyone who does family work deals with the family's method of organizing communication. The therapist must recognize which members in the family act as interpreters of family actions and family relations with the outside world. The family's choice of words and concepts is also important to note.

Obviously communication is not only verbal, but also nonverbal. In fact, families communicate much more powerfully nonverbally than verbally. A family develops a way of communicating to its members that is totally unique to its particular unit. Any outsider who becomes involved with the family will have difficulty understanding the subtleties in the way a particular family communicates. However, it is vitally important for the family therapist to understand how the family exchanges important information. Once the therapist has learned the family communication style, he needs to "plug" in to that style, rather than attempt to get the family to adapt to a therapy style of communicating. One way of doing this is to have each family member define important terms or concepts he or she uses during the interview. When a family member uses words like love, hate, sad, etc., he or she should be asked to explain what is meant by these words. In this way everyone learns the unique meanings a family member attaches to important emotional words.

The communication network of a family will often reveal the family role network. How the family chooses to express certain things about itself reflects what they value and what they consider important. The family member responsible for explaining family experiences obviously has been elected to this role in observance of the family power structure. It is important that the therapist recognize this power structure because it is usually parallel to the communication structure.

Differentiation of self

Differentiation of self (Bowen 1966, pp. 355–360) is a concept which helps to explain how an individual develops into a self in his own right. Differentiation is a person's ability to define himself as a self or separate entity. An individual moves over time from a relative state of undifferentiation to progressive differentiation. Birth is the beginning of the differentiation process. For a period of time, the child relies on the parents and his family for security and identification. From birth to approximately two years of age, the child is unable to distinguish or differentiate himself from his environment or caretakers. This stage is consistent with Erickson's stage of trust (Erikson 1963). If the environment is secure, supportive, and consistent, the child will move from almost totally personalizing the activities in his environment as a reflection of his own well-being, toward gradually separating himself from what is happening around him. When this process begins to occur, the child moves toward an identification of self as separate from his caretakers and immediate environment. The more insecure, inconsistent, or rejecting the environment, the more difficult this task. In other words, development of an individual sense of self is a continual process which moves from undifferentiation or fusion with one's environment, toward increasing differentiation or uniqueness, and identification of oneself as apart from one's environment. One way to perceive this concept is in diagram form (see figure 3).

As one can see, when the circle and the square overlap, there is not a clear ego boundary separation between the two people. Similarly, the infant is not able to distinguish himself from his parents or caretakers, so his sense of self or ego boundary is very much interconnected and fused with his caretakers. As the child develops more autonomy and a better sense of himself (which usually occurs when the child becomes more ambulatory and self-sufficient), he gradually develops an ego or identification that is somewhat separate from his immediate environment or caretakers. As the child continues to develop, he increases his sense of self. However, for a period of time his sense of self is still connected with his immediate environment (or "reactive" self).

In his attempt to be different from his environment, the child attempts to do things that are in opposition to what his caretakers or parents might wish. This opposition is the child's attempt to become separate from his parents. There are two major periods of reactivity in the child's attempt to develop differentiation: (1) from ages two and a half to approximately five; and (2) from thirteen to approximately nineteen. During these periods many families feel they have problem children. The children become obstinate, argumentative and, more importantly, different from their parents. Unless the parents can understand some of the child's behavior as an attempt to differentiate himself from his

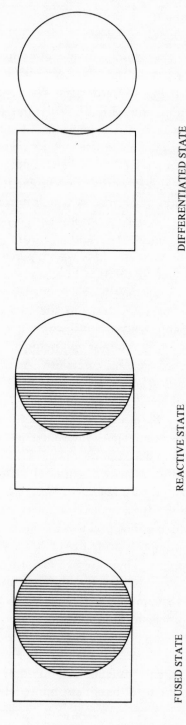

FUSED STATE

Almost no
emotional
differentia-
tion of self
from other

REACTIVE STATE

Self and other
define self in
reaction to
each other

DIFFERENTIATED STATE

(Ideal)

Self and other are
proactive, clearly
defined selves.
Little or no ego
fusion

Figure 3: Different Stages of Ego-fusion, from Undifferentiation to Differentiation

immediate environment, they will identify these reactive moves as symptoms of emotional problems. The parent who tries to convince the child not to be different or who pits himself against the child's attempt at differentiation can either prolong the child's struggle to find himself or create such a conflict that the child gives up his attempts to become an independent entity. The latter becomes a much more serious problem than the former.

The child who continues to struggle to be unique has the ability to eventually come to terms with who he is in relationship to his family. However, the child who gives up the struggle will become more seriously impaired and will have difficulty developing a clear sense of his own identity. Adolescents with no sense of self have trouble, as adults, becoming goal oriented, competent, and nonreactive in relation to the people with whom they are involved.

In a relationship where ego boundaries overlap, one finds a significant degree of personalization. Individuals who have difficulty identifying themselves as separate from others will tend to use others as a way of defining self. In these relationships there is much pressure on the other to be like, to agree with, and to support that self. Any attempt by the other to be different, to take a different stand, or to see the world in different terms will present a crisis and throw the relationship into some sort of emotional turmoil. If the other maintains a different stance, refusing to give it up to support the relationship, then the reactive partner will have to find some means to reduce that tension, either by finding another relationship that is supportive of these emotional needs or by making some differentiation moves which will redefine the relationship at a higher level.

Emotionally, a differentiated individual is able to define who he is, what he wants, what he thinks, what his goals are, and what he is prepared to work on (and not work on), in a way that is minimally influenced by others. Granted, all of us maintain some concern about what others think and are influenced to some degree by others, but the more differentiated the individual, the less his thinking is dominated by approval from others. On the other hand, the undifferentiated or fused individual is intimately affected by what others feel and think. Many decisions are made because of concern about approval from others. Much emotional energy is used thinking, feeling, and worrying about what others feel and think. The more undifferentiated the individual, the more controlled he is by his feelings and need for approval. Very few decisions are made independently of outside forces.

These two emotional stances, differentiation and undifferentiation, should be viewed on a continuum: when an individual is feeling calm, in control and confident, he or she will behave in a much more differentiated or self-oriented way. However, when an individual feels anxious, threatened, or emotionally shaky, the sense of self is impaired. The continuum is in fact punctuated by three general self-stances. The ideal, of course, is to be differentiated and clearly in control of self with minimal concern about approval. The second stance is a reactive or pseudoself stance. Here, a person takes a stand in reaction to another's demands as a way of demonstrating competence to a significant other. This stance is not differentiated because the other still has some control over self's decision; however, there is still an attempt to be different from the other. The third stance is the undifferentiated state in which the individual is unable to take a stance separate from the other; most of the individual's emotional energy goes into being like, and supporting the other.

These three stances are developmental. The third stance, the undifferentiated self, is predominantly in evidence during the first years of life and in the early teenage years. The second stance, the reactive or pseudoself, is in evidence in young adulthood when developmental tasks are geared to the individual proving that he is competent in his environment. If these two stances are "traveled successfully," the individual then moves on to higher degrees of differentiation. It is important to keep in mind that differentiation continues throughout life. No one achieves differentiation permanently. It is something we continually strive for throughout our emotional life.

When individuals leave the nuclear family, their level of differentiation and sense of self guide their choice of friends and a marriage mate. We most often marry people who are at the same level of emotional health and state of differentiation. If one leaves the family of origin feeling shaky and unsure, one will look for a relationship that will help make one feel more secure. It is also very likely that this sort of individual will find someone who needs to support another and make them feel good as a way of feeling good about their own self. For example, if you ask a couple how they found each other; what about the other was so attractive; the responses can be quite interesting. I remember one husband saying to me that he was attracted to his wife because she always made him feel good. She laughed at his jokes and made him feel wise, witty and competent. Turning to the wife, I asked her what she found in her husband when she met him. She reported that he really seemed to need her, that he made her feel good, secure and wanted. Later on in the marriage, they both discovered that they were not able to give freely to each other. The husband wanted his wife to continue boosting him up and making him feel good and the wife felt disappointed that her husband wasn't more secure and competent, that he continued to pressure her to carry the show, so to speak.

Relationships most often solidify when a couple discover they can fulfill each other's needs and emotional expectations. However, these needs and expectations change as the relationship progresses and usually one person changes more quickly than the other. When this occurs, the relationship begins to suffer because one or the other feels they didn't get the partner they thought they had. Changing needs and expectations are actually moves toward differentiation. Unequal rates of differentiation development within a relationship often cause a crisis. The one who resists personal differentiation will attempt to undermine or sabotage the other's progress. It is important that a therapist recognize this process because it is often at the root of a couple's decision to enter therapy.

If the therapist perceives this sort of situation, he can work with the individual who is making differentiation moves. This person will in most cases talk about wanting things to be different for self but will also display a degree of support to the other who is finding these moves threatening to the relationship. Differentiation moves within either individual affect both people in a relationship and therefore it makes sense to work with the husband and wife together.

If the therapist becomes involved with one member of the relationship and that person is working on self, there is a good likelihood that the relationship will end unless the other one makes corresponding moves. In my experience, when only one member is actively working on differentiation he or she may leave the relationship and become involved in other relationships at a higher emotional level. The member of the couple who remains more or less emotionally untouched except for a state of anxiety, will get involved with someone who is at the same level of differentiation. This change is related to the concept of *the emotional triangle.*

Emotional triangle

Bowen (1966) gives the clearest definition of how triangles operate:

> The basic building block of any emotional system is the triangle. When emotional tension in a two-person system exceeds a certain level, it triangles a third person, permitting the tension to shift about within the triangle. Any two in the original triangle can add a new triangle. An emotional system is composed of a series of interlocking triangles. The emotional tension system can shift to any of the old pre-established circuits. It is a clinical fact that the original two-person system will resolve itself automatically when contained within three-person systems, when one of them remains emotionally detached.*

When we talk about differentiation, we also need to include the concept of emotional triangle. The more undifferentiated or

---

*Dr. Bowen's writings have strongly influenced my thinking about the emotional workings of family systems. I would like to acknowledge his original contribution to the development of the following family therapy concepts: Differentiation of self, Emotional triangle, Thinking over feelings, Overfunction/underfunction reciprocity, Multigenerational perspective, and Unfinished business.

emotionally fused people are with each other, the more likely they are to operate in emotional triangles. One way for an individual to avoid working on self or looking at his own part within a relationship is by triangulation. Triangulation provides the opportunity to stabilize one's own emotional feelings about other through talking to a third person. The more anxiety there is in a dyadic relationship, the more likely one or both will move out of the relationship by involving himself or herself with another individual in order to reduce the tension level. The individual could be a therapist, friend, or family member.

The more fused the relationship, the more important it is for the individuals to maintain the relationship for their emotional survival. If one is holding onto a relationship for emotional survival, then the best way of reducing the anxiety is to avoid talking about the relationship or focussing on anything that might throw the relationship into question. In other words, one can triangle not only by moving out of the relationship to talk about it with someone else, but one can also triangle within the relationship by talking about anything but the relationship. In this case discussions about politics, religion, what is on TV or other people's problems are ways to avoid dealing with what is going on with self, other, and the relationship.

It is important to realize that triangles serve as a stabilizing influence by helping to keep the status quo in a relationship. They are a way of maintaining calm. The higher the anxiety, the more likelihood that people will talk in triangles; the lower the anxiety, the safer it is to talk about self. Awareness of triangles is critical in clinical work. Chapter 4 contains a discussion of how triangles can affect one's clinical judgment. Chapter 6 discusses the strategic use of emotional triangles to initiate change in family systems.

Thinking and feeling

One of the primary goals of family work is to help family members become more objective about what is going on around them. Individuals become too subjective to understand the events in their lives when they are emotionally involved with or take excessive responsibility for what is transpiring within the family. They therefore need an objective look at their situation. Therapeutic assistance is valuable in helping a family member see how his feeling is affecting his thinking. When feelings take over, a significant degree of distortion and fantasy occurs. To gain a better understanding of how this distortion and fantasy operates the following experiment might be tried with your own family: Ask family members to recall an event which was important to you. This event can be a positive or negative one as long as several family members were involved in one way or another. Have each family member write their memories of the event on a piece of paper and compare the reports. The perceptions of what had occurred will be significantly different. Some feel the event was positive, others may think it was unpleasant, and some may not even remember the event. Your perception of how family members feel may be very different from their actual reactions. You may discover that you don't know your family as well as you believed you did. The more conflictual a family, the more likelihood for distortions, misconceptions, and false assumptions to develop about family members. The more emotional the family, the more the feelings take over to color events in a personal perspective.

The more fused people are with each other, the more their feelings predominate. When anxiety is high and feelings are controlling thinking, a message sent is often not the message received. When a person is experiencing such a high state of anxiety that he feels frightened for his very emotional survival, he is incapable of hearing what is being said without coloring it to suit his feelings. As an individual gains better control of self and feels more confident, his thinking or logical processes will come more into play. It is also important to realize that people who intellectualize their feelings, and appear to deny them, are probably in truth overfeeling. The more frightened one is of feelings getting out of control, the more likely one is to keep those feelings under wraps. However this is a situation of feelings controlling self, rather than the other way around. On the other hand, when a person feels able to handle his own feelings, he will be freer to feel any way he chooses.

Overfunction/underfunction reciprocity

Relationships have to balance themselves in one way or another. The more differentiated and competent people are in relationships, the less they will need to have people around them to provide emotional support. However, in fused relationships which operate primarily in emotional triangles, an overfunction/underfunction reciprocity is set into motion. In other words, one member is usually perceived as more adequate than the other in a fused relationship. The adequacy of one member is balanced by the inadequacy of the other member. This concept is especially important because many mental health specialists work only or mainly with the family member who is defined as inadequate. When one gets involved with the more inadequate or underfunctioning member of a family and doesn't realize how that underfunctioning is sustained by another person's overfunctioning there is a limited possibility for change in the system. If a practitioner intends to work with an individual, rather than the family unit, he would be well advised to work with the overfunctioner in the family. This person is invariably more anxious and has more difficulties giving up the overfunctioning role than the underfunctioner would in becoming more productive. Typically, the overfunctioner overfunctions at about the same rate that the underfunctioner underfunctions. In order for the underfunctioner to begin functioning better, the overfunctioner has to give up some of the functioning. In many cases, the overfunctioner tries to do this but at the first sign that the underfunctioner is not going to function any better, the overfunctioner, who is the more anxious one, will begin to overfunction again.

It follows that in all families where there is a dysfunctional member, there is also a more functional member or members. These more functional members are locked into the underfunctioner to the extent that he has very little operating room to function better. Timing—when and how things should be done in a family—is an important dynamic in this overadequate/underadequate process. Family members can have different time frames for certain activities, decisions, or behaviors. When time frames are significantly different, one individual begins to be seen as lazier and less thoughtful than another.

Taking a multigenerational perspective

Nuclear families, both structurally and functionally, reflect many aspects of the adults' own families of origin. In order to understand the value stances, role distribution, and general attitudes family members have toward each other, at least a three-generational perspective is necessary. Figure 4 illustrates a three-generational perspective.

The experiences people have in their family of origin affect their expectations for their own children and determine how they will structure the sibling roles of these children. The family of origin has provided the individual with memories about a certain kind of relationship with his siblings and a certain role according to his sibling position within that family. As a parent, this person will either duplicate the structure he experienced as a child or will try to improve upon it in his own family. To understand how a family has organized itself structurally it is necessary to understand how the members deal with the various sibling positions in the family, for example, the role the oldest in the family plays in comparison to the youngest, and how the children fit into the family, etc.

By going back at least three generations, the therapist can gain a better sense of why certain problems are emerging in the family of procreation. The more problems that existed in the family of origin, the more likely there will be unfinished business being conducted in the family of procreation. Of course this depends on which members of the family of origin were central to the difficulties of that family. When there is one child who is in the central position of concern in the family of origin, the other

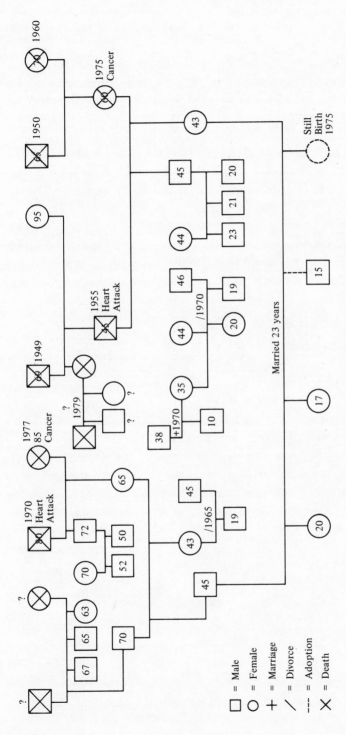

Figure 4: Example of a Multigenerational Geneogram

□ = Male
○ = Female
+ = Marriage
/ = Divorce
--- = Adoption
X = Death

77

children are not as emotionally involved and may be able to develop with minimal stress. By taking a three-generational reading, the therapist can discover who was of central concern in the family of origin.

A three-generational perspective also provides the family therapist with a better sense of the emotional level at which the parents operate in their families and helps him understand why certain problems are of concern to various members of the family. It is not uncommon to find that the father and mother have quite different concerns regarding family behavior. Many of these concerns are not based on what is going on in the present family but rather flow from concerns about their families of origin. It is therefore of the utmost importance to understand how the parents' families were structured.

Unfinished business

Unfinished business refers to emotional dilemmas an individual has not been able to resolve with significant others. The individual who has not been able to achieve a clear sense of his selfhood will be likely to search for other relationships that will help him to settle questions about himself. Unfinished business is related to the concept of differentiation, because the individual who is looking for relationships that will help him settle his unfinished business will be most attracted to someone at the same level of differentiation. The greater the unfinished business the more reactive the relationship will be. These individuals often have stormy, conflictual and unsatisfying relationships.

Carl Whitaker makes a strong case for helping adolescents work through the unfinished business they have with their families so they can be freed from fighting these battles in other relationships.

> If an adolescent leaves his family in a self-induced puberty ceremony of rebellion, if he breaks with the family without some group resolution of the problem of the symbiosis among them, if

he leaves without joining in overt family efforts to resolve his desertion—rather than by a therapeutic effort to relieve the individual in group stress—he is stuck with guilt and not free to investigate a new and creative life. He may then be compelled to reconstruct the old family, to work out that senior year in that graduating ceremony at work, at play, or in his marriage. [1975, p. 210]

A case example which illustrates how unfinished business affects perception follows:

Mrs. A, a 34-year-old woman, sought help because of severe difficulties with her husband. For the last several years in their marriage there had been constant bickering and fighting. According to Mrs. A, her husband had threatened suicide several times. Both partners had had affairs early in their marriage. They had four children ranging in age from nineteen to nine. I requested that Mrs. A bring her husband to the session. During the session there was much conflict and misunderstanding and a general lack of trust, all of which seemed to have been present in this relationship almost from the beginning. I decided to begin by asking about the family of origin rather than focusing on the present relationship problems.

Mrs. A said that her father was an uncommunicative type of person who never really cared for her and treated her mother very badly. Since the age of 15, she had very little use for him.

Mrs. A's mother had died of cancer when Mrs. A turned 16. As she talked about the experience of the loss of her mother, Mrs. A became very agitated and upset. During the six months her mother was terminally ill, Mrs. A discovered that her father was having an affair. Mrs. A was distraught when she made this discovery and began to act out. When her father discovered her behavior he became very angry and severely punished her. This enraged Mrs. A who felt that her father showed little compassion and understanding for what she was going through and punished her for what she thought was the same sort of thing he was doing.

After her mother died, Mrs. A cut off her relationship with her father. Throughout the years she had very little contact with him.

When they did communicate it was about inconsequential subjects. To demonstrate how uncommunicative her father was, Mrs.
A showed me a letter he had recently sent her. It was a one-page
letter about the care of her teeth. Mrs. A laughed when she
showed it to me, saying her father was not even a dentist.

When I inquired about the possibility of Mrs. A contacting her
father to try to talk to him about the difficult period surrounding
her mother's death, she became very upset and said it wasn't
possible; she was sure her father would never talk to her about
that. After several sessions of coaching, Mrs. A decided to write
her father and ask him about that period of time even though she
was sure he wouldn't answer. Several weeks after writing the letter
to her father, Mrs. A came in with a smile and reported that her
father had responded. She produced a five-page letter as
evidence.

In his letter the father explained that he was surprised that his
daughter had not understood the circumstances surrounding his
behavior at the time of her mother's illness. He said that he and
his wife had spent a great deal of time talking about the impact of
her terminal cancer on the family. He revealed that his wife had
insisted that he begin to go out with other women to help him
overcome the eventual loss. He said that they talked a good deal
about this and it was her wish. Mrs. A's father also said that when
he discovered that she was acting out, he had become very
despondent about what he feared was happening to the family,
and the punishment was his attempt to make things right again.
He said that until he received her letter, he was not aware of how
things were misunderstood.

This experience gave Mrs. A a new perception of her father. For
years she had held a grudge against him which had affected her
perception of all men. She had seen her father as insensitive and
uncaring, and felt that all men were basically the same, including
her husband. After this initial breakthrough, Mrs. A decided to
visit her father to try to get to know him better.

This example illustrates how resentment about early relationships, in which there was a significant loss at an important developmental period, creates unfinished business that spills over into present relationships. When Mrs. A allowed herself to perceive her father in a more positive light, and realized that her mother wasn't victimized, she was able to develop a different perception of members of her own family and of herself, which helped free her to perceive her relationships differently. Reconnecting with her father helped her diffuse the conflictual husband-wife relationship, and allowed her to reposition herself with both her husband and her children.

The concepts presented in this chapter add to a systems perspective for understanding how families organize themselves and behave emotionally. It is not the absence or presence of any one of these emotional processes which creates family problems. Rather, it is the degree to which these processes are used by the family to deal with conflict, relationship problems, and developmental crises that will determine the impact they have on family relationships. The therapist should be aware of how these processes affect a family and utilize the dynamics in a productive way to help the family move to higher levels of functioning.

In the following chapter the major interconnecting systems affecting therapeutic practice are presented.

4

THE MAJOR SYSTEMS AFFECTING FAMILY THERAPY

INTRODUCTION

The successful practice of family therapy requires that the practitioner have his personal and professional families in balance. Understanding other people's families without taking sides, forming alliances, or becoming overly involved in content is easier if one's personal family is in order. If a clinician has much unfinished business regarding his family of origin he should strive to be aware that this can influence his views of other families and affect his use of himself in practice.

A family practitioner should also have his professional family in order. There are two aspects to the professional family, namely, the immediate professional family and the larger professional family in the community. The immediate professional family is comprised of the colleagues the family therapist works with on a day-to-day basis. If the practitioner is working in a social agency, all the professionals in that agency belong to his immediate professional family. For the practitioner in private practice, consultants, supervisors, and the colleagues with whom he confers constitute his professional family. The larger professional family is drawn from other professionals within the community. It consists of those other professionals a client family has or is consulting to deal with their problems.

In my clinical work and consultation, I have found that professional families, like families of origin, can interfere with the practitioner's working freely and objectively with the clinical family. The following discussion details the importance of each of these systems for family work. Figure 5 illustrates how these three systems overlap in one's practice.

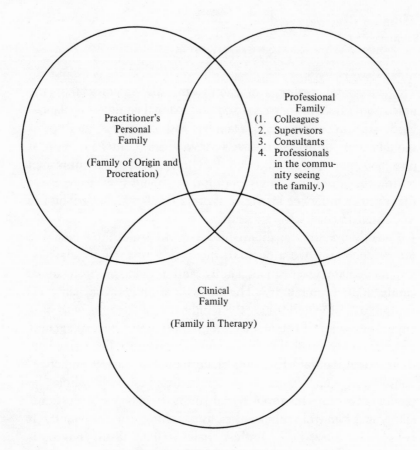

Practitioner's
Personal
Family

(Family of Origin and
Procreation)

Professional
Family
(1. Colleagues
2. Supervisors
3. Consultants
4. Professionals
   in the commu-
   nity seeing
   the family.)

Clinical
Family

(Family in Therapy)

Figure 5: Major Overlapping Systems Affecting
Clinical Practice

THE PRACTITIONER'S PERSONAL FAMILY

Everyone comes out of a family. When working with families, we are guided by our own definitions and understanding of how families should function as well as with the clinical family's definitions and expectations. Almost everyone believes he or she is an expert on how families should look and behave. This frame of reference helps us communicate with others about the concept of family; however, it also serves as a blinder. Many people come out of their families of origin with strong feelings about what to avoid and seek in family relationships. If these feelings and expectations are not under control, we are likely to attempt to mould other people's families either to resemble or be quite different from our own—a serious trap in either event. Family therapists should not superimpose their own expectations onto other people's families. By identifying with one or more family members as the healthy ones and viewing others as the dysfunctional ones, therapists bring their own unfinished business into the clinical situation.

Unfinished business consists of experiences from our most significant past emotional relationships which we have not yet finished working through. It is a form of projection, a way of trying to resolve difficulties in relationships that are important to us but that for some reason have been unresolvable at the source. These unresolved feelings are carried into our current relationships. People who have left their families of origin reactively, feeling a need to put a continent or an ocean between them and their families, have a fair amount of unfinished business influencing how they experience present relationships. People who have evolved from their families of origin as the overfunctioners, i.e., the ones who took responsibility for their families, will tend to overfunction in their current relationships. This of course has many implications for practice.

Clinicians who were overfunctioners in their own families often feel comfortable taking responsibility for the functioning of their clients. This can create a major problem in family therapy. One of the major goals in family work is to encourage the family to be its own expert. The therapist's job is to allow family members to help each other become more adequate, resourceful individuals. The more the therapist overfunctions, the less likely it is that the family will develop its internal resources. The therapist who becomes anxious and feels he must act to save the family could be interfering with the family's natural way of discovering its potential for change during a family crisis.

The family therapist may also be influenced by common myths about how families organize structurally and function behaviorally. The following list contains several such myths (Freeman 1976c, pp. 735–747). Belief in these myths prevents the therapists from moving naturally with the family and helping it recognize its internal resources.

Myth one: family structure is nuclear rather than extended

This myth is one of the more important ones. How we define the structure of the family is significant because it influences whom we see as being important to the family and whom we include in family treatment. For many years now, North Americans have viewed the family as a two-generational unit. The work of Parsons and Bales (1955) has strongly influenced this view. Their studies indicate that in an advanced industrial society, the most viable and flexible family system is the nuclear one. They describe the nuclear family system as a family made up of parents and children who do not have strong ties to extended kin and can at a moment's notice move where the labor market demands new labor. Since this initial work, many articles have appeared stating that the extended family is dead and that the nuclear family is the major family structure in North America. We have gone so far in this direction that family units that have close and significant ties with their extended families have begun to seem more dysfunctional and inappropriate in today's world than those families that have cut their ties with the extended family.

One clinical outcome of this myth is that we tend to look outside the family system to find resources rather than exploring extended family relationships that might be able to provide emotional, social, and economic resources to the client family. This position is analogous to the intrapsychic position for understanding the individual's behavior. For example, in working with an individual who does not have significant resources within himself to deal with his difficulties, we find it very difficult to move outside of the individual framework to rally resources that are natural to him, i.e., parents, brothers, sisters. When our framework moved from intrapsychic to intrafamilial, we were then able to do this. However, we've stopped at the nuclear, intrafamilial unit and have not looked at resources for the family outside of this unit. If we were to discard the myth that the family structure is nuclear, then our treatment strategies, theoretical frameworks, and research designs would include the impact of the extended family on the nuclear family.

Three research studies have dealt with the issue of whether family structure is nuclear or extended. A major study was conducted at the Jewish Family Service of New York (Leichter and Mitchell 1967, p. 210). This study dealt with the issue of kinship values in casework interviews. The agency workers were mainly first and second generation Americans, whereas the clients were newly arrived Jewish immigrants from Eastern Europe. One finding was that many of the families who came in for service valued becoming more involved with their extended families. The families saw their relationships with their extended families as being more helpful and supportive than the agency workers did.

The second study that questions this myth was conducted by Howard Irving in the Toronto Family Service Agency (1972, pp. 62–79). His goal was to discover where young families turn when they need help. His findings were quite revealing. He discovered that young families turn to members of the extended family first, either a father or a mother, brother, sister, or some other relative in the family. Next they turn to neighbors and other extrafamiliar figures, i.e., social agencies. Irving's findings were consistent with Leichter's findings in showing that young families continue to see the extended family as very viable for providing help and support when they are experiencing difficulties.

A third study conducted in London by the National Society for the Prevention of Cruelty to Children (Moore 1974, p. 30) revealed that mothers-in-law play a significant role in their children's marital difficulties. Their study showed that extended family members are involved when nuclear families are in a state of crisis. The study implies that one's framework for conceptualizing and working with families should include an understanding of the impact and involvement of extended family kin on the nuclear family.

The question one has to ask is not whether the family in North America is nuclear or extended, but rather what roles various members within a family constellation play to facilitate and at times handicap how a particular family unit operates. If we have a very limited concept of family structure, i.e., two-generational families, we tend not to ask questions about extended family and consequently are not aware of the natural resources that are available to family units.

What is crucial about the extended family is not the physical proximity of the family members to one another, but rather the emotional impact that family members have on each other. The old notion of extended family had to do with people living under one roof. Just a few of the questions that might be asked to begin to get a sense of what role extended family members play in the operating of the nuclear family are as follows: (1) Who are the most important people in your life? (2) Who can get you upset the quickest? (3) Who do you turn to first for help? (4) Who in the family do you spend the most time talking about? (5) Who has had the most impact on your own development?

Myth two: families are closed systems

The notion that the family is a closed system rather than an open one seems to be part of our belief system. Having given questionnaires to students learning to become family therapists, I have found that the great majority think that the family is a closed system. Many of the early studies on family behavior were done on schizophrenogenic families. Studies by Bowen, Lidz, Jackson, and Weakland were all conducted on families that were experiencing very serious emotional problems (Lidz 1960, pp. 323–345). These families were operating under a high degree of anxiety. They appeared to be fending off change and closing themselves off from new inputs of information and knowledge. Very few studies have been done on families that are not experiencing undue or extreme anxiety. I believe it is risky to use studies on dysfunctional families to describe the processes that normal families experience.

General systems research has demonstrated that it is impossible for a living system to be closed, that, in fact, the very life of a system depends on its openness. The issue isn't whether a living system is open or closed. What matters is whether the system is open enough to allow sufficient information and data into its boundaries to facilitate continued growth and development over time. It is hard to imagine any system, particularly a family system, being closed. There are no firm boundaries around the family system. What makes one family system different from another is the arrangement of roles, norms, and values that it observes to get its own job done as a family. Each family has a unique arrangement of its parts to the whole. It has its own role distribution governing how spouses, parents, and children position themselves in relation to each other. The family has its own normative setup governing what is acceptable and unacceptable behavior within the family and in the outside world. And each family has values, a network of "oughts" and "shoulds" about intra- and extrafamilial behavior. The above factors determine a family's boundary.

This boundary is permeable to inputs of new information. It doesn't necessarily follow that all information gets into the family, since part of the norm, value, and role structures of the family might exclude some inputs. Nevertheless, some information does come in. Each member of the family is a provider of new information. How people provide new information tells us about the degree of boundary openness. The dichotomy between open and closed tends to obscure the major issue of how a family grows and develops over time. To discourage oneself from seeing the family as resistant to change over time one should address the following issues: (1) how anxiety affects the family's ability to process new information; (2) who in the family is responsible for bringing in, interpreting, and transmitting new information; (3) the family's codification system for making sense out of certain symbols; and (4) what type of information a particular family needs to continue to learn about itself and its environment.

One has only to work with anxious families to discover that when the anxiety lessens, the family's ability to experiment and learn about itself increases. A clinical example of this dynamic follows:

The M family came in because they were concerned about the behavior of Mrs. M. The family consisted of the mother, age 52, the father, age 55, and an only son, age 20. At the beginning of the session, the family was quite anxious, and the only subject they were able to talk about was their concern about the mother's behavior. Up to this point, the mother had been hospitalized off and on for over eight years. It was quite obvious that the family was tense, anxious, and unsure of the meaning of having all members present, when the problem was "obviously" the mother.

At first, the family did not want to learn about itself and seemed to fend off any new ideas. However, as the session proceeded and the family members began to become more comfortable with each other and me, they became more curious about what each member of the family was thinking rather than concentrating on trying to figure out what was wrong with the mother.

The goal of the session was to reduce anxiety in the family in order to give family members the freedom to begin to think about themselves and the family as a whole, rather than fending off change by focusing on the identified problem. The therapist took the position that the family had the potential to change and actually wanted to change even though initially the family seemed to be quite unified in fending off any new way of looking at the problem.

This theoretical position has implications for how the therapist positions himself in relation to the family. If the therapist takes the position that the family system is a closed system, he will tend to see himself as the one most responsible for opening up the family system and will tend to do things for the family to open up the system. On the other hand, if the therapist takes the position that the family naturally wants to change and is basically an open system, he will try to tap the resources for change within the family. As the level of anxiety decreases, the family will begin to make its own moves at its own rate.

Myth three: families resist change and try to maintain the status quo

This myth implies a homeostatic model of family stability. Most of the writing on family behavior tends to be influenced by the homeostatic model. On this model, families are reactive systems. They fend off change, and have few mechanisms to help them grow and change over time. It is unusual to find an article in family literature that discusses the proactive elements within a family. Proaction is different from reaction in that it

> is used to designate an action that is not initiated by the confronting external situation, but occurs spontaneously from within. An action of this sort is likely to be a part of a serial program, one that is guided by some directional force, which in turn, may be subsidiary to a more comprehensive aim. As a rule, proaction is not merely homeostatic . . . . If successful, a proaction may be said to be superstatic inasmuch as it results in the acquisition or production of something new. [Murray and Kluckhohn 1953, pp. 10–11]

Thinking of families as proactive significantly affects one's theoretical and therapeutic work. In 1970, Speer stressed the need for a theoretical framework to deal with family change over time. He stated that the concepts of positive feedback processes, morphogenesis, and variety are important for providing a more tenable conceptualization of the family system in our society today. The concept of change needs to be emphasized in our attempts to understand family behavior. Most of the literature deals with the family's attempts to maintain stability rather than recognizing that in a rapidly changing society, it is the families that can deal with change who can provide the best insights into the functional aspects of family behavior. According to Speer,

> we need new concepts of family growth, self-evolution and restructuring .... Families need to be constructively responsive to change, able to change with change, and capable of learning to learn to give up obsolescent constraints .... One of the challenges confronting parents today is teaching children to be able to cope with unthought of and, as a result, unprogrammable situational and environmental changes. [1970, p. 274]

Speer is making a case for a morphogenic model of family behavior. In other words, we have to begin to see deviation-amplifying processes as essential for family growth and development rather than viewing them as dysfunctional. A status quo model would see positive feedback and deviation-amplifying feedback processes as a disservice to family stability, whereas a morphogenic model would highlight and emphasize the growth producing and sustaining processes that develop out of deviation-amplifying processes. An example of this point of view is found in Selye (1974, p. 32), who makes a strong case for the functional or healthy aspects of stress. He takes the position that life without stress is death.

It is not stress itself that needs to be analyzed, but the degree of stress any particular system needs in order to thrive. Stress serves as a propeller moving a system into action. In the old homeostatic model, stress is seen as deviant, undesirable, something for the system to fend off. In a morphogenic systems model, stress is seen as an important variable for moving a system into action.

Myth four: the family is breaking up

This myth ties in with the previous one. If we have a homeostatic model, family change is seen as a disruption and evidence of breakdown. However, if we have an open system concept that also allows for change over time, we view what is happening to the family today as a response to what is going on in the larger society. The family is changing because the needs of society have changed. In the past, the family's functions were tied in with the socioeconomic structure. The family was relied upon to prepare its members to serve in the economic structure of the time. The family of today no longer has this function. Society has taken over, through various institutions, school, military, etc., the job of preparing its members for the job market. The primary role of the family today is to meet the emotional needs of its members. If we use a turn-of-the-century model of family stability to analyze today's family, the family would appear to be faltering. However, if we recognize that the family is serving a new function and people's options for meeting needs have changed, then we will see that our model of the family must also change.

The latest census statistics indicate that people are getting married and divorced at a higher rate than ever before. Statistics also indicate that people are remarrying at just as high a rate as they are divorcing. What is the meaning of these statistics? In the past, it was unfeasible for many people to divorce. Today, the process is much easier, and one can guess that in the future the process will be even easier. The result is that people are divorcing and remarrying more frequently. This may be the product of an increase in one's awareness about what is best for oneself. The feminist movement has also had an impact here, in its message that women have needs of their own, and a right to develop other ways of meeting those not being met in the traditional structure. The census statistics indicate that people continue to see marriage as a valid and useful institution for meeting their needs. However, how the family system should be organized in order to meet individual needs is another question. The high divorce rate could be an indication of efforts to reorient the family system to meet individual needs rather than economic needs.

The following provides an illustration of how individual needs conflict with family expectations.

The C family came in because of general dissatisfaction with what was happening within the family and concern over manic behavior in one of its members. As the sessions proceeded, the mother of this family told us that when she got married, her mother put tremendous pressure on her to have children. She recounted experiences of family get-togethers where her sisters and mother continually asked when she was going to have her first child. Eventually she became so uncomfortable being around family and friends that she decided to become pregnant. Looking back, she saw this decision as a reaction to the stresses and demands put on her by her environment. She felt she would not want to put these pressures on her own children and that she could well understand if her daughters chose not to have children.

Now, one might say that the above illustrates that married people are deciding not to have any children because the family is no longer a viable unit. On the other hand, one could interpret young people's decisions not to have children as stemming from their belief that there are other satisfactions in life they wish to pursue. Thus one can see that the decision is not necessarily an attack on the family unit as such.

Myth five: the most stable relationship is a two-party relationship

Most people assume that the most common relationship is the two-party relationship. Early research by Bowen (1966, p. 356) has indicated that the most stable relationship is the triad. This is an intriguing idea for practitioners. It suggests a useful change in how we view two-party relationships. If one can sit back and observe two people in interaction, one would soon see that two people tend to talk about a third. There tend to be two insiders and one outsider. The outsider serves as the stabilizing element for the two insiders. The triangle serves to stabilize relationships between groups as well as individuals. The triangle was defined in detail in chapter 3. We all have experienced being caught in triangles in our own family of origin. Unless we are aware of how it affects how we deal with emotional tension we may allow ourselves to become entangled in emotional triangles in our clinical work. The concept of the triangle helps us to change focus from the two-party system to the significant three-party systems.

In my own clinical work, I've seen the triangle operate dramatically between professional groups. This occurred frequently in my earlier work in psychiatric hospitals. The usual triangle would be between the medical doctor, the nurse, and the social worker. Initially the basic two-party system, the "in" group, might be the nurse and the doctor with the social worker being on the outside. Time spent together between the nurse and the doctor would include talking about the social worker on the ward. They would say things like, "We really don't need a social worker on the ward, he just gets in the way with his crazy ideas." The doctor might say, "The social worker is just mucking up what's going on in the ward treatment plan." Or the nurse might say to the doctor, "The social worker tends to get overinvolved or underinvolved with the patients." In any case, the two have stabilized their relationship by having a scapegoat, the social worker. This can work out quite well until one or the other feels so much tension between them that talking about the social worker no longer serves to reduce it. When this happens, one or the other will make a move to the social worker. The nurse might move to the social worker who, being on the outside, is waiting for an opportunity to get on the inside. She will say something negative about the doctor, at which point the social worker will be more than willing to become involved. This places the nurse and the social worker in the "in" position and the doctor in the "out" position. Now this could go on for a period of time until the nurse and the social worker experience so much tension in their relationship that talking about the doctor does not stabilize it.

Then one or the other will make a move to the doctor. In this case, it might be the social worker. He might say something negative about the nurse. The doctor, being on the outside and not wanting to stay there, would agree with the statement. Now the social worker and the doctor talk about the nurse.

The basic difficulty in operating in triangles is that people talk about each other not about what is happening within the dyadic relationship. This helps stabilize the relationship but no new learning occurs. If one has ever been caught in a triangle, and we all have, one can remember feeling one's tension being reduced but not really learning anything new about oneself or the other or improving the relationship. Family systems contain the most intense triangles.

Jay Haley, in his collection of essays, *The Power Tactics of Jesus Christ* (1969, pp. 119–146), provides an example of how a schizophrenic child, who is expert in setting up and negotiating triangles in his home, begins to set up the same sort of situations on the ward when he is hospitalized. Triangles set up within the family are acted out in similar ways in other systems in which the family members are involved. By keeping the triangle concept in mind, one can begin to intervene in triangles as a way of changing family systems.

Myth six: it is possible to figure out the facts behind personal relationships—who is right and who is wrong

This is a myth that many family members cherish. When there is conflict within the family, family members try to figure out who is right and who is wrong. The harder they try to prove rightness and wrongness, the more the conflict accelerates. Very few people have been trained to become aware of process. One way to understand the use of conflict or the attempt to prove right and wrong is to see it as a way of defining process and seeing how people position themselves in relation to each other.

One of the most helpful procedures for working with families in therapy is to stay tuned in to the process and not get caught up in the content that people present. Families often come in with a story and try to get the therapist to figure out who is right and who is wrong, or to get the therapist to take sides. If you've ever tried to figure out a story, you begin to realize that it is an impossibility. If someone *can* convince you that his picture of the story is correct, then you have entered the triangle, and in fact everyone in the family, including yourself, becomes the loser. In looking at the process, the therapist should be tuning in to how individual members within the family use conflict as a way of keeping emotional distance. There are two main types of conflict. Nonproductive conflict keeps relationships pretty much the way they are. There is also functional conflict, which involves the renegotiation and reorganization of relationships. When one family member begins to make a move or change something that is important to him, other members of the family can become uncomfortable, and conflict occurs. In dealing with such conflict, one has to become aware of the processes that are going on within the family. Which member of the family is most comfortable with change? How is he positioning himself in the family to deal with that change? What are the other family members doing in response to that change? The issues (content) are not as important as how they are dealt with (process).

A story that highlights the issue of content over process tells of a famous rabbi in Russia who was well known for his astuteness and ability to resolve marital conflicts. A couple was having serious marital conflicts and decided to see the rabbi. The went to Kiev, where the rabbi lived. When they entered the rabbi's office, they found him there with his rabbinic student. The rabbi asked the husband what brought him in to see him, and the husband began to tell him all the things that were so terrible about his wife. When he finished the rabbi said, "You're right." Then the rabbi asked the wife what brought her in to see him, and she proceeded to tell the rabbi all the terrible things that the husband was doing, and when she finished the rabbi said, "You're right." At this point the rabbinic student was very confused and said, "But rabbi, how can the husband be right on the one hand and the wife right on the other hand?" The rabbi thought for a moment, stroked his beard and said, "You know something, you're right too."

Myth seven: you can learn about someone through the eyes of another

Many of us learn about other people not through direct contact with them, but by talking to someone else about them. Most of us who have done individual work can appreciate this problem. One member of the family comes in to tell us about the problems or the difficulties he or she is having with other members of the family. Many times we never get to see those other members of the family and begin to make assumptions and assessments about the whole family through the eyes of one member of the family. If we are fortunate enough to see the rest of the family or to see the individual who was talked about, we discover quite quickly that the person is nothing like the way he or she was described. In fact, it becomes even more complicated than that. When we see two individuals together, each seems different from when we saw him or her alone. When we bring the whole family together, all those individuals seem different from when we saw them in dyads.

In order to understand people, we have to see them in the context in which their behavior occurs. Each of us has a vested interest in seeing other people in a certain way. When someone describes someone else to us, is he really describing that person, or is he speaking from his need to see that particular person in a particular way? If we discard the myth that we can learn about someone else through the eyes of another, then we will begin to ask questions that encourage defining what is going on in the self rather than spending time talking about others. This helps us to work with individuals in terms of self-development. It cuts down on clients' using the time to ventilate about others, which makes it more difficult to learn about themselves. This myth relates to how the triangle operates. If a person comes in to describe someone else and we become party to that, then the two of us are "insiders" against the other, no matter how neutral we try to be.

Many members of nuclear families feel they know members of the extended family quite well, but after checking out whether what they feel is accurate, find out it is not. The legends or myths that we have about our extended family members serve as barriers that prevent us from learning about changes that have taken place in our extended family or discovering new resources that might be available. The following case example provides an illustration.

Mr. and Mrs. P both had older siblings who were considered black sheep, and their children, in turn, didn't want to have anything to do with their black sheep uncle and aunt. The 18-year-old identified patient (IP) of the family was considered very similar to the black sheep aunt and uncle. The more negative the parents were about their black sheep siblings, the more negative they were about their IP daughter. Consequently, the IP daughter was more negative about herself.

One of the things we worked with in this family was to get the parents and the children to reach out and do some research work on these two black sheep relatives. Our hunch was that family members would begin to see that the black sheep relatives were, in fact, not as bad or crazy as they thought, and in turn, would begin to see the IP daughter differently. As this occurred, the IP daughter would also change her picture of herself. In fact, this did occur and helped reduce the emotional intensity and distortions that were being acted out between the IP and the nuclear parents.

Myth eight: one family member is the "sick one"

It is hard to imagine a family where one member is hurting, and the other members are not experiencing hurt as well. The other side of this myth is that in order for one member of the family to be seen as dysfunctional, sick, or bad, other members of the family must be seen as functional, healthy, and good. Whenever a family member is seen as a problem, he or she is being compared to those "healthy" family members. In order for a family to have a serious problem, other members of the family have to be doing things to help maintain that behavior. Dysfunctional behavior can be seen as serving a certain role within the family. In order for that behavior or that role to be carried out, there have to be reciprocal processes occurring. One family that was defining its role structure told me that the identified problem was the warmonger in the family, while the father was seen as the mediator. It was an eye-opener to this family to discover that in order to have a warmonger, one had to have warriors, and to have a mediator, one had to have people who needed to be mediated.

Exploding this myth removes the focus from intrapsychic difficulties and places it on the network of social relationships that help to maintain or change a particular problem. Thus, we begin to look at the family as a system, rather than seeing an individual member as the sole carrier of a problem.

This approach makes it important to see behavior in terms of role structures, and to give the family an opportunity to define the reciprocal aspect of each role within the family. A way of assessing how other members of the family are involved in the dysfunctional behavior of a particular member is to ask the family members how much time they spend thinking, worrying, and talking about the particular problem. If a good deal of time is spent thinking, talking, and worrying about a particular problem, and by some magic that problem disappeared, a void would appear in the family. That void could become more of a problem than whatever brought the family in for help. Before a family can afford to give up a particular problem, something else, some other meaningful way of having the family use its time, must be found.

Myth nine: the "problem" member of the family is the one who needs help

This myth implies that when a family comes in with a defined problem, the center of attention should be the problem carrier. Bowen (1966, p. 351) has done some interesting work and writing about the role of the underfunctioner within the family. He takes the position that in order for someone to be an underfunctioner, someone must be an overfunctioner. In fact, many times the overfunctioner is more anxious and more of a problem than the underfunctioner. For example, you may see a family where there are complaints that one member of the family is not carrying his responsibilities. It might be as simple as parents saying that a child is not taking care of his room, that he leaves messes behind. If the complaining member is asked how long he can wait before he picks up after the child, he usually responds, "not very long." I had one father tell me that he was convinced that his son could never pick up his litter, so within a matter of seconds, he would pick up all the child's toys and clothes. When the child was asked why he wasn't taking better care of his possessions, he said, "Well, I know my father is going to do it, and he doesn't give me a chance to pick the stuff up myself." This is a simple example of how the overfunctioner dovetails with the underfunctioner to keep the underfunctioner underfunctioning.

One might consider working more with the overfunctioner or the "healthy members of the family" before one gets involved with the underfunctioner or the problems in the family. If the overfunctioner is the more anxious one, he will take over as a way of dealing with his own anxiety. Until that problem is dealt with, the underfunctioner is not going to be given enough room, opportunity, or time to experience new behaviors.

This myth has important implications for the health delivery system. Most of our services are designed to help the underfunctioners become better functioners without recognizing that there are other members within the family system or the community at large that are feeding into the underfunctioner role. At this point in my clinical work, I work much more with those members of the family who are not seen as the problem. I have found that when I am able to alleviate the anxiety of the overfunctioning family members, the others are able to begin to make moves forward.

PROFESSIONAL FAMILY

The professional family can be divided into two systems: the immediate or intraprofessional family, and the extraprofessional family. The difference between these two professional family systems is important. The intraprofessional colleagues one works with from day to day constitute an important resource. They serve as consultants to help the therapist become more objective in his work. The extraprofessional family, consisting of those professionals in the community who have been or may become involved with a client family, can interfere with effective family work unless efforts are directed toward involving them as a support system rather than antagonists.

It is generally agreed that family work is very difficult. It is a struggle to maintain objectivity and emotional distance from a family while at the same time remaining involved with the members. Family members tend to try to pull the therapist in one direction or another. Particularly during the early stages of family work, there is continual pressure to form alliances and triangles and to take positions. Consequently, it is difficult to practice good family work in isolation. It is helpful for practitioners to have colleagues with whom they can discuss their work and who will assist them in remaining objective. In addition, the use of videotape in family work can be helpful, not only in increasing effectiveness but also in aiding the therapist to recognize when he or she has become overinvolved in the family dynamics. The practitioner who has support from his colleagues will be likely to increase his creativity and competence in family work. However, the practitioner who works in a neutral or hostile environment will have to direct much of his energy into defending his practice or into maintaining an air of confidentiality about his activities. This stance would make it difficult for the practitioner to look objectively at his practice or to summon sufficient energy to maintain the emotional position with the family which it requires to progress in therapy. The energy required by a practitioner to defend his practice takes away from the energy required for quality family work. The point emphasized here is that family therapy requires a tremendous effort on the part of the therapist just to separate himself from what is occurring in the family.

The physical setup provided to the practitioner by the agency can be a source of support or, conversely, another hindrance to doing family work. Ideally, the interviewing room should be arranged to approximate a living room and should not contain a desk which separates the therapist from the family. The family members should be able to sit comfortably in a circle, and there should be a minimum of noise from the other offices. A well-equipped agency will also have videotape equipment available or a one-way mirror so colleagues can observe the therapy.

The second type of professional family is the external professional family. In my experience, it is unusual to have contact with a family that has not been seen by a number of other therapists. In fact, other professionals are often still involved with the family.

At the Vancouver child guidance center, a six-month study was conducted to discover how many therapists were involved with the clinic's families when they began treatment at the center. It was found that the average number was twelve, a staggering statistic. I suspect this figure is conservative. This phenomenon should stimulate the professional to ask about the impact all those services have on the family's view of itself and the energy the family expends in thinking about what it needs to do for itself, as compared to what others think needs to be done for the family. Since a clinician's personal unfinished business influences how he sees other families, it can be presumed that these other professionals will be responding in different ways to the family based on what they feel is in the family's best interests. It rarely occurs that all the other professionals see their contacts with the family as an opportunity to discover what the family wants for itself. If the family has to figure out what other people think is in their best interests and balance this with what they think is best for themselves they become confused and expend much energy arguing and talking about this with the professionals.

When a practitioner becomes involved with a family, part of his assessment process should be to find out who has been or is now involved with the family. The family's history with other professionals will strongly influence its expectations and fantasies about the new therapeutic encounter. Very few families or individuals who have had prior therapy are able to put aside those experiences to look at the new therapy in a fresh way. One of the most important tasks of the family therapist is to help the family acquire a sense of how this treatment experience is unlike previous ones. To accomplish this, the therapist must ask about who the family has seen in the past and enquire into the impact past therapies have had on the family's life. Families often refuse to enter therapy because they have had an earlier devastating experience. Strategies used to overcome these earlier negative experiences are discussed in chapter 5. The main point to be made here is that the way in which the family positions itself with the new therapist is strongly influenced by their previous experiences with other professionals.

The family that remains involved with other professionals can use this involvement as a means of distancing from the family therapy process in which the therapist is attempting to redefine the problem. As the family becomes more anxious about the family therapist's encouraging them to see their situation from another angle, they are more likely to move toward other practitioners who have essentially agreed with the family's definition of the problem. If the family therapist is not able to control this move, he may lose the family. The family is one of the hardest systems to keep in ongoing therapy. I believe one reason for this is that families seek out professionals they feel agree with their own definitions of the problem. One of the first tasks to accomplish with a family is the redefinition of the problem. Consequently, a knowledge of who the family is currently involved with in the professional community is vital if the family practitioner is to move beyond the first few sessions.

Several articles have been written which deal with the importance and difficulty of having some control over the involvement of other professionals with families. Auerswald's discussion of the interdisciplinary versus ecological approach provides an illustration of the competition between different therapeutic perspectives (1968, pp. 202–215). His article clearly illustrates the differences in approach between a systems therapist and a psychoanalytically oriented therapist working with a family in which there is a problem with an adolescent. An article by Hoffman and Long discusses the devastating effect of having a number of agencies and therapists involved in the life of a family (1969, pp. 211–234). Through a case study they illustrate how the various social service agencies and medical services dealing with the family's original problem created a bigger problem. When a systems therapist became involved, her first job was to try to remove the many agencies and professionals from the life of the family to enable them to get on with their own life.

The following interview illustrates how a family therapist can work with a family and the extraprofessional therapists who are currently involved in providing services to certain members of the family. This interview is presented in its entirety with commentary to point out how the family therapist attempted to integrate the goals and expectations of the family with the various positions taken by the other therapists. The interview will show how professionals take sides with various members of the family. Alliances and coalitions are formed with one or more members of the family. As these occur in the interview I will point them out and discuss how they can interfere with the family therapist's attempts to help the family use its own internal resources to work on its concerns.

The family being interviewed was referred to a university psychiatric hospital for assessment and possible hospitalization of the oldest son who was acting out in the home. There were five children in the family, namely, a son, age 17, two teenage daughters, ages 16 and 15, and two young children, a son age 7, and a daughter, age 5. The parents had been divorced for approximately two years and the father had remarried about six months prior to this interview. Prior to the divorce this family's home had been used as a therapeutic group home by the child welfare agency. Over the last ten years the family had had a number of professionals involved in its life. When it provided a therapeutic group home, several social workers and psychologists were involved in helping the family, particularly the mother, develop a therapeutic atmosphere for emotionally disturbed children. When the parents divorced and the agency stopped using the home, the mother maintained much of her involvement with helpers, because of the difficulties she was experiencing with her family, especially with the firstborn son.

The above history was revealed during the assessment interview conducted by a student psychiatric nurse. Because of the long-term involvement of professionals with this family and the ongoing involvement of professionals around the difficulties with the 17-year-old son, it seemed advisable to invite all the important professionals to the second session to determine how to proceed with the family.

As was pointed out earlier in this chapter, it is important before family therapy is initiated for the family therapist to gain an idea of the extraprofessional involvements. If these involvements seem to be significant to the family, the therapist should work with those other professionals so that they are supportive and in agreement with the family therapy process. The goal of this session was to develop a unified, consistent, and mutually supportive process with the other professionals. The reader will see that several of the extraprofessionals have taken sides with the mother in identifying all the difficulties of the family as resting with the oldest son. The job of the family therapist was to help the family develop a broader understanding about what was happening. An additional goal was to help the family recognize it has its own internal resources for working within its own system so that there would be a minimal need for continuing involvement of professionals in their life.

Interview with the C family and community therapists—foster mother, child support worker, psychologist and family friend, and school counselor

Student psychiatric nurse: I'll just go round, if that's okay, and just mention everybody's name. Mrs. R is a foster mother. Mr. G—

child support worker. Dr. A is a personal friend of the family and at one time the psychologist working with the family. Dr. Freeman is a family consultant who initiated this meeting. Mr. L is a school counselor from the school. Now I'll introduce the family. That's Steven, Sally, Tom, and Patty. What we'd like to do today and the reason we called you all together first of all, is to help us get a better understanding of the C family, and how we can give them some help. But we're really hoping that by the end of our first meeting, there will be—you will have a better idea of what all the help is that's available, and how to help the family decide how they want to use all these resource people that seem to be involved with the family. So that's what we're hoping is going to be the outcome. Dr. A mentioned that she has to leave about three-quarters of the way through. So if we're not finished by then she might have to get up and go. Okay? Are there any questions about what we're doing here? Okay. Dr. Freeman, do you want to begin?

Freeman: Well, maybe we should start with making sure we all know what's been happening. I watched one session last week so I've got a little bit of a sense of what you talked about. But my hunch is that each person has a slightly different sense of what's been happening with the family. Who wants to start that one off?

So far in the interview, the family and various therapists involved with the family have been introduced to each other, and a very general agenda for the session has been laid out. The family therapist now addresses the total group and asks a question to the professional family first. The family therapist has a choice whether to start the interview with the family itself or with the extraprofessional therapists. He elects to start with the extraprofessional family to get a sense of their perceptions of their involvement and how they define the concerns of the family. It also provides an opportunity for the therapist to check for alliances and coalitions that have formed between various members of the extraprofessional family and the client family. If there has been some side-taking or overidentification with one member of the family, it should very quickly become apparent as the members of the extraprofessional family share their perceptions.

It is important at this point for the family therapist to guard against scapegoating or overfocusing on one member of the family as the problem. He has to be able to monitor how much information he gets about individual members of the family and how much information he gets about how the extraprofessional members see their roles in relation to the family.

Mr. L (school counselor): I will if you want. Okay? I represent the school and I guess our first encounter was in August, was it, perhaps?

Mrs. C (mother): I talked with the principal before school started.

Mr. L: Ah, yes, about Tom's timetable coming into eleventh grade at the high school. We talked about this timetable and getting some of the things changed that he had set up with his timetable. So we set up a drama class for him, among other things, where perhaps he could get some more contact. And I guess, our further contact from there came when Tom started to have some problems in terms of keeping up with some of the work, in relating to some of the students in the school and so on. And since then our contact has been keeping track of his academic progress in school basically.

Freeman: Have you been involved with other members of the family as well?

Mr. L: No. Other than Mrs. C, the occasions on which we'd spoken on the phone, and then we had a meeting, I guess before Christmas.

Mrs. C: Yes.

Mr. L: Sally I know because she's also at school.

Freeman: There's no concern with Sally?

Mr. L: No.

Freeman: And the father?

Mr. L: No, this is the first time I've met him.

Freeman: This is the first time the two of you have met?

Mr. L: Yes.

Freeman: Well, how about some of the other people here?

Mr. G (child care worker): I've been working with them since August. And I've been involved with the family, within the family, at home during mealtimes, during activity times, that sort of thing. I've also been involved with the meetings with the school and that.

Freeman: The meetings? What sort of format does that take?

Mr. G: The meetings that Mr. L just talked about.

Freeman: So you've been involved actually with all the children.

Mr. G: Um hmm.

Freeman: So what do you see has been happening with the family?

Mr. G: Well, a lot of—everybody pitching in trying to pull the family back together again. From all members. From Tom also. Everybody else has helped out a lot too. Mother deserves very much credit.

Freeman: So things have been going pretty well from the way you see it.

Mr. G: Things have come a long way from when I first met them.

Freeman: How about a few of the others who have been involved with the family?

Dr. A (psychologist and family friend): Well, I'm in a curious position. I first met Mrs. C and the five children when there were three foster children as well in the home. It was a therapeutic group home, the best one I've ever seen. And at that point I was involved as a mental health psychologist because one of those children, who was a special care foster child, was referred to our center and my style then was to work with everybody in the family. And at that point the family comprised the children that you know, and these two children. So we met together as a family unit, and at that point I would say that the three oldest children who were most frequently in our conferences with two of the foster children and Mrs. C, were really working well together. There were the usual sorts of things that go on between brothers and sisters, but it was a really healthy unit. At that point Thomas was very helpful with this little boy, Pete. Pete was at that point I think about nine, wasn't he?

Mrs. C: Yes.

Dr. A: He was nine going on ten, and really Thomas, I think you were his hero. That was the time, remember, when you were reading C. S. Lewis books to Pete and I think Thomas was one of the people in the family who was helping to keep that boy pinned down to the ground instead of flying loose. That was about two years involvement, and a lot of things happened there. I think that—I seemed to feel that the family dynamics changed quite a lot and everybody—from my outsider's point of view, whether this is correct or not, it looked to me as if the kids started drifting apart from each other with the exception of the two little ones, and Sally and Patty always seemed to have been quite close. And I think that I watched Thomas periodically, from my outsider's point of view, drifting away from the close connection that there had been. And then, jumping a long time, I then moved away. For several months I was away in ——— and not in contact except in occasional crises. Then, I think, you (indicates Mr. G) became involved as a child support worker. I had by then renewed my acquaintance with Mrs. C on a more social and informal basis because I was no longer a therapist for the family. And we always sort of struck it off, hadn't we? I think we both enjoyed then becoming more friends, and since then I've become involved more as a friend. And that's been completely different. I wish I'd been able to be a friend before I was a therapist. I think I would have, I might have seen things differently. I don't know if you want me to go into my observations since I've become a friend.

Freeman: Well, how about with Mr. C?

Dr. A: Well, I just have met you (indicates Mr. C). We've just met, when was that, just before Christmas?

Mr. C: Before Christmas, yeah.

Dr. A: And that was over an instance where Mr. C was making a Christmas present to the children of skiing lessons. And coincidentally I just happened to be with the children's mother, and we had a financial arrangement to make because I happened to write the check. And so, that's how I met you, which is coincidentally, that you and I happened to be at the house at the same time.

Dr. A's role in the family is quite interesting. She makes it clear that she has moved from playing the therapist's role to becoming a personal friend of the mother. She also states that when she was involved with the family as a therapist she worked with the entire family. When the family therapist asks Dr. A if she had been involved with the father in the family, it becomes clear that she had not. This raises an important issue. Many extraprofessionals will state that they have worked with the entire family, but what that often means is mother and children or mother and problem child. Thus, it is necessary to ask specific questions about exactly who in the family has been involved with the extraprofessionals. As we go on in this interview we will see that the father has really been the outsider in this family for quite a while. The involvement of all the professionals with this family has been primarily with the mother.

It also becomes clear that Dr. A is a significant person in this family. The mother spends a fair amount of time consulting with her and values her opinion. Any change or new ideas that this family might develop will be screened and discussed in some way with Dr. A. Unless her role is clearly understood and she in some way becomes supportive of the family therapy process, it is likely that she could undermine any progress the family might make in redefining how it wants to work as a family.

Many times someone like Dr. A would not be involved with the family therapist and as a result the family therapist might not be aware of a possible reason for some resistance to doing things differently. As we go on in this interview, it will become clearer how aligned Dr. A is with the mother, and how much she has taken the position that the oldest son, Tom, is the real problem in the family.

Mr. C (father): I'm probably more of an outsider than anyone else to this current family setup.

Freeman: That makes both of us. Well, it must then be kind of interesting to you to see the different people in the family, people here involved with your family, I would imagine.

The family therapist aligns himself with the father momentarily as a show of support for the father who has been an outsider. As the interview progresses the family therapist encourages the father to become more active and involved with the family.

Mr. C: Well, I kind of feel suddenly transplanted in a fixed setting. Which is a little hard to adjust to and a bit hard to even participate, because I haven't really had any opportunity to do observations.

Freeman: Well, for you then, you actually haven't met some of these people. Like Mr. L.

Mr. C: No, I've only met Dr. A.

Freeman: And most of the information you'd get about members of the community being involved in your family, how would you find out about that?

Mr. C: I don't think I did.

Freeman: You don't think you did?

Mr. C: The only regular contact I had is with my two younger children, and I didn't feel it was right to use them as an information source at their age.

Freeman: And they didn't tell you anything about people who were coming into the family to help out in one way or another?

Mr. C: Not really, not really. The only thing they would sometimes mention is, like when I would take them out, is, Oh, that's Dr. A's car, or something like that. And the only other source and contact we had was the two months when Tom was staying with us in the summertime.

Freeman: And how much at that time would you learn about what was happening with the family? Would Tom fill you in?

Mr. C: No, not very much. I think we were mostly involved with our own problems at that time.

Freeman: Between the two of you?

Mr. C: Well, it would be the three of us. My wife and Tom and myself. And since the problems cropped up fairly early, that probably kept us occupied beyond the point where we could even look at the rest of the family setup.

Freeman: And if things were happening with your other children, that would not be something that you would be spending time on? Like with your daughter or the younger kids?

Mr. C: There's been a problem like where I mentioned I have had regular contact every two weeks with the two little ones.

Freeman: Right.

Mr. C: But I've had a great difficulty in working something out or seeing the big ones on a regular basis. Perhaps I was too busy with myself, putting my own life back on a straighter basis, and it could be that the big ones suffered from that. Although I'd have to say a lack of contacting is probably on both sides. Not that I want to attach blame to any side. It's just the reality, eh? And we have to face up to that.

Freeman: Your daughter wouldn't reach out and say, how come you're not spending more time with us? Did you get any of that?

Mr. C: Well, they wouldn't normally phone me or anything, unless maybe something happened that they would need me or— no regular or even periodic casual contact so to speak. But that's on my side as well as theirs. I find a great handicap the great distance between the two places. Like, we are about thirty miles apart and if I would go in the week and pick up say, Patty, or do something with her I have to spend three hours on the road to get her and bring her back and by that time, after coming home from work, it's just impossible. And every second weekend I have the little ones. And that leaves two weekends in the month. In the past I've felt quite strongly to devote some time to my new family now.

Freeman: And your new family would be?

Mr. C: Well, just myself and my new wife. But I felt a great necessity to straighten out my own life.

Freeman: So you have to find a way to balance these two demands.

Mr. C: I find it difficult. Yeah.

Freeman: When did you get remarried?

Mr. C: August last year.

Freeman: And your new wife's name is?

Mr. C: Maria.

Freeman: Do you have any children?

Mr. C: No.

Freeman: No children. So just the two of you. And you have an apartment, a home?

Mr. C: We just bought a home now. We rented a house before.

Freeman: So I'd imagine that one of the things you'd want to sort out would be how to balance these two things here.

Mr. C: Right.

Until the father was involved in the interview, the extraprofessional family identified Tom as the problem in the family. As the father shares his own understanding of what was happening in the family, it becomes clear that he has been an outsider for quite a while and was having difficulty balancing his commitment to his new wife with his commitment to his children. He points out that in the past he had been quite involved with his two younger children at the cost of being somewhat underinvolved with his three older children. He does not say the problem lies with his oldest son, but with how he can become more intimately involved with all members of his family.

So far the family therapist has monitored how much he has allowed the extraprofessionals to talk about Tom as a problem, and at the same time has tried to broaden the definition of the concerns with the family. The involvment of the father has helped in this. The family therapist now turns to the foster mother who has had Tom living with her for two months. Her personal life closely parallels that of the C family. It is noteworthy that she takes the position that it may be better for one parent to be less involved with the children when there is a divorce or separation.

Freeman: That might be something at least that we could spend some time on. Mrs. R, how about your part in the family?

Mrs. R (foster mother): Well, this is the first time I've met the children. I was there at the house one day, but just for a second. And I've had Tom now for just about two months.

Freeman: Two months?

Mrs. R: Um hmm. And I've had a lot of good . . . Tom and I worked things out and talked things over quite a bit. But I think Tom has gotten a lot better. In many ways I think he's improved. Once in a while he kind of slips back, but I think I see quite an improvement in him.

Freeman: How much of a family do you have?

Mrs. R: I have a large family, but at home I have one son.

The family therapist turned to the foster mother to see how much involvement she has with the total family. He finds out that she has only been involved with Tom. She states that she has had almost no contact with other members of the family. Her role then will obviously be to discuss what is happening with Tom. The family therapist, having begun to redefine some of the family concerns besides Tom, does not want to slip back to that focus. Thus, he changes the focus to find out more about the foster mother's background and how she understands family behavior in general. Without this change, the remaining part of the interview with her would be focused on Tom, and by the time she was finished speaking, the rest of the family would be refocused on their concerns about Tom. In contrast, the foster mother talks about the impact of divorce on family, which gives the family therapist a platform to involve other members of the family around how they have handled changes in the family, rather than around their concerns about the identified problem in the family.

Freeman: Some have grown up and left.

Mrs. R: Well, I had some foster children.

Freeman: Over how long a period?

Mrs. R: Well, since 1950.

Freeman: So you've been taking in foster children for twenty-nine years?

Mrs. R: Yes.

Freeman: Do they give trophies for thirty years? (Laughter)

Dr. A: Gold watches. (Laughter)

Freeman: They give you a gold coffee pot or something.

Mrs. R: That's right. No, we've had a lot of children, but a lot of our children go home. Derek is just fifteen. He's a foster child, I've had him since he was about two.

Freeman: Do you have any other children? Any natural children?

Mrs. R: Oh, yes.

Freeman: How many?

Mrs. R: I have three of my own and two adopted, and the rest are foster children.

Freeman: Three of your own, two adopted and then this large group of foster children.

Mrs. R: Don't ask me how many, because I really don't know— fifteen or twenty.

Freeman: How many living at home with you right now?

Mrs. R: Just the one.

Freeman: Tom and Derek and your husband.

Mrs. R: No, I'm divorced. Divorced in 1975. We separated in '74 and got divorced in '75.

Freeman: So from 1950 to 1974 you had your husband and your children. So this must be a new thing, your having a smaller . . .

Mrs. R: Yes, but it really wasn't that big an adjustment, though. The only adjustment was financially, actually.

Freeman: Now that you see all these people here, do you have any thoughts about what's going on?

Mrs. R: Oh yeah. Yes, I can see a lot of problems.

Freeman: Um hmm.

Mrs. R: And when you've gone through a divorce yourself I think you can see much easier than people who haven't gone through a divorce. And you have a child Tom's age. I think the divorce has had a lot to do with Tom's problems.

The foster mother now opens up the area of how divorce affects family relationships. Up until this time no one has mentioned the impact of the parents' separation and divorce on other members in the family. Since the foster mother has gone through this recently, she is especially aware of how difficult it is for the family once parents separate. Even though she minimizes the impact it has had on her, she still opens up an important area for the family therapist to explore with all members of the family.

Unless the family therapist gains a sense of some of the values and assumptions the other professionals have about family behavior and the interventive process, he will not be able to involve them as positive resources, and in fact may end up in competition with them. The family therapist encourages the foster mother to share her perceptions and her "wisdom" with the total group. He takes part of the wisdom to further help the family gain a better sense of what is happening to it and how it wants to use the various extraprofessional therapists.

Freeman: Do you think you could spend a few minutes, because you're in a unique position, sharing some of your thoughts, some of your concerns?

Mrs. R: Regarding Tom?

Freeman: And the family, and where you think things are going to go from this point on.

Mrs. R: Well, how would I say. Well, I think when there is a divorce it's really hard on a child unless you sit down and explain to them exactly what the situation is, which is really hard to do. But I think that Tom has locked himself into a closet so to speak, he doesn't want to hear. I think he was hurt.

Freeman: You mean by what happened between Mom and Dad?

Mrs. R: Yes. I think he's trying to be loyal to his father and loyal to his mother. And that's a hard situation for a child to be in. I'm sure a lot of people would disagree with me, but I think it's easier on a child if there's no contact with father or no contact with mother when the divorce goes through. I think until after the children are well adjusted to the mother or whichever one they're living with. I found that in my family. Everything was very hard to take. And if Derek had gone to see his father, I know it would have been very hard on me. And I think it would have been harder on him because he'd have been torn between the two of us. But luckily his dad didn't want to see him and he had no desire to see his father. So I had no problem with Derek. But I think Tom has got this problem and I think Tom resents me. He resents his mother, he resents his father. I think he resents everybody. He doesn't know who to blame, you know, I think Tom himself can pull himself out of this if he really wanted to.

Freeman: Any ideas as to what would be a good way of moving from this point on?

Mrs. R: Well, I think Tom needs a lot of love, but he also has to have an awful lot of discipline with that love, and you've got to have an awful lot of patience. To my own way of thinking he can make it, Tom can make it, but he's got to have help to make it.

Mrs. R has discussed now the negative impact she feels divorce has on the children. After she explains what has happened to her personally and discusses her own ideas about how divorce should be handled, she focuses back on Tom and talks about what he needs. The family therapist chooses to take her comments and observations about the impact of divorce on the family and use them to help the C family talk about how the various changes in their lives have affected the intrafamilial set of relationships.

At this point the family therapist has to choose which member of the family to start with. He decides to begin with one of the daughters and to get her reactions to what the foster mother said about the impact of divorce. The family therapist is taking the heat off of Tom by focusing on the changes that are occurring in the family system in general. It is important that the therapist not immediately turn to the identified problem after somebody in the group has talked about his problems. If he were to turn to the identified problem it is likely he would either not respond, or become very defensive. By turning to another member of the family, and asking a general question about how family change has affected the family, he effectively defuses the identified problem's role in the family.

Freeman: Sally? You're Sally, right?

Sally: Ah hah.

Freeman: You heard what Mrs. R said, about this difficulty of balancing being with your dad and being with your mom. She talked about Tom, but you also and your sister, and your other brother and sister are in the same sort of situation. What thoughts do you have about that?

Sally: Oh!

Freeman: It's a hard one?

Sally: I've sort of gotten used to it. You know, it doesn't bug me any more that much.

Freeman: At one time it bugged you more?

Sally: Oh yeah.

Freeman: Could you tell me a little about the time when it did bug you? What was the thing that bugged you?

Sally: Well, okay. At first it seemed like one of you (indicates her parents) was wrong and the other one was right.

Freeman: It seemed that way to you?

Sally: Yeah. And you don't know which is the bad one and which is the good one. After a while, you know, you figure it out. It's between them. It doesn't have anything to do with me.

Freeman: How did you manage to work that one through in your head, Sally?

Sally: Thought it over a lot. (Laughs)

Freeman: You thought about it a lot.

Sally: Yeah.

Freeman: Did you check it out with anybody?

Sally: No.

Freeman: You talk it through with Tom?

Sally: No, I don't think so.

Freeman: No? How come?

Sally: It never really occurred to me because before you talk to someone you've got to sort of be ready to talk to them. You know, it didn't seem like he wanted to talk about it.

Freeman: How about Patty? Did you talk it through with her?

Sally: No.

Freeman: How come?

Sally: About the same reason, I guess.

Freeman: You don't think she was quite as ready to talk about it.

Sally: Well, it just never occurred to me to talk about it.

Freeman: It never occurred to you.

Sally: No.

Freeman: Did either of them talk to you about what's happening with the family?

Sally: Not really.

Freeman: So you figured this one out, on your own with no help from anyone else.

Sally: I guess so.

Freeman: And you didn't share the benefit of that very interesting point of view with your sister or your brother. Patty, how about you? What do you think about what your sister is saying about what she saw as going on with the family over the last few years.

Patty: Well, I think it isn't really anybody's fault. I always thought of it as, you know, it isn't anybody's fault that the divorce happened or anything. It just kind of didn't work any more, so there just isn't anybody really that is to blame.

Freeman: Was there a time when you had more difficulty with that thinking or did you feel that right from the beginning?

Patty: Just in the first couple of months, but I never really thought . . . Like she says she thought somebody was the good one and somebody was the bad one. I always just thought of it, you know, I never really ever stopped to think of it like that. It just doesn't work that way anymore.

Freeman: So you become somewhat comfortable with there not being a good guy and a bad guy?

Patty: Yeah.

Freeman: Did you check that one out with Tom?

Patty: No, just like her, you know, I never thought to talk about it.

Freeman: Was there anyone you would talk about this with?

Patty: Not really.

Freeman: Now, Tom, how about you, what are your thoughts? You heard what Mrs. R said about her thoughts concerning your parents' divorce and the effect on your family. What do you think about that?

Tom: All of it can't be helped, because they didn't live together. And it's better to live apart than to live together like that.

Freeman: Did you think that right from the beginning, or is this something that developed, this thinking developed later?

Tom: I guess I thought that not right from the beginning, but I thought it later.

Freeman: Well, let's say at the beginning. How did you put together the fact that your Mom and Dad decided that they couldn't live together and were going to live apart?

Tom: How'd I put that together?

Freeman: Yeah. What sense did you make out of that one?

Tom: That it was bad.

Freeman: What about that did you feel was bad?

Tom: Well it wasn't exactly good either.

Freeman: What did it mean to you, though, personally, when your parents made that decision, that they were going to separate?

Tom: I didn't like it at first, but then I thought it would be better than if they were living together, that it would be even worse if they were still living together.

Freeman: How long had they been separated until the time you got that notion?

Tom: A month or two or something.

Freeman: A month or two. Did you check that one out with anybody? Did you talk to anybody?

Tom: No.

Freeman: No? How would you have liked . . .

Tom: I think I . . .

Freeman: Yeah?

Tom: I think I talked to my Mom about it.

Freeman: You checked it out.

Mrs. C: We have had a lot of talks about it, with the girls too, maybe they didn't verbalize it exactly in those words. But we have worked for the last two and a half years on the problem that when things like that happen, they have no need to attach blame. And we haven't really put it into those words, but, it sounds as if we never talked about it. We've talked about it a lot.

Dr. A: I was worried about that, too. I was sitting here listening to you talk about it and it sounds like a different family from the one I know.

Mr. G: Yeah. I agree with what you're saying, like I agree with that too. We never really talked about it outright . . .

Mrs. C: No, we haven't said those exact words. But we've always been careful not to blame anyone.

Mr. G: Not to blame. Yeah, right.

Dr. A: I want to check this out and see if you feel the same way. If there's one thing that I've noticed in this family both when I was a therapist and since I've been invited into the home, is that there's very open and frank discussion and I'm just having a really hard time. It sounds so intellectual, everything you're saying. And this family is not famous for staying on the intellectual level. There's a lot of emotional stuff, a lot of feelings I've seen expressed, and heard described and talked about around the whole issue. It almost sounds to me like it doesn't matter, this family breakup. You just put it aside, like what are we having for supper? We're having carrots and meat pie and that's it, no more discussion.

It's interesting that after each child talked about the impact of the divorce on him or her and stated that he or she came to the conclusion that neither parent was good or bad, the mother and the psychologist friend both become upset with the way the children were responding in the interview. The mother becomes somewhat defensive about what she sees as the children's lack of recognition about how she's helped them understand the impact of the divorce. Dr. A takes the position that the way the children are behaving in the interview is different from the way she observed them in the home. The family therapist finds it interesting that each of the teenage children is able to articulate how he or she perceives what has been happening to the family. However, it is also of interest that two of the adults in the session have a need to clarify how they perceive what is going on with the children. As we go on in the interview this process becomes more pronounced.

At this point the family therapist could lose control of the atmosphere he set if he allows the adults in the group to decide what it is permissible to talk about and how it is permissible to talk about important issues. Instead, he avoids picking up on what either the mother or Dr. A says, and continues to ask the teenage children questions.

Freeman: Tom, there's another question I wanted to ask you about what your dad said a minute ago, about spending more time with your two younger sibs—your younger brother and sister— and not with the older ones. What are your thoughts about how that worked out?

The family therapist makes this move and asks these question as a way of maintaining control of the interview and also to continue to broaden some of the concerns the family might deal with.

Tom: I didn't mind.
Freeman: Thinking back on it now, how would you have liked it to be if you could have turned that one around in any way?
Tom: It doesn't matter. I wouldn't have bothered to have turned it around.
Freeman: You wouldn't want to turn it around. Did you check that one out with your dad, how the decision was made?
Tom: No.
Freeman: No? Sally, how about you? The fact that your dad

said—remember you said that last week when I was listening to the interview, that he spent more time with the younger ones than with the older ones. What are your thoughts about that?

Sally: This is hard to explain. So. Okay, it's not so much not spending time, it's the...it's not physically being there. Even when he's there it's like he's not there.

Freeman: An example of that would be?

Sally: Okay, I've got a good example. When I think back on my life, right, I can never remember him being there. I can remember everyone else, but I can't remember him being there.

Freeman: Being there for you would be, what?

Sally: Sort of being with it, you know, knowing what's going on instead of just physically being there.

Freeman: Um hmm. How old are you, Sally?

Sally: Sixteen.

Freeman: In sixteen years, has there been any time you and Dad spent time alone together without other members of the family around? Could you remember, just the two of you?

Sally: I can't remember it, no.

Freeman: You can't remember the time . . . just the two of you going someplace together.

Sally: Oh yeah. I remember on my birthday, one time. On my birthday he took me out to dinner.

Freeman: Just the two of you?

Sally: That was nice.

Freeman: That was nice.

Sally: That was really a good time.

Freeman: How old were you?

Sally: Fifteen. Just turned fifteen.

Freeman: So it was your last birthday.

Sally: Birthday before last.

Freeman: Birthday before last, just the two of you went out to dinner.

Sally: Yeah.

Freeman: And that was nice. Patty, how about for you, the fact that your dad recently spent more time with your two younger sibs than with you? What are your thoughts about that?

Patty: Well, I feel quite comfortable with that. You know, that he spends more time because, he has a point, there is so much driving involved, so . . .

Freeman: Do you know how that decision was reached?

Patty: Which?

Freeman: That Dad spends more time with the younger ones than with the older ones.

Patty: No.

Freeman: Can you remember a time when you and Dad spent time alone together without other members of the family or . . .

Patty: No, I don't think so.

Freeman: You don't have a similar experience as Sally, where he took you out to dinner or somewhere, just the two of you? No?

Patty: I can't remember it.

Freeman: Tom, how about for you and Dad?

Tom: What?

Freeman: You and Dad doing something, just the two of you.

Tom: We went on a hike once.

Freeman: Where did you go?

Tom: I think it was called Lookout Mountain or something like that.

Freeman: How long was it?

Tom: How long?

Freeman: Overnight? Just a day?

Tom: Just a short walk, sort of a hike.

Freeman: Was it a day trip?

Tom: No, it wasn't very long.

Freeman: It wasn't even a day trip.

Tom: No.

Freeman: A half a day trip?

Tom: Yeah, about . . . well, altogether it was the whole day, but . . .

Freeman: How was it?

Tom: It was okay.

The family therapist has explored with the children what sort of relationship they would like to have with Dad. He took an earlier comment of the father about wanting to be more involved with the children and checked out with each one of the children what they would like. By asking questions, the family therapist has indirectly given some directives to the family. He has allowed the children to tell the family, especially the father, that they would like to have some more contact with him. Although the oldest girl in the family, Sally, was the most adamant about wanting to have more contact, the other two children, in their own quiet way, also indicated that would be a good idea. As we will see later on in the interview, the father begins to talk more about wanting to have some separate time with his older children away from the younger ones. This produces some conflict between the mother and father about how it should be done. The energy that the parents use in trying to figure out a way for the father to have more contact with the older children is greater than that they expend on any other issue discussed in the interview.

The family therapist has given everyone in the family an opportunity to talk about his or her perceptions with the exception of the mother, who has voluntarily participated at various points. He now turns to the mother and involves her in the interview directly. It is important not to wait too long to involve the member of the family who is most intimately involved with the family problems. During this part of the interview, the mother becomes eager to share her perceptions of what is going on in the family. Since the general discussion has concerned the impact of divorce and visitation decisions, the mother picks up on those issues rather than beginning with her oldest son.

Freeman: Well, Mom, I haven't spent much time talking to you. You've listened to everyone here talk. What thoughts are you having?

Mrs. C: I have a lot of thoughts. I think it has been an issue and the kids have been bitter, that they know that there is a formula in the separation agreement that their father should see them once a week. And I know that at the time the separation agreement was made, Mr. C was very eager to put this in and they were very glad. And I told them, you know, once a week you go out, and they were very happy about it, and it never came about. They haven't verbalized much about it. They have sort of, as you heard today, said, oh, well, it doesn't matter and it's better like this anyway and things like that. But there have been resentful comments, you know, on and off, put in. It was hard for me to talk about that with them because then I became the accuser of the other party. And it didn't really go into a big discussion but it has been there.

The mother immediately picks up on the importance of the father being involved with all the children in the family. She then talks about her other concerns about what is happening within the family, rather than focusing on the immediate concerns she is having with Tom.

Freeman: How would that sort of thing be affecting the family, would you think, now?

Mrs. C: I don't think it has damaged the relationship between the little kids and the big kids, which easily could have happened. I feel, though, that Thomas seems to have been displaced. I don't know whether I'm right. Now that's a guess I have, this has not been discussed with anyone. With the arrival of Steven. Thomas was ten years old at that time, and I had some difficulties after the delivery, and so often took care of the baby and grew quite close. In that year an awful lot of other things happened too, we had one foster girl leave who had been staying with us for two years. We started to build. One of the foster children went back right to day number one and became a baby himself, and it took a lot of my time and energy to look after that problem. And actually we had to come to an agreement that Thomas was more ... you know, that you (indicates Mr. C) were going to look after Thomas at that point. I think I remember that. That now it was the father's turn. But somehow events went like this: that Steven, the baby, became quite important and looking back I have the feeling that we never really paid much attention to Tom in that very important year. And from then on I remember that, staying with this relationship or with what happened, we started to build a house which took all of Mr. C's energy. He was very involved in it. Tom, who was ten or eleven years old, really tried to help, but Mr. C was so busy he didn't notice. Tom once went ahead and cut trees in a whole pasture full of trees that had been neglected. In other words, he desperately tried to be involved, help, but then maybe the project was too big or he was too little to be considered. And I have a feeling after a while he just gave up. From then on, by the way, our marriage . . . there were so many upheavals that somehow things fell apart. And when he was thirteen, I think, he left. So the marriage only lasted three more years.

Mrs. C, by being the last to talk in the group, has had an opportunity to reflect on what has happened within the family historically. It appears that she made some connections she had not made before. She describes Tom's behavior in the context of many changes that were going on within the family, such as marital problems, building a new home, trouble with foster children, underinvolvement of father with the children, etc. Looking back she reflects that Tom must have felt left out with the birth of the only other son in the family, at which time he had to move over to accommodate the second boy in the family. Not only did he lose his father and his mother-father relationship, but also his special place within the family. The family group has now moved from the beginning discussion with the extraprofessional therapists focusing on Tom to a discussion of the family as an historical unit that has undergone many changes. The therapist continues to support this broadened perception of what has occurred with the family. The mother goes on with a bit more detail about the impact of some of these changes on the family, and the therapist then turns to the children to see how they perceive these changes.

Mrs. C: That we first had all the troubles around that time. Also, remember right now, those were the first times that we had complaints from the school. Tom has always had very good report cards, but then he started having trouble cooperating. They started little physics projects, little science projects. And he was all right as long as he could do it on his own. But he had trouble cooperating. And we ran into a problem with the principal and I guess it was a rather rash decision, we took all the kids out and put them in a private school where we were hoping the principal who had Thomas's class would have a special eye on this problem, but he sort of forgot after a while and Thomas was permitted to do his own thing and started really moving away from other people and hid in books and wasn't seen much anymore.

The mother now mentions that Tom, with all the other changes that have occurred in his family environment, is also forced to change schools. The older children talk about how devastating this experience was for them, and how it increased their sense of social isolation from their peers, from their immediate family and from each other.

Freeman: Sally, you'd be the second oldest in the family, what do you remember about that period?

Sally: The people at the school were a bunch of loonies. (Laughter)

Freeman: Do you want Mr. L (school counsellor) to take that back? (Laughter) Go on.

Mr. L: I know the school and I agree with her.

Freeman: Could you give me an example so I know what you mean?

Mrs. C: Oh, you mean the Christian school?

Sally: Yeah.

Mrs. C: She means the private school that they went to.

Mr. L: Well, our school has it's share of loonies, too.

Mrs. C: Sally really very much resents our having made that decision, taking them out of the community school and into a parochial school.

Freeman: Is that correct, Sally?

Sally: Yeah.

Freeman: What about it did you resent?

Sally: Because it sort of took me away from reality because it was a sort of let-us-pray situation all the time. And it doesn't bother me, but all the time, you know, and . . . oh, the principle was wacky. I mean, he was smashed to the gills. And the first grade teacher, oh, she used to grab people by the cheeks and shake them. And they were all kind of strange. And all the kids there, they were all from this one church, and anybody that didn't go to that church was automatically out. You know, so that sort of just put all of us on our own. Because they were in this one big, oh, we go to this church, we're the best, you know.

Freeman: You were kind of an outsider in the school?

Sally: Also, 'cause they were Dutch. They thought they were the greatest.

Freeman: How about the friends and all you had in your other school? Was it difficult to maintain those relationships?

Sally: Sort of, because I only saw them at school, 'cause we lived way out in the sticks and it was about three-miles' walk to the next house.

Freeman: How did you understand the reasoning behind the decision to put you in the Christian school?

Sally: I thought it was religious reasons.

Freeman: That your parents wanted you to get more involved in religion.

Sally: Yeah.

Freeman: Tom, how did you react to this new school? What did it all mean to you?

Tom: I didn't really like it.

Freeman: As strong a reaction as Sally to the school?

Tom: No.

Freeman: What were the things about the school that you didn't like?

Tom: Oh, the same things Sally said.

Freeman: That you were an outsider?

Tom: Yeah.

Freeman: Did it take you away from a group of friends that you had before?

Tom: No.

Freeman: What was the major thing about the school that bugged you? The number one thing?

Tom: It was different from the other schools.

Freeman: Was there a certain difference that you didn't like?

Tom: Well, it's completely different.

Sally: I think the teachers were down on the students a lot too. They used to bang them around, you know, hit them, throw them against the blackboards, threaten them with all sorts of gross things.

Freeman: You say, Tom, everything was different. See, I never went to a school like that, so I have no framework to know what the differences are.

Tom: Well, like all their philosophies, you know.

Freeman: For instance, what?

Tom: Like it's, everything's for the Bible and that.

Freeman: What would happen if someone would question a philosophy of the school? Would that be encouraged?

Tom: That's different from other schools.

Freeman: From public school, you mean?

Tom: Yeah.

Freeman: But if someone questioned the philosophy, what would happen at the school, if you took issue with something?

Tom: Who questions it?

Freeman: No one questioned it? They all just accepted it? Is that true, Sally, too, that they just accepted what went on?

Sally: If you didn't accept it, you didn't say anything about it. Because they might smack you one or something. They did that a lot. That's the one thing I really didn't like, they felt they had the right to just hit anybody, you know, just when they felt like it.

Freeman: So there was no dialogue that went on between people, exchanging of ideas?

Sally: No, it was just . . . you go to school, you learn, you pray, and you go home. That type of thing. It wasn't . . . the teachers didn't see the students as people. They were just sort of objects.

Freeman: Would that be consistent with your experience with the school, Tom?

Tom: Yes.

Freeman: Were you in the same class, the two of you?

Sally: No.

Patty: I remember one thing that really bugged me. Actually, it didn't bug me till I was taken out of that school. At least twice a week, they'd always say, public schools are bad, they're evil, you know. Because of what they teach, because they don't teach the Bible or anything. Or because they teach the theories of evolution. And they were always, I remember, always . . . it was almost drilled through you, public schools are . . .

Sally: Wicked.

Patty: Yeah, wicked. That's the word. And this is the only right school that you can ever go to, you know. And one thing, as long as I was in the school I never realized what was going on. I thought it was really a good school, but when I came out I realized how much—like I didn't have any real friends there and I hardly ever got to see anybody or anything, and I realized how much I'd missed out, you know.

Sally: Coming out of the school and going into public school was really . . .

Patty: Yeah, it was almost like you'd been in a time warp. And I really had trouble adjusting and communicating with other people and making friends. It took quite a while to make some real friends.

Freeman: Did the three of you support each other? When you had this difficult time? Did you form kind of a team?

Sally: Not really, because another thing they did at the school was they sort of studied the grades, you know. All the good first graders stayed in one group, and all the really poor seventh graders stayed in the other group. People never stuck together except for the grade. It was all sort of groups. There didn't seem to be any real friends, really.

Freeman: Among the students.

Sally: No. At least not that I saw, because if there were any people who were put together, I don't think that they were really friends. I think they were just kind of like a gang.

Freeman: How about the three of you, what did you do? You would seem to be a natural unit, two sisters and a brother in the same school, not feeling a part of the school, kind of like an outsider. Did you join forces in any way? After school? Before school? During lunch?

Sally: After school we had to wait for a ride home for two hours.

Patty: (Laughs)

Sally: But that was about it.

Patty: I remember like with Marty, he and I always used to play with Marty, he was in my group.

Sally: Yeah, but you guys were in the same grade too.

Mrs. C: All these resentments were not there while they were going to the school. It was actually like having said, while they were there they felt quite all right, and the physical situation where we lived was so that you cannot have anybody over. And as the girls said, it was a very strict Dutch community who, we as parents did not know, looked down on Germans and were very— with a very cultural resentment which they brought over from years back. For instance, we found out later that Tom had been called Hitler. I watched him once at one meeting where he gave one of the fellows a terrible look. I would have died from that look. I took him aside . . .

Sally: Richard———. I don't blame him.

Mrs. C: Yeah. And I said, what was that? And Thomas said, just none of your business. So he did not confide in me the agony he was going through there. It was something that we could look on after we were already out.

Freeman: From hindsight.

Mrs. C: Yeah.

Freeman: Dad, did you know about your children's reactions to this experience?

Mr. C: No.

Freeman: So this is all new information, right now. Any thoughts about hearing your daughters and son talk about this?

Mr. C: I would feel that the situation is probably described quite properly, because now I know quite well that this particular religious group is quite fanatic in pretty well everything. But at the time we didn't know that. We were kind of fed up with the public school, and this seemed to be an alternative which was worth a try.

Freeman: But during the time the kids were going through this, you didn't get any inkling they were having a...

Mr. C: Not really, no. No.

Patty: Actually I was quite happy there while I was going. It was just ...

Sally: I wasn't.

Mrs. C: Yes, you were too.

Patty: You were.

Sally: Not really.

Patty: You never said anything.

Sally: I know. But the people there were awful.

Mrs. C: You think that now, but while you were there ...

Sally: Mom, do you remember that big thing with Chris that was going on?

Mrs. C: No.

Sally: And the other one?

Mrs. C: Well, that goes on in any public school, Sally.

Sally: Not like that.

The children are quite adamant that their involvement in this private school was a negative experience for them. Each child in his or her own way kept it to himself or herself. Patty is the only one who said that she was happy while at the school, but looking back realizes the impact the school had on her. Sally and Tom both state how difficult the experience has been for them. The mother takes issue with Sally and says that she was happier at the school than she acknowledges right now. The tendency to invalidate what the children say is quite common in this family.

After the children take a strong "I" stand on how they see things, one or another adult will say something that contradicts their stance.

Another interesting feature is the children's description of the isolation they experienced from the community and from each other. The mother states that it is a close-knit family that communicates about most things that are important. However, the children talk about not sharing many of their concerns with members of the family. The father in this family continues to be the outsider. None of the kids confided in him about their difficulties with the school. It seems clear that he has not been a resource to this family for a long time. Thus, one possible goal is for the father to become more available to his children as a resource. As the interview progresses this begins to occur.

Now, for a period of time, the extraprofessional therapists have not said much. They have been observing the family talking about how it has experienced life within and outside the family. Dr. A, who has been most intimately involved with this family on a personal level, becomes increasingly uncomfortable with the way in which the family, particularly the children, are discussing certain issues. She very forcefully brings the family back to focusing on Tom and goes into a long discussion about what she sees as the real problems of this family. She labels Tom as the problem, and comes up with a solution that she thinks would be in the best interests of the family and Tom.

Dr. A's emotional outburst, siding with the mother against the oldest son in the family, redefines the whole focus that the family therapist has been trying to achieve. Up to this point the family therapist has been successful in getting the family to talk about a number of issues that have been affecting it for years. He has been able to put the IP's problem in the context of the many developmental changes that have occurred in the family. However, Dr. A takes issue with this orientation, and makes a strong pitch for refocusing on Tom as the IP. This is a critical phase of the interview. As was stated earlier in the chapter, extraprofessional therapists, because of their own value systems and personal feelings about how families should operate, take sides with various members of the family. The emotional reactions of extraprofessional therapists can easily interfere with the family's coming to terms with how it wants to operate as a system. If the family therapist is unaware of how these various people have positioned themselves around issues, his efforts can be undermined. These pitfalls are illustrated in the following excerpt where Dr. A takes a strong stance, and the family therapist allows that stance to continue. After Dr. A gives a detailed description of the family problems and how she thinks they should be cured, the other members of the professional family begin to side with her and Tom is clearly brought back into center stage as the real problem in the family. The family therapist now faces the difficult task of bringing the family and the professionals back to the recognition that each member of the family has his or her own concerns. The father, the daughters and Tom have all expressed concerns about the total family. The mother has spoken adamantly about the importance of having the father involved individually with the older children in the family. Nonetheless, for a while Dr. A predominates.

Near the end of the interview, the family therapist is again able to shift the focus by helping family members formulate goals that involve family change rather than goals for change in one individual member. The major purpose of involving extraprofessional therapists in the session was to facilitate their reaching an agreement about who will work on what with the family. Eventually this goal is accomplished, but only after some struggle between the family therapist and several of the other professionals. The struggle over who is going to influence the orientation of the interview is not overt but occurs in an ongoing, subtle fashion throughout most of the interview.

Freeman: Well, anyway, it sounds like that school was an important experience. And you date the beginning of things not working out too well around that . . .

Mrs. C: Just prior.

Freeman: Just prior to that. And as the years have been going on things have been getting a bit more complicated.

Mrs. C: Yeah.

Freeman: Okay. One of the things we wanted to sort out was what has happened, what the family wants to happen, and who is going to work with the family, if anyone, to make sure that it does happen. Sitting here, I'm aware that there's one very important person not here, at least one that we know of, and that's your wife (indicates Mr. C), who might have something to say about what happens, especially in this balance thing that you talk about. Is there anyone else, you think, that should be here? Do you have any plans for bringing a new person into the family?

Mrs. C: No.

Freeman: No marriage plans, no engagement plans?

Mrs. C: No, don't have any plans.

Freeman: Any of you kids have anybody you're bringing into the family?

Dr. A: I would like to eject myself in a couple of minutes. And I wonder if before I go I could respond to something Mrs. R said.

Freeman: Okay.

Dr. A: I think that one of the things that I've been really impressed with, in all my capacities in association with your family, is that there is an enormous amount of love. It's a very warm, loving environment. And I've been there when there've been some terrific fights, and I've been there when there's been terrific jollity too. Sometimes those two things can happen at the same time. And I love this family, it's a wonderful, vibrant, very exciting environment. And I too think that you've done a remarkable job (to Mrs. C). It's the single most stable one-parent family I've ever seen. In that, there's all kinds of ups and downs, but certainly there's never been a lack of love. And I think that, as far as that goes, Thomas has never been left out. Sometimes I have thought to myself watching that it might be very difficult to love you, Thomas, in some of the behaviors that have gone on. Other times you're just as easy to love as anybody else. And I think that they've all really stuck together, which is remarkable considering all the things that have happened. Another thing I think is remarkable is that I've watched you (indicates Mrs. C) in the years that I've known you, go from what I would describe— and I think generalizations are really dangerous, but I'm going to level one at you—a very timid, inhibited, what I would call, typical German wife, to a really quite assertive and self-sufficient independent person. I know that's an evolution that you're still making. Nevertheless, to me, I've witnessed you really struggle with the difficulties of going from being a wife, and one of a pair, to being a topnotch, one person, more or less at the helm. And I really appreciate that you also encouraged a lot of democracy, which isn't easy. I don't find it easy myself, in my own life. And I certainly can see that in a big family like this it might be very difficult. So I think that there has been an immeasurable amount of love and always will be. I think this family will always consider each member as a close family member. As far as discipline is concerned, I've seen you go from, the whole gamut. Nevertheless, you're always in control. And I think that it's impossible to discipline you, Thomas. It's impossible to discipline Sally or Patty either, if they won't be disciplined. So I'm feeling that in response to this . . . you know, it seemed to me that there might be an implication that there maybe isn't enough love shown to you, Thomas. Do you think that I'm saying that . . . is that correct for you that there's a lot of love for you in this family?

Tom: Yes.

Dr. A: And I've seen you really love your family members too. I really appreciate that from all of you. And there's been some tough times, and I think it's hard to love each other when there are tough times. Nevertheless, I've seen you do it. As far as discipline is concerned, I've had a personal experience with that with you (indicates Tom), you remember when Patty and I were there. And my feeling is that nobody, unless they were willing to smack you hard enough that they might kill you, could physically stop you from doing what you want to do. And that certainly isn't happening in your family. I know in fact that you've done the opposite, you've done that to your mother. You've beaten your mother. But I know she's never beaten you. And I don't think it's possible. He's wild when he's out of control. And in those times I've seen you out of control, I've always been struck by the notion that you still were in the driver's seat. That you could stop that any moment you wanted. And I've watched you do it. In other words, I'm really puzzled over that as an adult who would like to be a friend of yours. I felt really sorry about it, seeing you kind of use your anger, and whatever that is that's coming out, to really hurt the people around you. But I've thought you maybe knew what you were doing. And that scared me sometimes. And I don't think that discipline, in the sense we usually think of it, is possible, whether in this family or outside it, so long as Thomas is going to buck the way he does. And I feel that that's something that's not predictable. I really enjoy being around you, I really enjoy it, when you're being what I call "you," I suppose I say that's you because I like to think of you as a 17-year-old kid that I've seen quite often. And there are times when I wish you were on the furthest corner of the earth, and wish I hadn't arrived at that moment you were being like that. And my feeling is that it's not going to work for Thomas within the family unit, because he won't allow it to work. And this family to me, you know the old thing about the rubber glove. I've seen you all turn yourselves inside out like rubber gloves to make it work and Thomas lies there like he's floating on the top of the Dead Sea not moving anywhere. And surely to God, that would never work for anybody. So, just... I had to throw in those... The only other thing I'd like... there are two other things I'd like to say. And one is that gradually over the years I've known Thomas, I think that I've seen quite a few people come to think that he's not very bright. That's amazing to me, because I've known you when I've seen how bright you are, and you're just as sharp as the rest of them. And this is a family of sharp cookies. You're a sharp cookie. And I've always wanted to ask you that, how come you're acting as if you don't have any brains? Gradually I've watched that, and I've wondered about that. Because always when we've talked about books and all kinds of things like that, it's no secret that you're just as sharp as a tack. So I've puzzled over that one. I wonder what you're getting out of, gradually acting dumb. Not talking, for example. I can remember hearing you talk and jabber away with the best of them. And this is a family of jabberers. (Laughter) The last thing is that I just have this feeling that anybody who wants out as much as I think you want out, I would encourage. I mean, I just think, why not? I think Thomas can make it on his own if—you know, being a visiting son for a while, until you make up your mind you want to come back into the family. This is one thing I've wondered about . . . maybe there's a little lack of faith. That may not be true, but I sense there's a little lack of faith in letting Thomas hoof it on his own, making his own meals, living on his own in an apartment or something like that. I even wondered why he was going into the foster situation. I thought, Thomas? He's big enough and ugly enough to stand on his own. How come he needs a foster situation?

Mr. C: If I may throw something in here, this is basically, what you say about Tom being able to make it on his own, is basically the same conclusion that I came to after being with him for two months.

Dr. A: Did you?

Mr. C: Yeah.

Dr. A: I'm glad to hear it.

Mr. C: I could not see him functioning in the family setup. It seemed to me myself, I had to make a decision at that point because it became impossible that he stayed with us, which was really hard for me to do. Because I could sense how much he needed me, and yet I wasn't able to keep him. I was quite upset when I learned that he was going back to Mrs. C. Because I could not see that function at that point. And I realized that perhaps he is maybe just not quite old enough, to be on his own.

Dr. A: Yeah, I feel that too.

Mr. C: But, I thought, he is going to make it, and that's probably the only think that might wake him up. I had the feeling he has to wake up to reality. And the only thing in my opinion that could maybe accomplish that, would not be a mom or a dad who is there anymore to do things for him. If he was forced to really take care of all his things for himself. And this I felt would be the only thing that maybe could check him up a bit.

Dr. A: I have to agree with that. And because this is such a close family, and because I think there are a lot of unresolved things between you and Thomas (to Mr. C), I'm glad to hear that your perspective is to try to figure out, as you say, how to get some balance. And I think that if Thomas, or any one of you, I mean Sally's been talking about the day when she's going to go out and live on her own, and yet I've never sensed that you would alienate yourself from the family. I just could never believe that. I know from watching each of you in the family that you'd always feel that you're a member of the family. I mean, Sally and I don't—I could imagine her living on her own now, she's so capable. And I can't believe that Thomas isn't too. These kids do more in this family. Mrs. C has done a fabulous job of training for independence, and Thomas acts crazy. I mean, not just out of hand, but he acts—and you notice I'm using that word, acts, he acts crazy at will. When he wants to it seems to me, and yet he's perfectly sane at other times. He can cook. He can do a great job of cleaning the kitchen and the toilet. I can tell you that. I'd hire him tomorrow. And if I were seventeen and harnessed in by all of these things that I've gotta work through myself, I think I might do better on my own, too. So there, I've put in my oar.

Freeman: Okay.

Mr. L: Could we speak briefly about the time that Tom was on his own, because I can use some observations on how he handled himself in terms of making the routine, of getting along. Like his job at that time was to get himself to school, and I don't know why that period of independence ended. My contact with that was a message, well a conversation with you (to Mrs. C), that Tom had moved out, with her sanction, and was now on his own, and she gave me the address and we monitored this. And then the next contact, other than with Tom, I guess was from you, Mrs. R, saying he's now with me, his independence period is now over. Okay, Tom, just from what I saw, from our school end, he had definite problems sort of keeping to the routine. Attendance, you know, as an educator I have to say that it's one of the key issues. It's how we uncover most of our problems because the guy who doesn't come to work is either not very happy or something. So the same thing with school. And the kids resent this very often. Why are you always calling our home and saying, where's so and so. But that is the first indication that something is not right. So he had problems keeping a schedule, he would arrive late. On several occasions I saw him. It was quite cold at that time, it was the beginning of the cold spell and he came in and his hands were very red, and I was alarmed thinking, you know, this fella at least needs someone there to say, hey, you know, wear your gloves. He was going through a time perhaps of initial bachelorhood, I don't know. Perhaps he needed a longer time at it, I don't know. But he was having difficulty coping. I remember worrying about him, if he was eating regularly, 'cause he didn't look terribly well. I remember one morning I saw, I had to drive downtown I think for a meeting of some sort with someone else, and it was almost amusing at the time. There was Sally sort of walking away from school, and there was Tom walking towards school. And there it is 10:30 in the morning when they should both have been in school. And I didn't stop or anything, they sort of met like this and went back.

Sally: That was the day when I had this little conversation with Mr. D, and Mr. D said, Bye bye. So I left.

Mr. L: Okay. But it was like a little vignette on the street there. You know, Tom is going one way and Sally going the other and they were meeting in between. And I thought if anything sort of sums up, you know, some of the situations this family has gone through. But I would like to hear at this point what happened during that period of independence. I'm not even sure how long it was.

Mrs. C: It was three weeks, I think. Two or three weeks. It so happened that where he lived, his landlady was very concerned that anybody would find out that she was making an extra income and she wouldn't accept checks. And she became very alarmed when somebody from the social assistance who were going to support Thomas, came to the door and she said Tom had to go. I also suspect that Thomas exhibited some of his crazy behaviors and that she became scared. I don't know about that.

Mr. G: There was that one incident over the furnace.

Mrs. C: Yeah, he had blown out the furnace. I mean, you don't usually blow out your landlady's furnace. Probably other things happened too, which neither she nor Thomas would elaborate on. We brought this back to Dr. P [the family doctor] and he felt that Thomas definitely for the time being . . .

Tom: I didn't do that on purpose though.

Mrs. C: Well, I mean, but you blew. I mean, you don't blow into a furnace.

Tom: I turned on . . . to see and the electric went out.

Mrs. C: Well, whatever it was it didn't work out. And Dr. P felt that he should definitely be in a room and board situation at that time. One social worker or whatever, came out with Mrs. R's address, and Dr. P felt that would be a very good placement until we made other decisions. Just to see how it worked out. That's how this all came about. And he definitely felt that Thomas needed as much strictness as possible, which Mrs. R is able to provide. But as Dr. A just said, if Thomas does not want to behave, all the strictness in the world is not going to do the trick in the long run either.

As the reader can see, the orientation has shifted from looking at what has been happening within the family as a whole to viewing Tom as the real problem. Dr. A's comments have influenced how the school counsellor, the family support worker and family members view Tom. They have moved from viewing him as making some progress to becoming more alarmed by his behavior. Dr. A is the first person who has raised the subject of Tom's violent behavior and his acting somewhat crazy. Following Dr. A's comments, the father quickly seizes on the idea of Tom's living away from home. The view seems to be that if Tom cannot be hospitalized, maybe he should be living alone.

The family therapist tries to regain the impetus he had created during the beginning of the interview by encouraging the family to look at what they can do as a family, and by again interjecting the father's concern about spending more time with all his children. Rather than make any comment, positively or negatively, about the statements of Dr. A, the family therapist tries to get the family to look again at how it wants to organize itself as a unit and what types of involvements the members would like to have with each other.

He ends the interview by getting a commitment from the extraprofessional therapists to support the orientation of the family working together as a unit to sort out how it wants to organize its set of relationships. Later on, in future interviews he deals with Dr. A's orientation, recognizing that for permanent change to occur Dr. A's involvement and support is necessary. Continuing to work with this family without somehow counterbalancing Dr. A's firm belief that Tom is the problem would probably result in failure. Only by bringing Dr. A into the session is it possible to obtain a true sense of the influence she has on the family.

At this point in the interview, the family therapist once again asks each member of the family who else should be involved in the sessions and what types of changes they would like to see occur in the famly.

Freeman: Now, Dr. P [the family doctor] is one person who's not here today, who is involved with the family?

Mrs. C: Dr. P, yes.

Freeman: Anyone else who is involved with the family who's not here today?

Mr. L: Dr.———from the school district is not here.

Mrs. C: No. I understood it as who had personal contact, because Dr.———only had . . .

Mr. L: He had not had personal contact with Tom. He had been over to the home, though, once, hadn't he?

Mrs. C: Yeah, that was when . . . I was not there, I was on holidays at that time. But it was very brief, as far as fifteen minutes or something. And as soon as Thomas saw Dr.———come in the front door, he walked out the back and it was really not a great encounter.

Freeman: Anyone else? Is there a social worker from the Ministry involved?

Mrs. C: No.

Freeman: So we're not missing anybody other than the Doctor.

Mrs. C: Dr. P.

Freeman: And he knows about the meeting?

Mrs. C: Yes, he was unable to come.

Freeman: And I mentioned your wife (to Mr. C). What knowledge does she have about all of this?

Mr. C: Not very much I would think. I think she has a somewhat basic idea maybe of what's going on. She had the two months with Thomas, but she's basically in the same boat that I'm in. That we cannot be there and look in.

Freeman: Would she have joined us if we had thought to invite her?

Mr. C: I think she would if she can get off work. I'd have to see how that would work out.

The student psychiatric nurse who set up the meeting did not think to invite Mr. C's wife. She had assumed that that person was not involved in what was going on. However, it would have been better to have Mr. C's new wife in the session as she would have been able to give an interesting perspective from her view of the family as an outsider. Mr. C brought his new wife to all the following sessions.

Freeman: What does she do?

Mr. C: She works in an insurance company.

Freeman: And she's met all the kids, everybody?

Mr. C: Yeah.

Freeman: And how are the relationships? The relationships as you see them? Are they confortable, or are there areas there that you're concerned about?

Mr. C: The little ones are quite comfortable. Sally and Tom and Patty can maybe speak for themselves. I don't know.

Freeman: Okay, let's give them a chance to do that.

Mr. C: I don't think it's quite that comfortable at this stage.

Freeman: That's how you see it.

Mr. C: That's my feeling . . . in some ways. In others maybe, yes. Which I think is to be expected as normal.

Freeman: You'd like it to be more comfortable? If it could be worked on?

Mr. C: I would definitely think so, but I think it takes some time.

The family therapist has regained control of the process. Through his questioning he is indicating that there are many issues that the family has to work on. Mr. C wants to be more involved with the children and for the family gatherings with his second wife to be more comfortable. Throughout the interview increased involvement has been one of Mr. C's primary goals and the therapist is able to focus on this to encourage the family to think beyond the goal of the identified problem.

Freeman: Tom, what are your thoughts about what your dad just said?

Tom: That's true, that it's uncomfortable for the older kids, I guess, and the little kids.

Freeman: Any ideas how it could become more comfortable for you?

Tom: Well, I'm not really uncomfortable, I'm just saying that it's more uncomfortable than for the little kids.

Freeman: But not too uncomfortable for you.

Tom: No. It's not even uncomfortable. I'm just saying it's probably more than the little kids' is, 'cause they're younger.

Freeman: They're younger. That would be the main reason that you'd think they'd be a bit more comfortable.

Tom: Well, if they're that young they don't really know much about the family thing anyway, so they're not uncomfortable.

Freeman: Sally?

Sally: What do you mean uncomfortable with? Uncomfortable about what?

Freeman: Ask you dad.

Sally: Uncomfortable about what?

Mr. C: Between you and Maria.

Sally: I don't think so. I get along pretty good with her.

Patty: I don't feel uncomfortable at all.

Freeman: Mr. C, there's something though that you're picking up that you'd like to see worked on.

Mr. C: Um hmm. As far as I'm concerned it boils down to trying to establish a way to reestablish contact with the three big ones.

Freeman: Yes, I guess that would be your major interest. What's your reaction to that? (To Mrs. C)

Mrs. C: Whether the kids are comfortable?

Freeman: No. The major objective is for Dad to become a bit more involved with . . .

Mrs. C: That would be nice. That would be really good, I think. I have made it my policy to totally stay out of it because it's very easy for me to be triangulated between the kids and between their dad. And they're all of an age where they can phone when they have something to say, and I speak when I have something to say, I will phone.

Freeman: So you're comfortable with a more balanced sharing.

Mrs. C: Yes, sure.

Mr. C: The thought I have to that is maybe sometimes they need a little encouragement to phone Dad.

Mrs. C: Oh, from you though?

Mr. C: No, from you.

Mrs. C: Why from me?

Mr. C: Because I'm not with them.

Mrs. C: Why don't you encourage them to phone you, you see? I encourage little kids to brush their teeth and say thank you and things like that. But these kids have already learned that. They're young adults. As we just said, they can be on their own.

The discussion that goes on now between Mr. C and Mrs. C is quite intense. They show more anger and disappointment with each other at this point than at any other time in the interview. Mrs. C seems to harbour a good deal of resentment about Mr. C being so uninvolved and passive in his dealings with the children. Mr. C continues to play the passive role and attempts to place responsibility for contact on his wife and on his children. However, as the interview nears its conclusion Mr. C begins to see that he has to take the initiative to have more contact with the children. Mrs. C has a little difficulty in hearing him say this.

Susan is quite adamant in her feeling that her father doesn't want to be more involved with her and expresses some of her resentment about this.

Mr. C: I don't know.

Mrs. C: So I as a mother should not say, well, it's about time you phoned your dad.

Mr. C: Sometimes perhaps.

Mrs. C: No. I don't . . .

Sally: I don't that that would be a very . . .

Mrs. C: I think the kids would resent it. Also, I resent it. I resent that very strongly. I do find that . . .

Sally: I phoned you a couple of times, just to talk to you.

Mr. C: Yeah, a couple of times. But I mean, I'm the same, I don't go to the phone and talk to you, eh? Unless I have . . .

Sally: So maybe you need us to remind you.

Mrs. C: Maybe you should ask Maria to tell you to phone.

Mr. C: It's the same thing.

Mrs. C: I mean, how would you feel about that? I mean, that's . . . then Maria and I become now in charge of your . . .

Mr. C: No, I don't mean in charge. I just mean that sometimes maybe it takes some encouragement from you too, or reminder.

Sally: But that's not . . . No, no. Then it won't be coming from us, then it's coming from her.

Patty: Yeah, It should be coming from us, right?

Mr. C: Maybe it would come from you under a little encouragement, I don't know.

Sally: If somebody really wants to talk to you, they don't need encouragement.

Mrs. C: I would like to make it really quite clear at this point. The time that I am responsible for the actions of the older ones, outside my home where I still am responsible, has gone. There were times, like Dr. A said before, where I felt responsible for everything that was going on. I don't do that any more. I am not God Mother or Earth Mother or something like that. People can think for themselves and they can act for themselves. And they are going to do that. Even the little ones. If Steven doesn't want to go, I am not going to tell him, you have to go because it's proper. This has happened once before. And I'm not also phoning you and saying, look, what are we going to do about this, Steven doesn't want to go, etc. Steven, if you don't want to go you speak to your father. I have nothing to do with it.

Mr. C: I guess you have to leave it then that we have a little opinion difference.

Mrs. C: There is a big change, and you will have to, I'm afraid, have to go along with it. I have nothing to do with that. I have nothing to do with my children's phone calls.

Mr. C: Well, I know that, then I don't have to expect it.

Freeman: Anyway, you do want to have more of an involvement as I hear it, with your three older kids.

Mr. C: Definitely. I myself feel very unhappy about the way the situation has come about. But I've tried to see whether it worked out that I could just sometimes take one of the big ones together with the little ones when they come. Because in the beginning I tried to find something that I could do with all of them and it just isn't possible. Even if I could find activities that we could still do all together, well, the one wouldn't be there or the other has different plans, or, so . . .

Sally: It's not just doing something. It's supposed to be that everybody's sort of, how would you put it, it's the being there, you know.

Mr. C: Well, but when you talk about the physical thing . . .

Sally: It's not just the, "let's go out".

Mr. C: No, that's not what I meant. Or maybe I didn't make myself clear. I didn't necessarily mean going out and doing something. Like what did we do when you were visiting last time, we played games or something at home. That is still an activity. But, I mean, you can't come visit me and just be there.

Sally: Why not?

Mr. C: Not talk, not do anything, not play or go somewhere? I don't know.

In this interesting portion of the interview, Mr. C expresses his struggle to figure out what to do with his older children. His discomfort in having them around without some structure is quite clear and could be connected with his eagerness to have Tom out of the home. His oldest daughter is trying to help him in this one. She is saying that it is okay just to be together. Mr. C has difficulty with this and is generally uncomfortable about how to relate to his children. It is probably more comfortable for him to argue with his ex-wife about whether he should be involved with the children than to actually have the responsibility of having the children with him. The whole issue about his visitation rights with the children, what to do with them, and who should be responsible for setting up their time together is an emotionally heated subject. It is interesting to see how quickly the family members drop their focus on the IP and begin to talk about an area that has apparently been a sore spot for quite a while. The issue of who should be involved with whom in the family and who is responsible for those involvements becomes a major topic of discussion for the family in future sessions. The importance of this issue is an eye-opener to the extraprofessional therapists who have not been aware of the importance of the father's role.

Mr. C: Not talk, not do anything, not play or go somewhere? I don't know.

Sally: Well, okay. If we show up there, right, and you don't have anything planned. If somebody ... Okay, if two people really get along, if one person just walks into the house without warning, right, and just stays a couple of hours, it's not going to just end up that you just sit around in a chair and stare at each other and do nothing. You're going to figure out something to do. So that's no excuse to just say I can't think of anything to do that's suitable.

It appears that Sally has a much better sense of the quality a contact can have than her father does. She conveys the important message to him that just having a short contact without anything planned can be satisfying to his children.

Mr. C: But I can't quite see what we are talking differently about.

Sally: I'm just saying that what you just said is not really a very good excuse to say that you can't come up with anything to do.

Mr. C: Well, I'm not trying to make an excuse. What I'm trying to say is that first I tried to find things that I could do with all three of you together and that just never worked out.

Sally: As part of our not getting together?

Mr. C: Yes. And also other reasons like distance problems and time problems. Well, what I at this point feel might work out better is what I just started when I invited you to come. Just seeing if it would work out if one time I would take Patty when I have the little ones, or I take Thomas and you. Rather than try to get the whole family together.

Mrs. C: Could we—I have a few misgivings about that. Sally made the observation when she and Maria were playing monopoly with you, that the kids were totally on their own in their room and they were smelling feet. Which is sort of a gross entertainment in a way. Could you maybe when you take the big kids put your full attention on the kids and not have the little kids in the background, just on a one-to-one. Because the little kids are not getting anything out of that because you play monopoly, and the big kids are sort of caught in the middle between the little kids and you. This is the impression Sally got anyway.

Mr. C: Well, this, what I was trying to do is kind of compromise.

Mrs. C: Why a compromise? I think, if you do this once a month, with one child, one of the bigger ones, one younger adult, let's put it like that, without putting too many things under one hat, the older kids would much more appreciate it and not just feel like a tagalong with the little kids. And the little kids would not feel that they are sort of now superfluous and have to

be on their own. I mean, that's the suggestion I have to make. I
don't know how you kids feel about that, but I feel if I would go to
somebody then I would feel much more appreciative if in all that
time, this time would be fully devoted to me.

Mr. C: I realize that fully, but I am the one that has to face up to
the distance problem, pickup and delivery times.

Mrs. C: Well, I just thought, maybe . . .

Mr. C: Like I said, to get somebody to my place I spend three
hours on the road.

Sally: Is it that much of a problem to see your kids, though, that
you're going to worry about your gas?

Mr. C: No, it's not the gas, it's . . .

Sally: Oh, your time?

Mr. C: And this is why I thought as a starting compromise,
because I am already every second weekend doing this, to take
one of you with the little ones. I fully realize that.

What I think the father is conveying here is his discomfort with
a one-to-one relationship with his older children. It seems to be
more comfortable for him to have the young children around and
to devote some attention to them without having to get intimately
involved with his older children. Unfortunately the older children
interpret this as meaning their father doesn't care about them.
They have difficulty recognizing his discomfort in knowing how
to relate to them as they get older. The family decides that one of
the major goals for future sessions will be to work on what type of
relationships each can have with the other.

Freeman: Let me just break in here, because it sounds like there's
a lot of need to talk about how to organize your time. This is a
good place to pinpoint where some of the work might take place.
I am wondering who should be involved in those sorts of
discussions, which in itself becomes an interesting question.
What family members should be involved in discussion about how
the family is going to organize its relationships? Dad, do you have
any suggestions about who should be involved? In ongoing
sessions around how the family's going to manage?

Mr. C: I would feel, the family itself.

Freeman: All these people here?

Mr. C: Plus perhaps my wife, and the social worker or whoever is in touch.

Freeman: (To Mrs. C) Are you agreeable?

Mrs. C: Oh, yeah.

Freeman: And Patty, are you agreeable to that?

Patty: (Nods)

Tom: Who will actually be with the family?

Freeman: Well, we'll decide on who that person will be. But in terms of just the family right now, who in the family would meet.

Tom: Yeah. The whole family.

Freeman: So the family is in agreement that everyone here should continue to meet, including Mr. C's wife.

(The family nods affirmatively.)

Freeman: Now, how about the professionals who should be involved.

Mrs. C: I think if we could continue sessions like this with you it would help.

Freeman: Well, how would the rest of the professionals here feel about that?

Mr. L: I think that's a good idea. I have only been involved around Tom, but I can see how there are other issues in the family to work on besides Tom.

Freeman: Mrs. R?

Mrs. R: Well, anything that would help Tom make a better adjustment would make sense to me. I can see how important the father's involvement is in the family, and this session was quite an eye-opener for me. I would be willing to continue to have Tom in my home, but the more involvement he has with his family, I guess, the better it would be.

Freeman: Mr. G?

Mr. G: Well, I think things generally have been getting better, and I'm happy I had a chance to meet Mr. C and . . .

Freeman: Well, let's stop the session now and we'll set up a meeting for next week to meet with the whole family and Maria, and we'll continue talking about how the members of the family

can stay involved with each other. I will keep the other professionals informed as to the progress that is being made. In terms of
any decisions about who should live where, I think they should
be made after we have a number of sessions and discuss how the
family members want to be involved with each other. I think out
of these discussions a natural decision will be made as to living
arrangements for various members of the family. I hope this is
okay for you, Tom.

Tom: (Nods)

Freeman: And Mrs. C?

Mrs. C: Yes. I can see where we need to have a few more
sessions before any decisions are made.

This interview provides an example of a typical session involving extraprofessional therapists. In these interviews it is important
for the family therapist to remain in control of the process. He
must be aware of alliances, triangulation and scapegoating, all of
which are likely to occur when a large group gets together. Each
extraprofessional has developed his own assessment and point of
view about what is best for the family, and based on his contact
with a particular member of the family, will have developed
treatment strategies. Often there is no one in the community who
has an overall perspective of the family. I think it is essential for
the family systems therapist to organize the extraprofessional
therapists' involvement so that a coherent, unified approach can
be taken in which all members of the family are involved and
individual and collective needs are respected.

Chapter 5 discusses how to begin family therapy. The preceding interview represents a beginning interview of a preliminary
nature in which it was necessary to obtain the agreement and
support of the extraprofessional therapists. The following chapter
contains a beginning interview with a family in which all the
important intrafamilial members were involved. It discusses how
to set up such an interview and contains a transcript of an initial
session.

5

BEGINNING FAMILY THERAPY

FAMILY THERAPY STARTS BEFORE THE INITIAL INTERVIEW

A common belief is that the family therapy process begins with the first interview. In actuality, the process begins with the first contact between the therapist and a family member. Usually, one family member will call the therapist for help, upon the recommendation of the family doctor, a social agency, a friend, or a neighbor. The family member who requests the help often has his or her own opinion about what type of assistance is required. This person is also likely to be the one who has traditionally taken responsibility for dealing with problems in the family.

Making a decision about who should attend the initial session is the first important therapeutic maneuver. This decision is based on the information the therapist elicits from the family member who calls for help. During the initial conversation, which is normally by telephone, the therapist must ask questions about family composition and be able to identify which family members are most intimately involved in the concerns the caller expresses. The following is an example of an initial telephone conversation.

Caller: (Father) Are you Dr. Freeman?

Freeman: Yes.

Caller: I received your name from our family doctor who said that you worked with families who are having trouble with their children.

Freeman: Yes.

Caller: Well, we are having difficulty with our 16-year-old daughter. She has been getting into trouble in school and we have not been able to manage her at all.

Freeman: Could you tell me a little bit more about your concerns?

Caller: Well, she has been expelled from two schools and now the newest school is threatening to expel her. She is involved with a very bad crowd of people and my wife and myself are just not able to control her.

Freeman: Can you tell me who else is in the family?

Caller: We have two other children besides Patty, our 16-year-old.

Freeman: What are their ages and sexes?

Caller: Our youngest, Johnny, is 13 and he is doing real well, no problem with him whatsoever. And Sally, our 15-year-old, is also doing very well in school; she is the opposite of Patty. We fortunately have no trouble with our younger children. Our major concern is with our older girl, Patty.

Freeman: How about your wife?

Caller: Well, she is so exasperated and upset about what is happening with our daughter that she immediately breaks down and cries whenever she thinks about it. The reason I am calling is because she is too distraught about the whole thing to get involved.

Freeman: Have you seen anyone else about the problems that you are having? Is anyone else currently involved with the family?

Caller: We have been involved with the school and the school counsellors and we have seen a child psychiatrist for Patty but none of these things seems to have helped; actually things have gotten worse over the last couple of years.

Freeman: Who in the family has been involved with these various helpers?

Caller: My wife and myself and Patty went to the child psychiatrist but Patty refused to talk to him. She said it wasn't her problem and she didn't want anything to do with him. We sent her a couple of times alone but she refused to talk to the psychiatrist at all.

Freeman: How about the school counsellors?

Caller: My wife went to talk to the school counsellors but the only thing they told her was that if we weren't able to control Patty more effectively, they would have to expel her from school. They weren't helpful at all.

Freeman: Has the whole family ever been involved together in talking about some of the concerns that have been happening?

Caller: No, never, I don't know why we would want to do that. We are not having any trouble with the younger children.

Freeman: Well, for the first session, why don't you and your wife come in together to meet me. I can get a chance to talk to both of you about how you see what is happening with the family and then we can make a decision about who should be involved. How would that be?

Caller: I think that is a good idea. I'll come in with my wife.

This conversation typifies the situation of one family member being concerned about, and trying to get help for another member. If the therapist handles the call well and makes the correct decision regarding who should attend the first interview, the conversation begins to help the caller redefine the problem. In the foregoing conversation, the therapist could have suggested that the whole family attend the first interview. However, the therapist decided that the parent subsystem should first be given an opportunity to feel comfortable with the practitioner before exposing their children to this stranger. In the long run, the therapist will be able to provide more support to the entire family if he has the confidence of the family organizers, i.e., the parents. Once this comfort is developed between family therapist and parents, the parents will be more likely to allow the therapist to see the whole family.

Most parents experience much anxiety about their problem child and generally feel guilty and responsible for the problems within the family. Consequently, it is understandable for them to resist the idea of involving the entire family with the therapist. Parents often fear that the involvement of an outsider may only serve to undermine the efforts they have devoted to solving the problem. However, when the parents and the therapist have a chance to meet before bringing in the children the fears can be allayed, and the parents usually become more willing to allow the therapist entry into the family.

In the illustrative telephone call, the therapist elicited information about family composition and the caller's perceptions about the involvement of various family members in the previous treatment encounters. If the caller had said that one or more family members was presently in therapy, then the therapist might have decided not to get involved with the family at all. If the caller had information that a particular therapeutic structure had been unsuccessful, i.e., seeing only the problem child or seeing parents and the problem child, then the therapist might decide to avoid a similar structure. I have seldom seen success in cases where the parents bring only the problem child to therapy and leave the nonproblematic child(ren) at home.

In summary, the therapist should obtain basic family information before setting an appointment for the first interview, or even before deciding whether to become involved at all. Below is a checklist of information which the therapist requires.

1. Who are all the family members? (Discover the age and sex of all family members and others living in the home.)
2. Have any members of the family experienced previous therapy? What kind? When?
3. Which family member is most anxious or overinvolved in the expressed problem?
4. Which other family members are peripherally involved?
5. How long has the problem existed?
6. Who is willing to attend therapy sessions?

This information is the minimum that the therapist should have before deciding who to invite to the first session. Many times a referral will come to the family therapist from an agency or a family doctor. The referral source will indicate a certain view of the problem and may often suggest who should be involved in the therapeutic process. Sometimes therapists take the referral at face value and proceed to work with the family on the basis of the referring information. I caution therapists against this. Much referral information does not reflect the strengths and resources of the family. The referring agent may have only been involved with one member or have accepted the family's definition of the problem. It is unusual for the referring agent to have an understanding of how the family operates as a system.

It is essential for the family therapist to make his own decision about who should come to the first session. For this reason, when an outside agency requests that I see a family, I suggest that they ask the family to call me to set up the first appointment. The motivation for getting involved in the family therapy process should come from the family. Then, when a family member calls, the telephone conversation can be used to begin to help the caller gain a different perspective of who is involved in the problem and who should be included in the first session.

IN THE BEGINNING

The basic family structure involves two parents and their children, but there are endless variations on this theme. There is a growing number of blended or reconstituted families, composed of children from previous marriages of either spouse and possibly one or more children from the new marriage. Another family constellation is that of the single parent. Less common but increasingly prevalent are homosexual couples with children. Because of the growing divorce rate and changing norms and values, the family therapist cannot assume he knows the structure a family has organized for itself. It is consequently necessary to ask the contacting family member to give his views about who is included in the family. This information will help the therapist choose which family members to begin with.

In handling the initial family contact the therapist has to be especially sensitive in dealing with the caller's anxiety. It is my belief that anxiety is greatly increased if the therapist begins by disagreeing with the caller's definition of the problem. It is wise

for the therapist to use the caller's definition as a base for helping
the caller gain a wider understanding of what is occurring with a
family. The problem is naturally causing distress and concern
throughout the family. Even if the caller is convinced the problem
rests in one member he is able to see that everyone in the family is
under some stress and concerned about the problem.

The behaviors the family displays during their initial contacts
are good indicators of how the family deals with discomfort and
anxiety. Alliances, coalitions, triangulation and scapegoating are
all in evidence during the initial phase of family therapy. If the
caller insists that the problem be handled in a certain way the
therapist is alerted to that person's position in the family behavioral patterns. Everything which occurs from the moment of
the first contact provides clues about how amenable or resistant to
change the family will be.

The most common behavioral pattern occurring during the
first telephone contact and the first several sessions is scapegoating. The role of the identified problem is to help the other family
members focus their anxiety on a known concrete problem. The
reduction of anxiety through scapegoating helps the family
members maintain some sort of balance in their relationship. The
more anxious family members are about their personal relationships, sense of well-being, or feelings of competence, the more
resistant they will be to looking at their own needs and concerns.
The therapist has to keep a systems perspective on the family
problems while at the same time reassuring the individual
members that their own needs, goals and struggles for differentiation or autonomy will be recognized and supported.

There are six basic types of problems family members initially
present as concerns. These all reflect family system disruption
and have implications for how the family has developed its
homeostatic balance.

1. *Personal problem:* an adult family member might be concerned
   about himself, i.e., anxiety, depression, a general feeling of
   inadequacy.
2. *Parent-child problem:* there is conflict between a parent and one or
   more children.

3. *Child problem:* the child is experiencing difficulty in school or the neighborhood.
4. *Sibling problems:* the siblings are having undue conflict with each other and the adults don't know how to handle it.
5. *Extended family problem:* a member of the extended family is ill or a behavioral problem to the family.
6. *Husband-wife problem:* there is marital conflict.

The type of presenting problem will influence the therapist's decision about who should attend the first interview. If the initiator of the contact defines the problem as resting within himself or herself and indicates a desire to work individually then it would not be necessary to involve the family in the initial stages. The time may come, however, when change in the individual begins to have repercussions in the family, often negative repercussion. At this time, other family members should also be seen. When there is a parent-child problem, it is important that both parents become involved in the therapeutic process at once. The child(ren) may be involved later. If the child is having problems in the school or community, it is also important to involve both parents from the start and possibly other members of the family at a slightly later date. It is very unusual for a child to be having difficulty without it somehow being interconnected with relationships within the family. If the problem involves undue sibling conflict it is important to involve the entire family. Many times when siblings are having serious difficulties within their relationship, it is a reflection of something going on between the parents.

If the problem is with a member of the extended family the therapeutic structure will have to be expanded to include additional family members. Extended family problems, such as poor health in aged members or in-law overinvolvement in nuclear family matters, involve many members of the three-generational family. When other family members are involved in the therapy process they often serve as a resource to the family and help share responsibility for dealing with the problems.

Lastly, when adults want to improve how they relate to each other or how they organize the family structure, it is not necessary to include the children in the therapy process. If the adults accomplish their goals, the rest of the family will also benefit. The adults will create an atmosphere that allows the children to behave differently. (However, I think it is important that the therapist meet the entire family once in the early phase of work with the couple in order to get a feel for the group as a whole.)

This approach may be confusing to people who view family therapy as a process that always includes the entire family. There are times when this is important and also many times when other therapeutic structures are necessary. In systems thinking it is important to influence change by helping to restructure the way the system behaves. The adults of the family are the most important subsystem to consider for system change. If the adults have a relationship in which they do not need scapegoats or use the children as a way to stabilize their own relationship, then probably the children will not be negatively affected by their parent's difficulties. When husband and wife are having difficulties in their own relationship and try to resolve them by involving the children, serious emotional or behavioral problems may show themselves in the children. This makes it more likely that they will need to be involved in the therapy process. Often, in this situation, the job of the family therapist will first be to help the adults learn how to deal with their problems without involving the children. If the therapist can accomplish this goal then most often the children will be able to get on with their own lives and it will not be necessary to see them.

For example, one family I worked with was composed of five members: two parents; and three children, identical twins, age 24, and a 19-year-old girl who was the designated problem. At the end of the third session the parents said that they couldn't carry through with their plans for their own lives until the youngest child shaped up. At this point, the 19-year-old turned to her parents and told them she wasn't going to take on responsibility for their lives and that she was tired of being used as an excuse by her parents for not doing the things they said they wanted to do. It is very unusual for the identified problem child to be able to say this sort of thing; however, it does illustrate how the family maintains a certain balance. In this situation the therapist's job is to help one member make a move irrespective of what is going on with other members in the family. The result is most often an improvement throughout the family.

In summary, there are no set rules about who should be involved in the therapeutic process. Some take the position that you can only do family therapy with the entire family. Others take the position that it isn't who you involve but what framework and what strategies you bring to bear that are critical. One of the principles of systems thinking is that in order for change to occur the most important and powerful subsystem has to be involved. Once change occurs here it flows throughout the entire system.

The next section will discuss how to conduct the first interview. Families are probably the hardest systems to maintain in therapy. One of the reasons is that therapists have difficulty in turning the first interview into a positive experience for all members.

CONDUCTING THE INITIAL INTERVIEW

The first session determines the course and direction the family therapy will take. During this session, the family will usually decide whether it wants to continue in therapy. As was mentioned in the previous section, the decision about who should attend the initial interview is made at the time of the first telephone contact. When beginning the first therapy session it is crucial for the family practitioner to be aware of the phases the family goes through during the initial session. In the beginning the family has not yet identified the problem as being a family one. The family members will most often come into the session feeling anxious, uncertain and often confused about why they are there, especially if they are convinced that no one is involved besides the identified problem. How the family's anxiety and fears are dealt with during this session will determine to a great extent whether the family will continue to work as a unit.

The first session can be divided into four general phases: (1) warming up or becoming comfortable; (2) defining the problems; (3) reframing the family's thinking about the problem; and (4) commitment to work as a family. These phases overlap and at times certain family members are in a different phase from others. It is not unusual, for example, for one family member to be in the problem-defining phase while the rest of the family has moved into the reframing phase.

The warming-up phase occurs during the first five or ten minutes of the initial interview. Family members will be testing whether this setting will be a safe place to talk. Coalitions will be observable between various family members. Family members will be quiet or talkative, depending on how they handle their anxiety and discomfort. The question of trust and safety will be paramount in almost all of the family members' minds.

The therapist's goal during the first five or ten minutes of the session is to demonstrate to the family that this is a safe, nonthreatening place to be. One cannot expect family members to risk talking about their concerns if they are going to be attacked for it. At the beginning it may be helpful for the therapist to explain briefly why he requested the family's presence. He might start out with some simple, structured questions. For example, what each member of the family wishes to be called. This conveys that the therapist will accept each person as an individual on his or her own terms. The family members may be asked their ages and what they were told about coming to the session. These questions are asked with several purposes in mind. They are attempts to reassure the family that no one is going to be asked to talk about threatening things before they're ready. They give recognition to the fact that family members are individuals with their own identities. These questions provide some structure and comfort during the warming-up phase by giving each member an opportunity to participate in his own way in a nonthreatening manner. For example, the question which asks what message family members received about coming to the first session is a concrete one, but also indirectly provides information about how important messages are communicated. In contrast, direct questions about how the family communicates may be felt as threatening at this point. Members might react by feeling criticized or feeling they need to defend another member. The warming-up phase is also a crucial part of each succeeding session. I have found that no matter how often I have seen a family, it is important to use a few minutes of each session to develop some sense of comfort before people can involve themselves in issues.

The initial session may provide the first opportunity the family has had to sit down and discuss something. If this in itself is a new experience, the therapist can help the family use it in a productive way. The positioning of the therapist within the family during the first five or ten minutes becomes important. Does he ask the overinvolved member of the family, the one who called him on the telephone, all the questions? Does he start with the one who is recognized as the problem in the family? Does he try to get the silent members to talk first? How the therapist structures this phase will affect how the family moves into the second phase of the first session.

The best way of moving from the first phase to the second phase (defining the problem) is to be in control of the process. The therapist exercises control by not allowing the family to criticize or blame one member for the family's problems; by not letting one member of the family talk for another; by asking questions that allow each person to talk for himself or herself; and by asking for each member's perceptions about why he or she is there that particular day. If the therapist is successful in guiding the process in this way, the family begins to change their thinking about what they want to work on.

As this occurs they move into the third phase of the session, which involves reframing the problem. During this phase members begin to think and talk about the problem in different terms. At this time it is important for the therapist to pay special attention to the following dynamics. (1) Which family member originally defined the problem? (2) How do members relate to each other and how does the family as a group react to the therapist? (3) Which family member tries hardest to control the problem? (4) Who offers explanations about how the family operates as a social system? From the moment of first contact, the therapist is learning about the family. How the family moves through the first three phases in the initial interview will determine its commitment to work as a family. This occurs during the fourth and final phase of the first interview.

Families return for additional sessions because the first session with the therapist was a positive experience. If the family's view is positive the therapist has achieved the most important goal of the first interview. The family therapist is responsible for maintaining a safe, comfortable atmosphere where there is a minimal amount of scapegoating. The therapist has to start with the family's definition of the problem and at the same time strive toward getting the family to rethink how it might work as a unit to deal with it. There are many strategies the family therapist can employ to accomplish these important goals.

From the beginning, the therapist emphasizes through his questions that no individual is to blame for the family experiences, and that each family member is important in his own right. He also emphasizes the importance of the family as a unit and points out how that unit is affected by its history. For example, the parents' experiences in their families of origin affect how they perceive their present family and may be the reason certain problems are particularly distressing to them.

The initial interview which follows illustrates many of these goals and strategies. The interview was with the R family, a single-parent family, consisting of the mother, age 39, and her three teenage sons, Steve, age 19, Peter, age 17, and Jim, age 15. The mother initiated contact because she was concerned that Jim, the identified problem was becoming a serious behavioral problem at home and at school. She had called a child psychiatry service where it was suggested by the psychiatric resident that she come in with all her children. The following transcript of the first session is divided into phases to illustrate the process which occurs during each of the four phases discussed above.

Phase one: warming up

The session began with the mother and her children signing the videotape consent forms. During the discussion about signing the consent forms the therapist had a chance to talk with each one of the boys and the mother about the video equipment and the studio. This process helped them become more comfortable with the interviewing room and the therapist's presence so that they were generally more at ease by the end of the warming-up phase. After they signed the forms, I started the session. The transcript starts with the beginning of the second stage, defining the problems.

Phase two: defining the problems

Freeman: I am new, obviously, to meeting all of you. Judy (the psychiatric resident) has met some of you or talked with you on the phone, so actually this is kind of a beginning for us all and maybe you can fill us in on what is happening with you.
 Mother: Well . . .
 Steve: Well, we've all been separated, except Peter, Jim . . . and my dad. My mom has been on her own and I have been on my own and now we are trying to make—you know, we have got a house and we are trying to get back together and stuff, that is where the problem is . . . that is generally where the problem lies.
 Freeman: Two of you have been living away from Jim?
 Mother: Their father is an officer in the military and we moved around a lot. We had been married eighteen years I guess when we agreed to separate when his transfer came in. He was transferred to Oakland so at that time I drove across country with Jim. The two boys went ahead. I got everyone settled there and I came up to Seattle where I took my RN training and just finished in April. The agreement between their father and myself was that when I finished school and got registered, that I would take over the responsibility of the boys. And this happened on the nineteenth of June. I wrote my exams on the twelfth so we all came up. He has never really had much responsibility of the boys,

it was sort of pretty much left to me. So to suddenly put him in with three boys, you know teenagers, it was a big jump for him and I think his way of coping with it was, you don't fool around and I won't bug you kind of thing, and we will live in a more or less kind of harmony. And this is the type of philosophy he had down there. But it is not my philosophy. I feel that we are a family and we do things. I mean we don't have to spend twenty-four hours a day, but there should be a general caring, and if you care then you are concerned and if you are concerned then you voice your concern. You don't say, do your thing and I will do mine. And then also ... over the past ... Jim had spinal meningitis when he was three and was put in a hospital with visiting hours for one hour on Sunday. This was a very difficult time. He was there for a month and when he came out he not only had physically suffered a loss of weight, but mentally I think it had a tremendous and profound effect on him. He was never really the same after. For two years we struggled along, he seemed to be very aggressive and very violent and so when he was five I talked to his father, and I said, you know, I think you should seek some kind of help because I can't cope anymore. And so he went to Dr. ———— in Bellingham, who is a child psychiatrist.

Freeman: Now you are going back how many years?

Mother: I am going back to when Jim was five.

Freeman: Which would be how many years?

Mother: Well, he is fifteen now.

Freeman: About ten years ago.

Mother: Yes. And Dr. ————, I think we had about six or eight visits with him, my husband saw him once or twice, the rest of the time it was either myself or with Jimmy. And Dr. ———— told me at that time that Jim had quite a high IQ. That he was a hyperactive child that needed few rules but very high fences and that certain rules shouldn't be broken. So he put him on Dexedrine and it seemed to put him almost into a totally lethargic state and I didn't like that. He also told me it was something that he wouldn't outgrow, that it is something he would have to cope with. So it was my decision after six months that I would take him off the drugs and we would try to work together and he would learn to control the problems that he seemed to be facing. So during the next, oh, up until a few years ago, Jim and I worked kind of—we worked together closer than I think his father worked—and we tried to when his temper flared, I tried to encourage him to go into his room until things cooled. And endless little things and for the first time really when we left Virginia four years ago, he got his first good report card. And you know, it really looked promising. Now, I sort of blame myself because I left at the wrong time, maybe I should have left now as opposed to three years ago for Jim's sake because maybe I didn't give him a chance to sort of put into practice the things that we worked so hard on, and so I think it is the last three years and the feeling of having to take care of himself and be responsible for himself really. It seems to me that if someone makes, if Jimmy makes a comment, I immediately feel hostile for some reason and I don't understand it. Peter can make the same comments and I don't have the same feeling. And even in discussions with Jim, when he and I will discuss, oh, anything, even generally, I usually feel hostility and I don't understand it, why? I don't know whether the other boys feel the same way or not, but this is my feeling so I felt that if we all came here that somehow, maybe it is deep rooted to before or maybe it is just hard to forget things that are said and things that are done. You know, I go wild, I can't cope anymore with arguments and shouting. What can I do? I have no authority other than my word. They are all bigger than I am. You know, if I tell Jim to stay home, he can leave. I have no recourse, except their caring for me and a certain degree of respect, but how long will that work? It won't necessarily work forever, so I felt that before we get to the point where Steve doesn't want to come home and Peter doesn't want to come home and Jim doesn't come or I don't, we should see what the problem is all about and maybe get to the root of it.

Freeman: Let's go back to just one comment you mentioned about the different reaction you have to Jim as compared to Peter. How about as compared to Steve? Is there a difference in . . .

Mother: Yes.

Freeman: The same comment . . . it's the same for the two of them but different reactiveness in terms of Jim? Is there anyone else you are involved with who can produce the same . . .

Mother: My brother Bob.

Freeman: Your brother Bob. He can produce the same sort of reaction that Jim produces in you? Anyone else besides your brother Bob?

Mother: No.

Freeman: Where is your brother Bob?

Mother: He's in Calgary. He's my youngest brother. He's five years younger than I am.

Freeman: So how old would he be?

Mother: I'm thirty-nine, and Bob is thirty-four.

Freeman: Bob is thirty-four and you are thirty-nine and he could do the same sort of thing? Could you give me an illustration of how your brother Bob could produce that?

Mother: He is an authority on everything, he is . . .

Steve: He is very belligerent. He is very . . .

Mother: He makes a lot of money. He has rings that dazzle you and I can never understand . . . he is such a good person himself, why does he need all of those things? Why does he need the penthouse? He took my sister and myself to San Francisco to see the penthouse, and the best restaurant. I mean, I love him the way he is. There is no need to show me that he is successful. I mean I wouldn't care if he was a bum on the street. So this sort of thing with my brother really bugs me. It is this . . . he is so insecure in himself that he feels he needs these things as transportation into acceptability. It's the feeling I get. You know? And very belligerent, extremely belligerent.

The above segment of the interview lasted about ten minutes. It illustrates the family members' different perceptions of the problem. When I asked the family what had been happening to them, the oldest son, Steve, immediately defined the problem as their readjustment to living together. He stated that the family—his mother and his brothers—had been living apart and now were attempting to get back together. The mother quickly redefined the problem as the difference between her and her husband's attitudes and values regarding the raising of children. She also elaborated on the developmental and physical problems experienced by her youngest son. She goes on in great detail to identify Jim as the problem. Not until the end of her description did she make reference to the difficulties she is having trying to reunite her family. The most insignificant feature at this point is the difference between the mother's defining the problem within Jim and the oldest boy's defining the problem within the foursome. The therapist does not reinforce the mother's definition of the problem as Jim but rather focuses on one of her comments and asks her to explain what she meant. The mother had said: "If Jimmy makes a comment, I immediately feel hostile for some reason and I don't understand it. Peter can make the same comment and I don't have the same feeling. And even in discussions with Jim, when he and I will discuss, oh, anything, even generally, I usually feel hostility and I don't understand it."

Of all the mother's remarks, this appears to be one of the most significant. Her reaction to Jim is different from her reaction to other members of the family. Usually a comment like this is an indication of unfinished business in the family of origin. There is something about Jim that stirs up the mother and makes her uncomfortable. In her mind, it is Jim's fault that she gets stirred up this way. However, in checking this out with the mother, she very quickly identifies her younger brother Bob as having much the same impact on her.

The therapist immediately refocuses the interview away from Jim by asked the mother to talk about herself and the things that personally upset her. This allows the mother a natural opportunity to discuss her extended family and her behavior within that structure prior to the birth of her children. Such explanations are enlightening for the therapist but also usually serve to provide the children with a broader understanding of the caretaker within their own family structure. This is often reassuring for the children, especially the identified problem. One of the messages that get communicated is that the session will not be used simply to talk about the identified problem.

As the interview continues the mother talks about her family rather than her concerns about Jim:

Freeman: What does Bob do for a living?

Mother: He is in the insurance business. But he didn't get out of tenth grade. First he was a prison guard. When he got married, he decided he wanted to go to the university. He won scholarships throughout the whole of university. I mean, he didn't get through tenth grade simply because the system didn't conform to Bob, and you have to conform to Bob. He doesn't conform.

Freeman: He had difficulty fitting into the system?

Mother: Very much so. Very much a loner. He has no friends, he has no—my older brother, Bill, is like Steve, easy going, he is a teacher.

Freeman: How old would Bill be?

Mother: Bill is three years younger than I am. So kind of easy going, he doesn't care what he wears. To me, if you don't like me in my grubby clothes you're not going to like me in my good clothes. And my mother's feelings toward my brother Bill are similar to mine toward Steve. And my feelings toward my brother Bob are the same as hers. And Bob spent the last ten years sending my parents on trips, buying them things, everything to buy their approval. He hasn't. But not in the same way Steve hasn't. If you can understand what I mean. And it's really tragic. I see it, and you know, that Bob is only himself when he isn't buying people.

Freeman: Do you know if your brother Bill has the same reaction to Bob as you have?

Mother: Well, you see when I was married, Bob was eleven, and my brother Bill was fourteen, and I was away travelling so I never got to know them well, and I've seen them maybe on one or two occasions in twenty-two years.

Freeman: He is the youngest in your family?

Mother: Yes.

Freeman: All right, so there is Bill and then you have a sister.

Mother: Yes. I am in the middle.

Freeman: And you.

Mother: And two younger sisters.

Freeman: So your older sister would be how old?

Mother: My older sister is five years older than I am.

Freeman: Which would make her forty-four. Her name?

Mother: Ruth.

Freeman: And then?

Mother: Susan.

Freeman: How old is she?

Mother: Susan is eighteen months older than I am.

Freeman: That would make her forty-one.

Mother: Yes.

Freeman: And your two sisters, do they have the same reactions to your youngest brother?

Mother: My sister Ruth does.

Freeman: The same as yourself?

Mother: The same, oh, I can't speak for them, but there is that aggressiveness, the feeling of disharmony. My sister Susan is another story. She is a very, very quiet, sensitive person who had a great deal of psychiatric treatment here with Dr. ——— She lived here for twelve years. She has a feeling that my mother can't make mistakes. When Susan wanted to go to a convent, my mother said she would burn down the Catholic church so Susan has had a lot of feelings. She always envied me because I was outspoken and aggressive and she wanted to be that way, but people said that she was so good when she was quiet that she was torn between doing what she wanted to do and giving the impression of being good, a nice little girl. She always had friends. I didn't. I was bad. I mean really a bad kid in growing up. Teenager, I wasn't quite that bad but growing up I was bad.

Freeman: How about when you were Jim's age?

Mother: Jim's age? I was going out with fellows. Always got along with men, fellows, much better. I didn't get into trouble. I didn't get along with my mother because she and I are very similar. And

I can see my problems a lot in Jimmy. I can also see myself in my brother Bob. Things that I know, areas of improvement ... that I should work on that I see in Jim that I find irritating.

Freeman: Those would be the areas that would get you going.

Mother: Oh yes. Very much so.

The mother has made a move away from identifying the problem as being Jim to beginning to identify her own part in what has been going on in the family. She is able to see that some of what she brings into the situation is influencing the way she sees her immediate family. The therapist is still defining the problems to be worked on, but has very gently begun to reframe the family's thinking about the problem. He is beginning to move into phase three of the first interview.

Up to this point in the initial interview, the therapist has spent most of the time talking with the mother, who is the most overinvolved, anxious member in the family. However, he has been able to move the mother away from talking about the identified problem and toward talking about herself. This refocusing paves the way to the appropriate involvement of the identified problem because the tension of scapegoating has been removed. If this tension is absent, the person who is seen as a problem will be more inclined to contribute during the session. The timing for involving the identified problem in the session is important. If the therapist turns to the problem member after someone has criticized him, or identified him as the problem, the usual response is defensiveness, anger, or silence. In contrast, if the identified problem is involved as a functional member who has comments and ideas about the family, he is apt to involve himself more and respond much more favorably.

The therapist's choice of questions is based partly on what information he wants to elicit. His questions also serve to create an atmosphere of safety. The family quickly learns what type of information the therapist is seeking. Many families fantasize that the therapist only wants to know about the things that haven't worked, or about problems they have been having. Asking about positive aspects of the family, i.e., the things that have worked, provides reassurance that therapy can be a positive experience. This experience helps move the family into the third phase, where the major task is to reframe the family's thinking about the problem.

After the mother has identified some of her own concerns about herself and her reactions to various family members, the therapist involves Jim by inviting his response as an information giver about his mother and the rest of the family. The therapist wants to demonstrate to Jim that he is interested in him not as the problem but as a family member who has opinions.

Freeman: Jim, were you listening to your mother talk?
Jim: Not really.
Freeman: How about your Uncle Bob?
Jim: Yeah.
Freeman: Do you get a chance to spend much time with him?
Jim: No, not really, I don't want . . .
Freeman: I didn't hear that.
Jim: I don't like him.
Freeman: You don't like him. Would you agree with your mom's evaluation of your uncle? How do you see him or do you see him in different ways?
Jim: (No response)
Freeman: How about you other uncle, Bill?
Jim: I don't really know him too well.
Freeman: Who would you know the best besides your mother, your brothers and your father? Who are you closest to?
Jim: I think my science teacher down in Oakland.
Freeman: Your science teacher?
Jim: Uh huh.
Freeman: Is he someone you would see as a person you are more involved with than other members of the family?
Jim: Uh huh.
Freeman: Uncles, aunts, grandparents?
Jim: Yes.

At this point, the therapist realizes that Jim is not going to offer much more. However, he has accomplished his goal, which was to involve Jim as a legitimate member of the family with his own opinions. Now the therapist moves on to the other two members of the family, Peter and Steve. He asks each one of them to give their feelings about what their mother has just said. The therapist balances between asking questions about the family and asking questions about their individual goals and aspirations.

This balance is especially important in work with families that have teenage or young adult children. Developmentally, young adult children are making moves to leave the family and many experience great anxiety about being in family therapy. Much of this anxiety is developmentally connected with their own struggles to leave the family. They often feel that family therapy is an attempt to keep them within the family. I have found that teenagers who are beginning to make plans to live on their own are the hardest members of the family to keep in therapy. It is up to the therapist to demonstrate that their individual needs will be recognized as well as family concerns. The following portion of the interview illustrates how the therapist attempts to help Peter and Steve talk about both their family concerns and their own hopes and goals. (The session is still in the problem-defining stage, but is gradually moving into the stage of reframing the family's thinking about their problems. While the therapist is questioning Peter and Steve about how they see the family, he is also asking them questions about how their personal concerns relate to family concerns.)

Freeman: Peter, how about you? What thought do you have in listening to your mom?

Peter: She sums it up pretty good. That's about it, you know. The problem—I don't see why you should be using background or something, you know. That is why ... but, I don't see the problem as Bob or Bill or stuff. It's more a family thing. I mean everyone feels sort of uneasy when Bob comes in, he's got a pushy way about him of showing you his $2,000.00 ring, flashing it in your eyes and stuff, but . . .

Freeman: Do you agree with your mom's picture of Uncle Bob?

Peter: Yeah.

Freeman: But you say that the problem rests with the four of you or the five of you, including your dad?

Peter: Yeah. My dad would walk out before he would sit down, you know. We'll sit down and discuss something and all it is, is a two-hour debate and nothing solved. All there is, you know, a talk session. I hate to say you're the last resort but that's what it comes down to.

Freeman: Who is debating, when you say it's a debate?

Peter: We all are, because we all have a point of view. Everyone, you know, is trying to show their point of view and push it at the other person. And trying to say well, you don't see my way, you don't see this, you don't see that. Of course you don't, you aren't them.

Freeman: Can you give me an illustration of a problem where that was happening?

Peter: Well, there were so many of them. Mostly those little picky comments that fired things up, you know, the little sparks that fuel the whole fire.

Mother: I think that this morning for example, I set my alarm but the clock was wrong. It rang, but it rang a half-hour late. Peter and Steve had classes this morning and they got up at 6:00. Well, it was raining and the day didn't look so hot so they decided upstairs that they wouldn't go to classes, we would all go in together. Jimmy didn't set his alarm, which he usually does, thinking that everyone else was going to wake him up and, you know, this developed into a . . . Jim got very angry because of this. I mean, total misunderstanding and disorganization.

Peter: We're building a house and right now it's only half completed. We're suing companies, there are a whole lot of, you know, headaches and. .so that's all.

Freeman: That is an additional stress?

Peter: Yeah.

Mother: Oh yeah.

Peter: University for us and a new school, high school for him. She is working. There are a lot of problems. And this is just one more problem, and you know it's hard to cope with.

Peter has now expanded the problems to be worked on. He talks about the many changes the family is experiencing, and the new structure in the family. The family, for the first time, is without the father; they have also experienced a change of environment. All of this, according to the middle child, has contributed to the stress the family is experiencing. Thus far, Peter has not focused on Jim as the major problem, as did his mother.

Freeman: Peter, how old are you?

Peter: I'm seventeen.

Freeman: And you go to university?

Peter: Yes.

Freeman: And what faculty are you in?

Peter: I am in first year Arts. (Laughter) He's in forestry (pointing to his oldest brother, Steve).

Mother: Steve thinks it is a yo-yo course that Peter is taking.

Freeman: And your long-term educational goal? Your main goal?

Peter: There were times it seemed I wanted to be a disc jockey, you know, the whole bit. But I was always in the middle somehow, it seemed to come out that way. (Peter goes on to say that his goals in university are to take a law degree.)

Freeman: How about your relationship with Jim? How has that been?

Peter: Well, it's constantly strained. We spent three years together when I was in Oakland with my dad. Steve was there one year. And there were hard times, you know, constant conflicts and stuff but it seems like when Jim is together with me, like when we are alone, things aren't too bad, you know.

Freeman: Just the two of you alone.

Peter: Just the two of us, yeah, you know, things can be mildly peaceful. But when more people come in and stuff it seems things get hostile. You know, the center of attention moves around to different people in the conversation and it makes it very ... things go somehow wrong. (This is a very interesting insight of Peter's. Without his knowing it, he is talking about triangulation. Peter mentions how difficult it is for him to have a relationship with Jim independent of other people. He says very clearly that if he were alone with Jim, there would be fewer problems.)

Freeman: Do you get to spend much time, just the two of you without other people there?

Peter: Not usually. Up here of course there are four of us. We have two dogs and, you know, there isn't much chance for us two to be alone. Whereas there was in Oakland. I had my car, so I never stayed home anyway. And maybe it was out of choice. Why be somewhere when there is going to be conflict when you can go where there isn't, so you know, I used to drive. Which is my dad's opinion, too.

Freeman: What?

Freeman: Why stick around, you know, when it is so hard, when you can go somewhere and be with your friends where it is easier.

Steve: Why hang around and have to be hassled.

Peter: Right. And Jim couldn't drive so he was left alone and he wasn't hassled either. Which is one solution.

Mother: So Peter went his way and his father went his way and Jim spent a great deal of time alone.

Peter: Maybe it was wrong but at the time it was a temporary solution. I had things to do, and you know, commitments, and I went to school and stuff, so ...

Mother: And I think there were times when Peter, you know, felt bad that Jim was left alone and he would take him places with him. But like it's an older group. You take a 14-year-old brother with 16-, 17-, 18-year-old kids and it's difficult. Because even though there is the same years between Steve and Peter, you're in a sort of different group, peer group thing. So Peter found it difficult. His father didn't approve because he felt that Peter's friends were a bad influence on Jim.

Peter: My friends . . . things they did conflicted with my dad's views of how you should grow up, teenage antics and stuff. And so he got mad sometimes and Jim would be affected by things, you know, my friends did, and I did.

Freeman: How about your relationship with Steve?

Peter: We get along pretty good. We come out on the bus every morning to school and meet for lunch and stuff like that.

Freeman: Do you ever get into any hassles between the two of you?

Peter: No, I drive his car all the time, he pays insurance and everything and he doesn't complain which is nice. So everything is pretty good. (Laughter)

Steve: He's my mechanic (pointing to Peter).

Freeman: He's your mechanic? Well, how would you put things together, Steve? You listened to your mom and how she . . .

Steve: Yeah. I spent, I guess out of all of us, the most time with my grandmother, so I saw Uncle Bob and Uncle Bill a lot, you know. And, like, what she says is pretty well true, you know, like it seems like there is a competition between them. Like one day I helped them move Bill's furniture to some house around the corner and Bob kept reminding him that he was helping him, you know. And that he had never been paid back for anything that he did for him and stuff like that. So it was just competition. So I guess what she said in my experience is pretty accurate.

Freeman: Do you find yourself getting annoyed with your uncle or are you able to just let it go?

Steve: No, he came for a visit when I started university here. He came to visit my mom on Thanksgiving and they spent Monday with me. We went down to the park and the beach and stuff like that and his wife sort of, like, wants to do that sort of thing. I saw a different sort of person altogether than what I was used to. That was really the last time I saw him.

Freeman: And that other part of him you find a bit more interesting and enjoyable?

Steve: I found that I had a good time with him because he would take me out to dinner and stuff and just the way he acted I thought was humorous and it was funny, and I had a good time, like that. (Steve seemed to be the least reactive to Uncle Bob of all the members of the family. Diagnostically this could be important in that he might be able to see things a bit more objectively than other members of the family. In fact, as therapy continued, Steve did manifest the most objectivity.)

Freeman: You're the oldest. How old are you?

Steve: I'm nineteen. I'll be twenty in November

Freeman: You'll be twenty in a couple of months?

Steve: Right.

Freeman: And you're in fourth year university?

Steve: No, I'm in second year.

Peter: Actually, I'm turning eighteen in October, too. (Laughter)

Freeman: How about you, Jim, you are going to be sixteen soon?

Jim: Uh, huh.

Freeman: Okay, we'll give you all an extra year. (More laughter)

Mother: Not me please, I'll go back a year.

Freeman: Then this is your second year here, Steve?

Steve: Yeah. I've been out here two years or so.

Freeman: So you're most used to what's going on here?

Steve: Yeah.

Freeman: How did you become interested in forestry?

Steve: Oh, I don't know, I like outdoors work so it was either garbage man or forestry. (Laughter) I don't know, I'm not even sure if it's the right field. Maybe in three years' time I can answer it better.

Freeman: So you're not as clear about where you want to go professionally as your younger brother, who's talking about going into law.

Steve: Oh, I have goals like he does, you know, like I have set goals. Like I want to get into recreation or something like that where the pressures of the logging industry aren't on you. I mean, there are a lot of pressures in logging 'cause it's push the bucks . . . and I want to get into recreation and that's where I am gearing all my courses to. You could give that as the thing I would like to do.

Freeman: Sounds like you like to be out of doors a lot. Working outside. And not an office job or anything like that.

Steve: No, I don't like that.

Freeman: Well, Steve, how would you describe what is happening to your family?

Steve: I'm not sure. Like, when I left, like I graduated in 1975 from high school so when I came up here to university, I used to go down south every now and then. And like once I went down at Christmas and like I seemed to be annoyed by everybody. And like I figured that it was just, that I was myself and I had adjusted myself, you know, to everything else so that when I went down there to Oakland, there were constraints again, and you know it was hard. Well, I don't know what to call it. But it was just hard to be there for an extended period of time. You know, someone is used to being by himself. It's just like a single guy going to his mother's place or grandmother's place for dinner and all of that. That's the only connection I had with these guys until, like, this year. My mom wanted to be in a place with everybody and everybody going there. I thought it was a good idea, you know. 'Cause, Peter's older and I like to spend a lot of time with him. And soon Jim will be driving and stuff. You know, so we could sort of get together and do shit, you know. Like I sort of wanted to be closer to my brothers. Because I really missed them and the two years I was here and stuff, so . . .

Freeman: So you saw that as a good opportunity for the three of you to begin to get your relationship together.

Steve: Um, hmm, 'cause I, like, remember running for the bus, like, I'm always late so I remember running for the bus with Peter and he's always on time. He was only late because I was late, right, and stuff like that and Jim seemed like he was always four years younger than me so when my mold was changing, then he was forced to change 'cause he would come with us, you know, so we would go and play football, the three of us would. So it's just sort of hanging around with us. So I, you know, now that we are all older, our ages seem to get closer when you get older so I would do it again, and that was fun.

Freeman: So, if you looked at the next year or so, how would you like it to be between the three of you, just you and your brothers?

Steve: In this next year, you mean?

Freeman: Yeah.

Steve: I was looking for, you know, closer relationships on a more stable basis. And, like, when I was down in Oakland it didn't seem that bad, when I lived there for a year. And it wasn't nothing like that TV series, *My Three Sons*, you know; it had the same characteristics with like a sheep dog and stuff, but it wasn't anything like that perfect, but it was good. I enjoyed it. I get along with my dad really well.

Freeman: How about you and Jim then, how would you like that to be?

Steve: Well, I think I have always gotten along with him except certain things I say, you know, and certain things he says, annoy me. I used to be able to let it just pass by, but I don't know why it changed, maybe it's because I've been gone for two years and everybody that says anything to me I take immediate offense. But also I guess there was a major outburst when my girlfriend was around. Maybe she, being an outsider, it's hard for everyone to mix in sort of thing.

Freeman: Does she spend a lot of time with the family?

Steve: Yeah. I think the last few months that we have been together, like a majority of time, like over fifty percent.

Mother: She's not very happy at home. Her family are of German extraction and . . .

Steve: But that has got nothing to do with it.

Mother: No, but they have very high standards and they don't compromise.

Steve: She stayed at our place for about a month and a half, I guess. Because she got kicked out of the house.

Freeman: What is her name?

Steve: Carol.

Freeman: And how old is she?

Steve: She's eighteen.

Mother: Nineteen.

Steve: No, nineteen.

Freeman: So, the last several months it sounds like she has been part of the family.

Mother: Uh, huh.

Steve: Not several, about three.

Mother: Six. First of July, really.

Steve: Since these guys came up here, yeah. Four months ago.

Freeman: The last four months then she has really been, part of the family. If I said, let's bring in all the members of the family, Carol then would be included.

Mother: Carol would be sort . . . sure.

Steve: I guess she sort of instigated a few things, too. Like we are aggressive talkers, right? I guess it stems from my dad . . . the guy who yells the loudest gets heard sort of thing, so whenever we have had discussions, it is a rip-roaring discussion and she would get upset when Jim would talk to me rough.

Freeman: More upset than you would?

Steve: Oh, yeah, it wouldn't bother me. We're trying to put a point across and our skulls are thick as the next guy's so we are going to talk loud, you know. It wouldn't bother me, you know. I could see where it bothers them with her interfering, though.

Freeman: So Carol is, she has had some opinions on what is going on, Steve?

Steve: Probably, she would have some opinions, yeah. She would probably have different opinions because . . . she doesn't know these guys that well. And they don't know her that well.

Freeman: All right, it sounds like Carol should be here. That is an interesting perspective. Is there anyone else that has been living with the family.

Mother: No.

Phase three: reframing the family's thinking about the problem

The therapist has now moved into the process of reframing the family's thinking about the problem. So far, each member of the family, except the identified problem, has defined the family's concern slightly differently. The mother sees the problem as between her and Jim, but much more within Jim. Peter has labelled the problem as an adjustment to the four members of the family living together, coupled with the stress of a new environment and a new home. Steve has indicated he doesn't know his brothers as well as he would like and finds that his girlfriend at times interferes with the way the family deals with conflict. The therapist takes the position that Carol, who is involved in the emotional triangles of the family, should be present. This position encourages the family to rethink how various members interact with each other.

Now that the interview has progressed for some time without anyone talking about Jim as the major problem, the therapist can direct his attention to Jim and ask him what he thinks should be worked on in the family. If the therapist has been successful in shifting the family's view of the problem, the identified problem should now be more willing, and able to participate less reactively in the session.

Freeman: Jim, have you found it a difficult adjustment moving here?

Jim: Not really. It's just the environment's different.

Freeman: Like what sorts of things in the environment?

Jim: Well, you have to worry about what is happening here and I didn't have those concerns in Oakland.

Freeman: In Oakland you were more looking out for yourself?

Jim: Well, just in the way things were set up down there. My dad went to work really early. Peter was going to a different school than I, so everything was just like living alone.

Freeman: I see. So you have a family but it was what, really like a collection of individuals?

Jim: Yes.

Freeman: Very little time together; no real connection? You would be in the house but each person goes their separate way.

Jim: We were just living together.

Freeman: A convenience, a physical place.

Jim: Well, it seems that everyone wants to be all buddy-buddy here and it just won't work that way.

Freeman: You don't think that it's going to work, this buddy-buddy business.

Jim: No.

Freeman: What do you think is going to get in the way?

Jim: Well, the fact that I've been, that I have had two years of just doing . . . holding up my end, and the same with Peter and all of a sudden we have to change when we get up here, and Steve had two years of just about the same thing. It's just too much of a change for everybody.

Freeman: So in the last three years you've adjusted to going your own way.

Jim: Yes.

Freeman: Doing your own thing and taking responsibility for yourself.

Jim: Yes.

Freeman: And now you feel the pressure is to kind of fit into a family unit where you don't have as many freedoms to come and go as you please.

Jim: Well, I can leave anytime I want to; it's just that . . . somebody, everyone, is, I guess we're supposed to try and it just doesn't work. 'Cause you don't have to try when it's just yourself.

Freeman: Well, if you were to design the ideal living arrangement for you right now, what would it look like?

Jim: Just living by myself.

Freeman: In an apartment?

Jim: Uh huh.

Freeman: Okay.

Jim: Just some place where I could be alone.

Freeman: And you feel that would be most comfortable for you?

Jim: Uh huh.

Freeman: How about the types of relationships you would like to maintain with the rest of your family members? Let's take your brothers, for example. What sort of relationship would you like to maintain with Steve. Say during the next year. What would you like it to be?

Jim: Well, I will have to see them for the next three years, but after that I'll be gone.

Freeman: You would be about nineteen three years from now.

Jim: Yeah.

Freeman: So you say for the next three years you see yourself being in contact with Steve. What form would that contact take?

Jim: Well, I have to live with him.

Freeman: Well, why would you have to live with him?

Jim: He lives in the same house I do, my mom feels very strongly it should be the same way it was.

Freeman Well, let's just kind of fantasize for a moment. Say you're able to design your own living arrangement and just for the sake of discussion, you had your own place. Then what would you like your relationship to be like with Steve? Now you're not living together but you're in the same city.

Jim: Well, there's no need to have contact.

Freeman: That's right.

Jim: Then why would I want to?

Freeman: Well, that's what I'm asking, I don't know. I heard Steve say that one of the benefits he sees is that the three brothers would be able to spend more time together.

Jim: Well, that was seven years ago. You can't go back seven years.

Freeman: Okay, how about Peter? Do you take the same position with Peter?

Jim: Yeah.

Freeman: How about with Mom?

Jim: Well, I have to leave home sometime.

Freeman: Uh huh, and with Dad? He's the only one now who isn't in the same city. Any plans to have any contact with him?

Jim: Not really.

Freeman: Does he have plans to come up and visit? Or do you have plans to go down and visit?

Jim: Oh, I ... When he went back East, I went with him. I didn't know if it was going to achieve anything. I doubted it, but I still went with him.

Freeman: In other words you go to see him, but you don't think he has plans to come?

Jim: No, I doubt it.

Mother: He is planning to come sometime.

Freeman: He is?

Mother: He's in Oakland so he'll probably come for Christmas.

The therapist now is clearly in the reframing stage. Each one of the boys has identified a major portion of the problem as being the adjustment of living together and the different expectations of the mother and the father. They each said the father was less emotionally involved with them. The mother has made a stronger case for family unity and family activities together. This has created some conflict within the foursome. Jim does not see himself as the problem, nor do his two older brothers. Jim has also made it very clear that his goal is to become somewhat independent of his family.

Later on in this family's treatment, Jim manifested the strongest commitment to working with his brothers and his mother. However, in this first session, he is taking the position that he wants out of the family. The therapist is not discouraged by this reactive position but encourages Jim to pursue his thinking by fantasizing more fully about his ideal situation. This establishes his support of Jim as an individual. It would have been a mistake at this time for the therapist to make a strong pitch for family unity. This is the mother's need more than the teenagers'.

The next portion of the interview contains the mother's last effort to focus the problem on Jim. Up to this point, the therapist has moved the family from defining the problem as resting within one of its members, to looking at the whole family unit as being part of the problem. However, the mother appears uncomfortable with this concept and reintroduces Jim as the problem. The therapist's management of the mother's anxiety is crucial. If the therapist sides with the mother in her scapegoat attempt, he loses the gains he has already made. If he resists the mother's attempts but doesn't explain to the mother why the focus should be on the family, then he loses the mother and possibly the family.

Freeman: (Turning to the mother) Is there any chance the father can become involved in the family sessions? (To the whole family) I'm just wondering if there is a chance I will get to meet Dad.

Peter: He's not the type you would say to, "Hey, Dad, let's go and see a psychiatrist."

Mother: No, I talked to him on the phone. I told him what I was doing. What really brought all of this to a head was that Jim took an overdose of pills, which to me was a signal. "Look I've got a problem, help me 'cause I can't cope anymore."

Freeman: And when was this?

Mother: This was about two and a half weeks ago. And it upset me very much that I hadn't picked up, you know, cues that he had been giving out that I had maybe misinterpreted the severity of the problems that he had, so when I called their father and told him what had happened, he said, "My kids don't need a shrink." His attitude is that if you got problems you don't talk about them and they eventually go away, or push them aside.

The therapist perceives this explanation as an attempt to redefine the problem as being in Jim. She explains the role the father plays in the family in a negative way. By this stage, it is important for the therapist to have a diagnostic impression of the family as a unit as well as an understanding of the funtioning level of each of the individual family members. If the therapist has successfully gathered these impressions, he won't experience the anxiety that would cause him to focus on Jim's pill taking, since he would realize that Jim is not depressed or seriously disturbed. So far, Jim has maintained his functioning in the family at the same level as the other members. The therapist avoids picking up on the mother's focus on Jim's pill-taking episode. He instead asks the mother a bit of background information about the father's family.

Freeman: What is your husband's rank?
Mother: He's a major.
Freeman: How old is he?
Mother: He's forty-three.
Freeman: Just for a moment, let's get a picture of who is in the family. On Mom's side of the family, we've gotten a picture of Bob and Bill and Susan and Ruth. Who on the father's side would be involved in the family?
Mother: You see it's difficult because we moved around a great deal and neither my family or their father's family really had that much influence on any of us.
Freeman: That's because of the military?
Mother: Because of the military and two years here and two years there, and this sort of thing. He is from a family of all boys, four boys, he's the oldest of four. There is a span of maybe every other year and then they skipped a year and the youngest boy was born. The father never remarried again after the mother died. The youngest boy was fifteen months old when she died. He raised he four boys. He was thirty-four when he married. So he was about forty-four when his wife died, so he raised these children and because I guess the boys had no one else, they knew whatever Dad said was the beginning and the end. His father was the authority on everything and I think the only thing that might have influenced the boys with regard to their father's family was that they never write. They made it very difficult. They would make person-to-person calls so they wouldn't have to talk to me if John (father of the family) wasn't there. They would make sort of unpleasant remarks about me, and I don't know whether it was in the presence of the boys but they heard me voicing opinions on it. And so I think that this was the only thing that you guys would have very much to do with.

Peter: Steve and I went across country. We flew across and we stayed there a week. And the picture I got of my uncles and aunts on my dad's side is a very different one from my mother because we were John's kids, you know. We seemed to be okay. I got along with them really good. When I was there they never made funny remarks about my mother so I didn't take offence, but I got along with them. I wouldn't mind going back.

Freeman: You would like to see them?

Peter: Yeah, I don't know whether I would fly all the way out there just to see them but, yeah, I would like to.

Mother: They're shouters, too, aren't they?

Peter: Uh huh. Well, they all are. Paul is the head of the policeman's union or something and he used to bang his fists and be heard and stuff, so they're all very loud and stuff. That's the way they are so, you know, they're all that way.

Freeman: So you two, did you say, went across country and got a chance to meet some of your father's family? Jim didn't?

Peter: He was younger. That's when he drove across with my mother when we moved to Oakland, you see, that's when we all sort of . . .

Freeman: I see.

Mother: And Jim just spent two weeks with John. They drove across country and on about the eighth of July, he met the brothers all living within two or three blocks of the house that John and I bought. So Jim would have had two weeks of seeing them.

Jim: We didn't live in the house they were living in.

Mother: No, I know that. I just said that the house that John bought is within a three-block radius.

Freeman: Of the rest of the family?

Mother: Of the other brothers.

Freeman: So they have stayed together.

Mother: Very much so.

Freeman: And the oldest is the one that has been away from them.

Mother: Yes. But they have always called back and forth a lot.

Freeman: But physically they were closer together than your husband was.

Mother: Oh yes, yes.

Peter: I think my grandfather, I guess had a tendency to, you know, how older ones are the father's favorite, usually the firstborn, it's like . . . no, I can see it. When they're together my dad gets on better with Steve than he does with me and Jim. And I guess it's maybe the same way with my dad and my grandfather, who never would say it was, but my other uncles will say it of course, you know.

Freeman: He was the favorite?

Peter: Dad, being the firstborn.

Mother: And I know John made a statement to me when Steve came up here. Like Steve had been spending time down there for the three months, and when Steve left, John said that his only reason for doing anything was that, he said that, "In my mind, I only had one son." This was his feeling about Steve. He missed him terribly. Maybe because in retrospect it was like his father and himself, when his father died.

Freeman: What was the year that the father died?

Mother: His father died in 1967.

Now another concern in the family arises. Peter mentions that his father favors his firstborn son, just as his grandfather did. We have also learned that because of Jim's hospitalization at a young age, the mother has been very involved in acting as his caretaker. This leaves the middle child, Peter, neither here nor there. Steve had his father; Jim had his mother. Even though the presenting problem was Jim, continued therapy uncovered the fact that for years, Peter has felt left out. And in fact his way of coping with stress in the family is to remove himself. In the early part of the session, he clearly stated that if there is conflict in the family the best way to deal with it is to leave, to go somewhere where conflict is not present.

As the family was encouraged to talk about the extended family, they quickly and comfortably moved away from their concerns about Jim and his pill taking. The mother's talking about Jim's pill taking seemed to be a move to redefine the problem as Jim. The therapist continues to find out more about the extended family, using this strategy to continue reframing the family's thinking about the problem. The family does this comfortably and talks more about the impact of other family members on the functioning of the family. This redirection reinforces the idea that the problem is in the entire family fabric, rather than just one member. This focus prepares for the therapist's move into the fourth and final phase of the first interview, which is the phase in which the family may make a commitment to work as a unit.

Phase four: commitment to work as a family

Freeman: Now I'm just looking at the time and we have to stop in a few minutes. This was really a chance to get to know you, meet you. There are a thousand more questions that I would like to ask but we just don't have the time right now.

Peter: Are these sessions every Monday? Like this?

Freeman: Well, that is what I would like to spend the last few minutes on. Actually, two things. One is, get a bit clearer notion of what you hope would happen if we continued these sessions, what your expectations would be both individually and as a family. And then how often we are going to meet. So you can take really the next ten minutes and deal with those issues. Maybe we can start with Steve. What do you hope could happen or come out of ongoing sessions like these?

Steve: Well, I knew what I wanted, but I never knew what everyone else wanted. You know. So maybe they would help that way.

Freeman: Do you get a sense of where other members of the family want to be?

Steve: Yes, I would like to make this year a little easier too, because this is the hardest year for me. Second year, you know. It's the heaviest load. So, I guess I'm short of temper when I get home and stuff. You know, long day, I get home about 6:30 to 7:00 so you know, if it's something that I'm doing that I don't realize, then I would like to find out.

Freeman: Okay. Carol. Do you think it would be a good idea to have her?

Steve: I could ask her. I guess she's been a big part of what has been going on. You can if you want. I mean, you're the expert. If you think we should, it . . .

Freeman: On Carol you're the expert. (Laughter) Okay, let's leave that one open, think about it and see what . . .

Steve: Then it's up to me?

Freeman: Yeah. And up to the family. It would be fine with me if you think that there is an issue. If she were living in the home I would say it would be very important to have her, but if she's not, if she's coming in and out, I think I'll leave that up to the family.

Steve: Okay. I'll see if she can come and then you can get your impression, you know . . .

Freeman: And get a sense of her.

Steve: Yeah

Freeman: How about you, Peter, what were you thinking?

Peter: I was trying to remember the questions. The first one was . . .

Freeman: What were the expectations?

Peter: Maybe I'm pessimistic or even prejudiced, but I feel that Steve and I get along fine together and my mother and I get along fine together, but I don't feel I get along with them around Jim. And maybe, I don't know whether the fault lies with all of us, but I feel that the fault is really Jim, you know. And so I can live with Steve, I can live in the same house with my mother, but it's too rough with Jim, you know, I can't. I can't study and everything else. I mean, doors slamming, you know and stuff.

Freeman: Do you think that there's any way that this could help sort it out? The conflict between the two of you?

Peter: Help sort it out?

Freeman: Yeah.

Peter: I've been trying for . . . I'm seventeen, almost eighteen, hasn't worked yet. Maybe God will come down and help, but I don't think so. So I don't know.

Freeman: Would you like it to be different?

Peter: Of course I'd like it to be different, yeah. But when I was moving up here I was debating moving in here with the family because I didn't know if it would work. I didn't know how much problem it would be and everything else. But my mother needed help in the house and stuff so, I thought it may be better if I go . . .

Freeman: I don't know, I'm just thinking if sibling relationships can work out now it's like money in the bank for the future. If you think about relationships now, especially at your age when you're all adult, it's like an investment in terms of what relationship you'd like five years, ten years from now. And if you've got a lot of fantasies about each other, if they don't change they'll simply lock you into relationships. And that seems sad to me. Anyway, that's just a thought I had. If you have these concerns now and work them through, you're really opening up relationships. That's why I'd like to spend some time just on your relationship with your brothers. How about you, Jim, what would you like to see happen? What would your expectations be?

Jim: Well, I don't really like my dad too well, we didn't get along this time. I don't want to go back East. And my mother violently feels that it won't be the way that it was in Oakland. So that I would, for the next three years anyway, the only door that there is is the one that we're really getting into right now. But after three years then I'm just going to university and I'll be out.

Freeman: Do you have any long-term educational goals?

Jim: I want to be a marine biologist.

Freeman: A marine biologist. How did you get into that?

Jim: I just sort of decided I wanted to do this.

Freeman: So, if I hear you then, since you're going to be living with the family for about three years then you feel you have to help reduce some of the tension, these hassles.

Jim: I could live very well without it being the way it was down in Oakland. I mean, it's no problem with me about it. One person trying while the other person doesn't just makes a nervous wreck of everybody.

Freeman: It doesn't work. Mom, how about you, what are your expectations?

Mother: I guess my whole idea about getting a house and stuff ... I mean, Steve and Peter could have gotten an apartment. But home and family mean a great deal to me, and as I've told the boys all along, the day may come when all you have is each other. So it's important for me to have them together for this year. You know, I feel maybe that to hold the fragile strand of the family together again because there are ... oh, so many things that you can do, you know, as a group. I mean, I don't expect to spend every free moment with the guys, but like we're all interested in sports and things like this. I run, the guys like to run and things like this and so there's a lot of things we can do and I feel that they've missed out, I really feel they've missed out over the last three years.

This is a typical example of a first interview. The interview has been divided into the four phases of the initial interview: (1) the warming-up phase; (2) defining the problem; (3) reframing the family's thinking about the problem; and (4) the commitment to work as a family.

These phases are in evidence during the entire beginning stage of the family therapy process. Each session contains these four phases. Gradually, with each succeeding session, the family focuses more quickly on matters other than their initial concern with the identified problem. As this occurs, they begin talking more about individual concerns and about how the family is functioning as a unit. When this shift in focus has solidified the family has entered the middle stage of family work. This stage is evidenced by the family's acceptance of a new definition of the problem and by each member's assumption of responsibility for his or her own part in the family.

The next chapter will discuss the middle phase of family therapy.

6

THE FAMILY THERAPY PROCESS: BEYOND THE FIRST INTERVIEW

THE MIDDLE PHASE OF FAMILY THERAPY

The middle phase of family therapy is characterized by the family's ability to recognize that by working as a unit, it can better meet both individual and group needs. During this phase, there is less scapegoating, blaming and reactive behavior. Individual members begin to take more responsibility for their own behavior, and the family acts more as a resource for itself. Anxiety and ambivalence about being in family therapy decreases, and the therapist is not as likely to be put into the position of mediator, ally, or expert.

Often in this period the family begins to feel quite positively about what is happening within the family; the crises and difficulties that brought them to treatment are no longer of great moment. Many families terminate at this point, which is unfortunate because the family has not integrated sufficient change to withstand a new crisis. The task of the therapist during this phase is to help the family identify or further define issues and concerns they can profitably work on.

At this stage the therapist may need to be very active, asking questions that stimulate the family to identify subsystems within the intrafamilial and extrafamilial networks to which the family could direct their attention. Discussion of relationships with extended kin can help identify productive areas for work. For example, if things are calm between parents and children in the nuclear family, there may be some valuable work that could be accomplished by focusing on the relationships between the adults and other extended family members.

In one family I worked with, the father moved from working successfully on his relationship with his daughter to desiring more involvement with his oldest brother, with whom he had always had a poor relationship. As he made a move toward his older brother, his wife began reevaluating her relationship with her older sister. As the parents worked on their extended families their children's relationships with each other, which had been extremely conflictual, improved in a parallel fashion.

It may be crucial during the middle phase for the therapist to introduce new issues to the family. Systems theory maintains that there is a need to have new information entering the system which helps the system learn more about itself and its connections with the outside world. The more dysfunctional a family the more likely it is to be cut off from the outside world, i.e., extrafamilial relationships. It is not unusual for a family that is experiencing severe intrafamilial conflict to have few resources available to itself. Most of the effort members of these families expend goes toward struggling to get others in the family to meet their needs. If these members themselves are very needy they tend to resent demands to meet others' needs, and serious conflict, dissatisfaction, and anger result. Once the family is able to branch out and begin to make contact with other systems, it finds other viable resources beyond its own intrafamilial boundaries. Once this occurs, family members loosen up their demands and expectations that other members will meet all their needs. This extension of boundaries is the major goal during the middle phase of family treatment.

The middle phase of treatment is the heart of the family therapy process. The new resources that are built into the system, the redefining of what constitutes family, and the new options and choices open to the family and its individual members become clear during this stage.

PRACTICE PRINCIPLES FOR THE MIDDLE PHASE

The following principles of practice help the therapist move a family into and through the middle phase of therapy. Although useful from the beginning, they are especially important in helping a family become a resource system of its own.

Using process over content

The family's approach to therapy is content oriented. That is, the family presents its stories, issues, and concerns for the therapist to deal with. How the therapist handles this content is the critical factor.

The therapist should be wary of getting too focused on content issues. Rather, he should view the content as providing illustrations of how the family members position themselves in relationship to each other. The content clearly indicates how the family uses issues to deal with intrafamilial relationships. From the therapist's point of view content is important because of the response it elicits in any particular family member and in the family as a whole.

The stories family members tell are important because of what they reveal about the storyteller. The story in itself does not explain what is going on in other members of the family. However, it does illustrate concerns the storyteller has about himself. The family therapist should encourage the individual who is sharing some content to explain what makes that content important to him. The therapist who is able to free himself from preoccupation with content can listen to it more comfortably without taking positions on its correctness. This stance permits a refocusing on process, and the individual is given the opportunity to express what is going on that makes particular issues important. This process helps to diffuse the family emotional system by moving family members away from having to defend and justify themselves in reaction to another member's story.

In summary, the important point to remember is that content defines process and the therapist's use of process will determine content. The therapist should control process by viewing content issues as expressions of concerns about self, rather than statements about others. In this way he frees himself from taking sides and offers the family new ways of understanding old content issues.

Helping the family to restructure

Families that come in for therapy commonly have either an overly rigid boundary structure, or a weak boundary structure. In helping the family restructure, the therapist's goal is to help the family get a sense both of itself as a unit, and how it relates to the outside environment. A rigid boundary structure does not allow individuality to flourish; the therapist's task here would be to soften the boundary structure. In contrast, if the family's boundary structure is weak the therapist will work with the family to strengthen and clarify its boundary structure.

The basic goal is for the family to see itself as a unique unit which can both provide resources from within and utilize resources from without. The goal for the family is to be resilient, flexible, and receptive to energy from the outside which keeps it vital and functioning. The task of the therapist is to encourage the family to use its own strengths and resources, and to help identify additional resources outside the intrafamilial system.

Using a multigenerational concept to help expand family boundaries

This idea originated with Murray Bowen (1978) and deals with how the extended family can help the nuclear family develop a better sense of itself as an historical unit. Helping family members research their roots, reconnect with lost family members, and generally use family as a resource system are the basic principles in this area.

One of the tasks of the therapist is to help the family obtain a sense of its own history. A common characteristic of problem families is their isolation from their extended families. When asked about their involvement with parents, uncles, aunts and siblings, many family members will say that it has been years since they have had any involvement with these relatives. Yet they will often show very strong emotion when they begin to talk about these family members. One way of helping a family to develop a better sense of itself is to encourage members to reconnect with some of their lost relatives. These reconnections have several implications. Often there is a fair amount of unfinished business in these old relationships. The chances are high that the conflicts in these relationships will be acted out and repeated in the nuclear family and other relationships. The nuclear family may be indirectly helped by having one of its members reinvolve himself with an extended family member and resolve some earlier problems. Their resolution may relieve the need to act out a particular conflict in the context of the nuclear family.

Recently there has been a resurgence of interest in family history and genealogy which reflects the strong need for this connection with one's past history (A. Haley 1976). It has been theorized that the better one's sense of personal history, the fuller is one's sense of self. Thus, the therapist can use the extended family and a three-generational perspective to help expand the family's boundaries.

Introducing new information to redefine the problem

One of the tasks of the therapist is to help the family expand its ideas about its functioning by teaching its members new concepts about family behavior and helping each member define individual concerns. The teaching of systems concepts is helpful in this regard. The following concepts can help families view behavior differently: (1) role structure, and how it can limit flexibility and options; (2) alliances and coalitions, and how they create conflict, and barriers to members understanding and knowing each other; (3) family loyalties, and how they can serve as a barrier to family members using outside resources more effectively. These concepts can be shared with the family members to help them get a better sense of how they are operating as a social system.

In the middle phase of family work, the teaching of systems concepts is especially helpful. Since family members are less reactive during this phase, they are better able to hear new ideas and concepts about family behavior and respond to them in a more positive, proactive manner.

Using humor to help diffuse an intensive emotional situation

Humor may easily be one of the most helpful methods of helping the family get some distance from its own misery. Once a family laughs a little about its dilemma it has developed a handle for dealing with it. The ability to use humor as a therapeutic strategy is one that should come naturally to the therapist, and, of course, the use of humor should always be appropriate. If the therapist is basically comfortable with humor, the chances are that he will be able to use humor to help the family become more comfortable and feel more in control if its situation.

Using the concept of emotional triangles to restructure the emotional system of the family

This concept was developed by Bowen (1966), who postulates that the triangle is the basic emotional building block of any social system. When systems are under stress, they naturally develop triangles as a way of dealing with it. When the therapist enters a family situation he is automatically put into a triangle position. How he uses the emotional triangle is crucial. The early efforts of family members will focus on convincing the therapist to take a triangled position within the emotional system. They will tell the therapist stories to attempt to get the therapist to take sides. As was mentioned in chapter 3, it is important for the therapist to be aware of how the family uses stories to structure their relationships. When the therapist uses the triangle in a positive way it helps the family members relate to each other differently. The therapist enters the triangle but is in control of his part within the triangle. When a member of the family tells a therapist a story about another family member the therapist enters the triangle. He can deal with this in several ways: (1) by encouraging the individual to continue the story, thereby becoming part of the triangle; (2) by asking the storyteller questions about himself in relation to the story; or (3) by encouraging the storyteller to direct his story to the family member he is talking about and tell him what concerns him about his behavior. In each of these maneuvers the therapist uses his part within the triangle to produce a different set of experiences between the twosome. When the family becomes aware of how it uses triangles to avoid relationship intimacy and conflict, it can begin to find more functional ways of relating.

Taking 'I' positions to help family members differentiate themselves

This principle is related to the use of triangles. One of the therapist's tasks is to position himself as a clearly defined "I" (one who does not take sides) in relation to family issues. When the family is under stress, it will increase its efforts to get the therapist to take sides on issues. If the therapist yields and takes a side he has become triangled and loses effectiveness. On the other hand, if the therapist is able to be somewhat detached from the issues, but involved with the family, he has taken an "I" position with the family. The main idea is that the therapist shouldn't become a party to secrets, coalitions, and alliances, or view certain members of the family as right, wrong, sick, or healthy. If he can avoid these traps, the family will be freer to explore new ways of looking at each other and defining the family process.

Taking a research stance to help family members learn about themselves in the outside environment

Only the family can teach a therapist about itself. In turn, as the therapist learns about the family, the family learns more about itself. The therapist who thinks he must put all the pieces together and inform the family about itself is overfunctioning. The family will tend to be passive in response. When the therapist takes the position that he can never really know a family, he will naturally begin to ask more questions and make fewer statements. When engaging in this process, the therapist should allow himself to become a rich bank of new information. This information will teach him not only about this particular family, but about families in general. Correspondingly, the family, by sharing its knowledge about itself, will begin to hear things they haven't heard before. Through this process, the family becomes more knowledgeable about intrafamilial needs and extrafamilial expectations.

Going with the energy

This therapeutic strategy comes out of research in social systems behavior. There is a tendency in systems to oppose that with which one feels uncomfortable. For example, if a family member is silent in a session, the tendency is to encourage the silent member to talk. If a member is combative, the tendency is to discourage the combativeness. Opposition to the behavior can easily become a source of reinforcement for it.

By "going with the energy" the therapist can often quite easily resolve difficult therapeutic dilemmas. For example, the therapist may encourage a silent member to continue his silence, and take the position that the silence is an indication of his involvement in the therapeutic process. It then becomes difficult for the silent member to remain silent. Once the opposition is removed, the motivation to continue the struggle is lost. An analogy is a tug of war in which both sides pull against each other. If one side lets go, the other side collapses and the struggle ends. Similarly, if the therapist redefines resistance as positive and healthy this takes the power of the resistance away and the resistance ends.

Going with the energy is easily one of the most powerful strategies to use in a therapy session. Rather than avoiding the anger, the discomfort, or the conflict, the therapist can go with it and encourage the family to understand it differently by not making it the same old issue. This principle was illustrated in the interview contained in chapter 5, when the identified problem, Jim, said he wanted to leave home. My strategy was to encourage him to think about it and to ask him to fantasize what it would be like, rather than try to convince him that it would be a good idea to stay at home. Once I encouraged the very thing the family had been discouraging, his interest in maintaining that position lessened.

Supporting the more functional members

The tendency in therapy is to become concerned and involved with the least functional member(s) of the family. If the therapist defines the therapeutic task based on the functioning of the least adequate member he can bring the whole family down to a lower level. However, if he encourages the most functional members of the family to continue their level of functioning he defines the family at its highest level. In the beginning of family work I try to identify those family members who are the most flexible, re-silient, and creative, and the least anxious about change. I then use those family members as an impetus to help restructure and redefine the family struggles. It is helpful to have the more functional members of the family present during the family sessions. They will often encourage less functional members to move up. In contrast, if the process is geared toward the less adequate members, it becomes more difficult to build on the resources naturally available to the family.

The ten preceding principles are the major practice strategies used to help move the family through the phases of therapy. Some of these principles will be illustrated in the following interview, which is the sixth session with the R family, whose first session was reported in chapter 5. The family is now in the working-through phase of family work.

Besides illustrating certain practice principles, this interview demonstrates how differently the family deals with its concerns and its relationship structure when it has moved from the beginning phase of family work to the middle phase in which they are beginning to see themselves as a more resourceful and functional unit.

Freeman: Maybe you can fill me in on what has been happening.

Mother: I think it has been that we seem to have conflicts every two weeks or so but basically I see an improvement. Jimmy's really putting forth an effort. Peter hasn't changed much. Peter's very easy to get along with basically, anyway. Steve is a mess. I don't think he is putting forth any effort. But I excuse him because he's got a heavier thirty-six hours this year. He's got a girlfriend that, you know, puts pressure on him to see her and he feels obligated to stay home. These things make life very difficult. Plus he likes to go out and cut wood on the weekends to make some money. So he is under a very stressful time and he doesn't want to be hassled, although he is inclined to drop comments which provoke other people. It is such a stressful time for him and he just wants a bit of peace and quiet and harmony, you know. You got to pick up his clothes, wash his clothes, do everything for him because ...

Freeman: How about your life? Apart from the boys, what is going on with you?

Mother: I am changing jobs tomorrow.

Freeman: Is that something you have been planning to do for a while?

Mother: Just for a month. I am going to be a nurse out at the penitentiary, at the hospital. It's sort of a challenge. I am kind of excited about it. I've never done that kind of nursing before. It's more psychological nursing because they are basically well, so I am anxious to start. It will alternate, and I am on five weeks of days. You spend another week with the psychiatrist when he is dealing with the problems of these people. So ... I am sort of looking forward to it.

Freeman: Is this the kind of nursing you are interested in, psychiatric nursing?

Mother: No, not psychiatric nursing. Not people who have mental problems. I am interested in people who have social problems, but not mental problems. I don't like caring for people with mental problems. I find it very unnerving, very. When I was at a psychiatric hospital I saw people in there with kinks that I have and I know it's all a matter of degree but I get nervous . . . I really do. I think primarily because my father had a nervous breakdown, my sister had a nervous breakdown and had psychiatric care. One wonders what is keeping you from going over the brink. So if I stay away from it, keep it out of my mind then I don't have to really consider it. But these people out there, some of them have extremely high IQ's, very bright people, and yet I don't know really what to expect and this is where the element of excitement comes in for me.

Freeman: Do you think the difficulties you feel your dad had influenced your wanting some distance from that?

Mother: Oh, for sure.

Freeman: How would that work, how would the difficulty your dad had and your sister had have an impact on you as a person?

What is interesting so far in this interview is how quickly the mother leaves her concerns about her boys after initially evaluating them quite differently from how she evaluated them at the beginning of therapy. Now she says that Jim, originally the identified problem, is doing the best, whereas Peter and Steve are not doing quite as well. She is able to move comfortably to talking about herself and her own concerns. She introduces concerns about her work and her family of origin. Most importantly, she begins to make a connection between experiences in her extended family, her work situation, and her relationships with people in general. Clearly, the mother has moved into the middle phase of work when she begins to think more about her family of origin experiences and their impact on her as a personality.

Mother: My father had a nervous breakdown when I was about ten. I was very close to my dad and it frightened me as a child of ten to hear him cry. He used to cry—I mean cry—from the toes right up, like I had never heard before. And that used to upset me very much. And my sister of course, all of her problems happened when I wasn't even with her, but . . .

Freeman: Was this after you left home?

Mother: Oh, yeah. When she came out West there are things she told me about shock treatment and things . . .

Freeman: Was it explained to you what your dad was going through when you were ten?

Mother: No, no. I didn't know really until I went into nursing exactly what. And even now I don't know. I don't think the doctors in those days were that liberal with information so I don't think that my mother knew anything except that he had a nervous breakdown. So, no, it was never explained. I never knew really exactly what nervous breakdown meant.

Freeman: Having been ten, is it kind of hard to go back all those years? I am curious how a ten-year-old put that experience together, seeing a father at a very stressful time.

Mother: It was a terrible thing.

Freeman: Was there anyone you could turn to for support?

Mother: Oh, no, I think it was just, like, things were different. People weren't outspoken, people told you things and you accepted it as the way it was. He cries because he is sick. And that was the extent of it. I don't remember really a day-to-day existence with him being sick. I just remember the crying and I mean, in those days it wasn't a sort of macho thing to do, to ever cry, so just, every time my father cried it was just . . . and it was crying like I had never heard before or since. Just a desperation, almost. Then I think it endeared him more to me as I grew up. I recall being close to him before but not in the same sort of way. And then, of course, my mother had to take on the responsibility of home, and she never gave it back to my dad, so my dad always became like a star boarder, with little or no responsibility except earning a living in the house. My mother is a very strong person.

Freeman: So at the time you were ten there was a shift?

Mother: Oh, definitely.

Freeman: In the relationship between your mother and father.

Mother: Oh, for sure, for sure.

Freeman: Did your brothers and sisters ever get together and talk about what was going on?

Mother: Oh, no, we never had those kinds of discussions. Not in our house. No, never.

Freeman: Do you think it would have helped—again, going back to that period—if your brothers and sisters had spent more time with each other trying to deal with that issue, what was happening with . . .

Mother: Oh, for sure. From my perception now and the way that I think, sure. If that kind of thing happened to my family circle now, by all means we would. Because I think ignorance, too little knowledge is bad but I think ignorance is even worse. Even when I deal with patients every day I say, "Why are you here?" "Well, the doctor said I need an EEG, do you know what that is?" I think people have a right to know when it affects their lives.

Freeman: Do you think it makes it easier?

Mother: Of course it does. Basically. Generally. You get people who can't handle the truth so you have to kind of go at it slowly, but with the kids, knowing how to and knowing them well, I don't think they would be content. I think they would ask.

Freeman: You think so.

Mother: Oh, yeah, for sure.

Freeman: Your sister, when she had her difficulties, did she turn to any of her brothers and sisters?

Mother: She was out here on her own.

Freeman: Did she write?

Mother: She wrote to me all of the time. Yes.

Freeman: Did you know when the difficult time was going on?

Mother: I knew, but not the extent. She didn't ever write the extent of the thing that she suffered. It's only been since then when I have had a chance to talk to her. I think she is still ill. Oh, she is a weak, weak person with no self-confidence and tends to be influenced tremendously by my mother. Now what is fabrication and what is fact I don't know. I can't sort it out because I could go to my mother and say, "Marilyn said this," and my mother would deny it. Over the years I have found my mother is inclined to shape things a little rather than admit it. So there is a conflict. I don't know the full story.

Freeman: So, of all your sisters you think she is the most vulnerable.

Mother: For sure.

Freeman: Any hunches as to why that one?

Mother: Oh, yeah. She was the middle child of the three girls.

Freeman: Sort of Peter's position.

Mother: Oh, yeah. But Peter's more outgoing, the way my sister never was.

Freeman: Tell me, was she real quiet back in childhood?

Mother: She was always very quiet and my mother used to say, "Oh, you are such a beautiful child, you are so quiet and so good," and I was bad. I demanded a lot of time and attention. And I remember my sister telling me, about six years ago, she was always so envious of me, because I was the kind of person she really felt she was inside. But people kept saying how nice and quiet she was, so in order to get their attention she stayed nice and quiet. But something inside her was screaming, "I am not good and I am not nice and I am not quiet." It was the first time she said anything. My mother favored my sister because she reminded her of her mother who had died when she was thirteen. And Marilyn told me that my mother had always said, "Look, when the kids are all gone you and I will get a place to live in, I will take care of you, Marilyn," and even to this day, at forty-one years old she doesn't understand why my mother broke her promise. My mother didn't leave my father and they didn't find a place. I mean, it's really—I was frightened when my sister was talking to me like this. I couldn't believe that she hadn't faced the reality of life at forty-one years of age with three children. And I am not equipped to deal with problems like this. I have always shied away from them.

Freeman: So, when she tells you this, what gets going inside of you?

Mother: I panic inside.

Freeman: You want to get away from it.

Mother: Oh, yeah, yeah, because I don't know how to handle it, and I don't know what to do. This is why we are here. I leave these things to skilled people, you know.

Freeman: What do you think she wants from you when she tells you about those things?

Mother: I guess she wants someone to listen to her.

Freeman: Not to do something more than just listen?

Mother: Yeah, and maybe looks to me for guidance, because she said to me, "You're so strong and things come so easy for you." Which I find hilarious because I fight tooth and nail for everything I get.

Freeman: You don't see yourself that way, the way she sees you.

Mother: No, oh, God, no. She said, you know, "You went to school and it was so easy." You know those were the most difficult years of my life, going back to school. She says, you know, "You've got a house and you are supporting the kids and it seems so easy for you." This is how she sees things. She is not realistic and she doesn't see things the way they really are. But she is envious of me and envious of my supposed strength of character. She doesn't think she has this. That is why I am most uncomfortable.

Freeman: Do you think it helped you to be in rebellion and acting out a little bit?

Mother: For sure. Even in my adult life.

Freeman: That is your strength, so you see it as a positive thing in finding out who you are and what you are.

Mother: Yes, getting things done.

The therapist has been using the three-generational perspective as a strategy to help the mother identify areas that she finds uncomfortable in her own life. The mother points out that in her own family there was an intense triangle. When her father developed "his nervous breakdown" she was ten years old. She identifies that period as a time when there was a shift in the relationship structure in the family. She moved toward her father while her mother moved toward her sister Marilyn. The mother identifies this as a difficult emotional time in her life. She was confused and received little information to help her understand what was going on. She was left on her own and moved toward an alliance with her father, with strong loyalty ties toward him and an antagonism and confusion toward her mother.

She understands her sister Marilyn's developing difficulties because of her middle position in the family and in some ways connects this with Peter. Later on in the interview we see that Peter in many ways felt he was in a similar position between his younger brother, Jim, who had a favored position with the mother, and his older brother, Steve, who had a favored position with the father. Peter's way of dealing with this was to find activities outside the family, and to shut down his expectations for family intimacy. The family is just beginning to identify this pattern.

The therapist has been attempting to help the mother define areas of unfinished business in her family of origin and see how they are affecting her current life. In the following excerpt, the therapist moves with the mother and other members of the family to uncover how family of origin experiences have been influencing their perception of what is going on in the nuclear family.

Freeman: When you think of your three children here in terms of this need to find themselves and the struggles they have to go through, how would you relate it to what you experienced with your middle sister and your dad? If your three boys began to rebel in ways similar to how you tried to, how would you . . .

Mother: I would let them. I don't know if they agree or not . . . but, from when they were thirteen I said, you are old enough to question. If I tell you something, go to bed at ten, and you don't agree with it, tell me why. Maybe I don't see things in the same way you do, so let's discuss it and perhaps we can compromise.

Freeman: You see that as an important thing, compromising so that all people win?

Mother: Yeah.

Freeman: You don't think it is all right when only one person wins?

Mother: There are some things I won't compromise on. Because it goes against basic principles of mine, like lying and stealing. No, under no circumstances. If you do something, you bear the brunt. No. I won't compromise. But on basic living things, I feel if the boys want to explore, by all means.

Freeman: How about this one then: between having someone who keeps things in and tries to make things good and nice and smooth, and someone who lets things out and fights what is going on. Which of the two are you most comfortable with?

Mother: The outgoing one.

Freeman: So, the other one, you would be a bit more uptight about?

Mother: I don't understand it. Someone who works their problems out by themselves and makes a decision on their own quietly and—if I have a problem, the whole world knows about it, the better to resolve it.

Freeman: So, in your family, who kept things in more, who was the one who did not let the family know what was going on?

Mother: Marilyn, I think basically. But we weren't a conversing family, when I look back, but then times were different. You didn't have family discussions. Your family told you to do something and you did it. There were no questions. And I don't think it is fair, I don't. You did it. It was much different then than it is today. I don't think you can really compare times. I was aggressive and I was outspoken and I said it's not fair. But I still ended up doing it. And I could rant and rave all I wanted.

Freeman: But you did rant and rave.

Mother: Oh yeah.

Freeman: I am just trying to figure out where you got that gumption to rant and rave. Where did that come from?

Mother: I don't know.

Freeman: And your middle sister didn't have it? You both came from the same parents.

Mother: I don't know, I really don't know. I don't think any of them, of all the children, are as vocal as I am.

Freeman: And they see you that way too?

Mother: Oh, yes.

Freeman: So, of these three guys, who is the most vocal?

Mother: It is hard to say, because they are all ... There is something I really admire in each of them. Tremendously outspoken, all of them. Steve is not so shy that he can't call Carol's mother over some small problem like her getting in at midnight. I was very proud of him when he talked to her on the phone saying what his feelings were. Peter's the same way in talking to his girl friend, very honest and I find it very admirable. Jim too. He is very outspoken, not afraid. I find this a very admirable quality in them.

Freeman: So you see that as a good, positive, strong thing.

Mother: Oh, for sure. Nobody walks over them.

Freeman: Jim, what do you think about what you mother is saying?

Jim: I don't know ... I think it's ...

Freeman: When you hear her talk about her own sister, your Aunt Marilyn, and your grandfather, and the struggles they had, did you know about that?

Jim: No, they are not my family.

Freeman: Not your immediate family?

Jim: It's none of my business.

Freeman: Well, just picture yourself being ten and your dad going through this sort of thing that your mom's dad went through. How do you think you would have put it together, if it's possible to project yourself into that position.

Jim: (Laughs) I don't know, when I was ten? I guess I would tend to shut it away. I don't remember that much. I don't pay that much attention. I knew there were a lot of quarrels, a lot of fights, but I can't seem to remember anything. I guess I just went outside or just sort of shut it away. So I think I tend to do much of the same thing.

Freeman: Kind of shut it out.

Jim: Uh hum.

Freeman: When your mother was talking you smiled once and said "Syracuse". Did you get a memory to come back?

Jim: No, she is talking about parallels between Peter and Marilyn. Well, in Syracuse Peter was just about like Marilyn. You know, Peter was sort of quiet. Then something seemed to snap and he seemed to change when we went to Oakland.

Mother: No, a year before.

Peter: A year before.

By this point the family has made some interesting moves. Jim begins to identify Peter as having some of the same features as his mother's middle sister Marilyn. Prior to this the mother had only casually mentioned a connection in sibling position between her sister and her son. But Jim brings it home by saying that Peter's behavior was similar to his aunt's. It provides an example of how the mother's discussion of her experiences with her family of origin stirs up other members' thinking about their own family experiences. The therapist moves between two time dimensions, the past and the present. Once Jim introduces his concerns about how he saw Peter's behavior when they were younger, the therapist can use this as an opening for helping the three boys talk about their experiences in their own family. He begins with Jim, who in the past has been identified as the problem, but by now has made the most moves in terms of repositioning himself in the family. Jim quickly identifies Peter as being like his mother's middle sister. He makes the connection and begins to talk about one of the things that made him uncomfortable about his brother, Peter.

The family is now in the middle phase of the middle interview and the therapist moves the focus away from the mother and her experiences to the boys. He begins to check out if there are any triangles and alliances in the family similar to those the mother identified as existing in her family of origin. It is usual when there are only three children in the family for one to be on the outside of the triangle at any given time. When the therapist started with this family, Jim was on the outside and Peter and Steve were on the inside. Now that the family is in the middle phase of the therapy, these triangles should not be as much in evidence. In addition, the triangled set of relationships change over time. The therapist should check to see who is currently on the inside and how the configuration has changed. The mother clearly defined the alliances of her family of origin as consisting of her and her father on one hand with the mother on the outside, and her mother and middle sister on the inside with her father and herself on the outside.

The therapist has also been encouraging the family to share their concerns with each other. The mother's explanation that she was frightened about having so little information about what was happening to her father brought home the importance to the family of their sharing information, without the therapist's suggesting that this be done. Rather, the therapist encouraged the mother to talk about how important she felt it was, based on her experiences in her family of origin. This provides an example of how to utilize a family member's ideas about what is good for the family, reinforcing them by encouraging the person to talk more about them. The therapist could have introduced the importance of sharing information, but the message is more powerful when a family member is able to state the need for it in his or her own terms.

The interview now picks up with Jim talking about how he sees his brother Peter.

Freeman: Jim, how do you see Peter as being like Marilyn?

Jim: Not really outgoing, didn't like sports or anything like that. He sort of gave the appearance of being whiney and always sort of complaining, really moody. All round sort of whimpiness, there is no other delicate way to put it.

Freeman: Those are your memories of it anyway. What, six years, five years?

Jim: No, this was when I was nine or ten and Peter was eleven or twelve.

Freeman: How long ago was that?

Peter: Five or six years. (Laughter)

Freeman: Steve, you're taking issue with this?

Steve: Yeah. It might be because I'm older. I shared a room with Peter and went to the same school with him. Jim was in a different school. So I saw him more and knew his friends better. And I don't think he was shy, because he was vice-president of the school. I don't think he was shy. I don't think he was shy, because he was popular and anybody who is shy isn't popular.

Mother: I think what Jim means, Steve, is that in public school, the little school on the base, Peter was very quiet. He had one friend. When he went into ninth grade . . .

Steve: This is what I am talking about.

Peter: This was in seventh to eighth grade.

Mother: When was he king of the carnival?

Steve: He was vice-president in seventh grade, king of the carnival in eighth grade.

Peter: King of the carnival! (Laughter)

Steve: Speaking of rebellious, when Peter was rebellious, and this was an example, he didn't tell my mother about his team business and he went to a dance in his hockey shirt. He was having his picture taken and my mom would have made him get all dressed up and he knew that. So he didn't tell her and he went in his hockey shirt.

Mother: And there is his picture on the front page of this magazine and Peter in this dreadful hockey shirt with the crown on and . . .

Steve: That's sort of rebellious.

Peter: We used to play hockey, remember?

Steve: Yeah.

Jim: Remember when you didn't want to participate in sport so you sort of got out of it by your . . .

Peter: You take a specific account and try to apply it to generalities.

Jim: No, I can remember when you were whining to Mom about that, you couldn't go to the dance and went stomping upstairs. And all the time you were stomping upstairs.

Peter: I remember times when that happened with you. You were playing hockey, you didn't want to play anymore. You'd hit

The therapist has assessed how the sibling relationship developed over a seven- to ten-year period. He discovered that Jim and Peter were conflictual and competitive with Steve being the older, somewhat more observant one. Jim's perception of Peter differed from Steve's. Steve saw Peter as much more competent and successful in his peer relationships. Jim, on the other hand, viewed Peter as somewhat inadequate and shy.

The therapist uses the siblings' discussion about their relationships as a way of helping them express how they would like their relationships to be in the here and now. The past relationship structure is a safe place to evaluate how the siblings would like their relationships in the present. The therapist got the overall sense that the siblings basically got along with each other and were observant of each other's behavior.

In the following excerpt the therapist takes the family back to what went on in the mother's family of origin and in her relationship with her husband, and tries to connect these areas with how the family is currently using itself as a resource system.

Freeman: Peter, how would you fit into that one yourself? Let's go back to being ten. Your mother said she was having a difficult time when she was ten and didn't have anyone to talk to. Now picture yourself in a setting with your dad where he's have a very difficult time and isn't able to manage his own affairs. How would you manage it?

people with the stick and go whining in and mom called you in the house and wouldn't let you play anymore.

Jim: Well, that's aggressiveness. You weren't aggressive at all, you . . .

Peter: You wouldn't let him go to dances, so I kept pestering, hoping she'd change. But she didn't, that's right.

Freeman: Well, let's turn it around and get off the word shy and into this very intriguing difference between the middle sister and yourself. One holding it in and the other letting people know what's going on with you. Are you saying that helped you get through?

Peter: One instance sticks out in my mind. My mom and dad were having a really big argument. And I remember her saying she wanted a divorce and stuff and she was crying in her room. I remember Steve saying, "Come on, let's get upstairs and leave them alone." Its hard to say, you don't know what is going on so you are very confused. I don't know how I would have reacted if my dad would have had a nervous breakdown. I don't think my mom would have, or my dad.

Jim: It's not that he's strong, it's that he won't let it happen.

Freeman: Did you turn to Steve at that time during that period?

Peter: Yeah. I always found it easier to be with Steve. Sure we had arguments, but it is always easier for Steve and I to get along better than I ever got along with Jim. That is why it has always ended up that Steve and I share the room, not Jim.

Jim: They do mean things to me when I am alone with them.

Freeman: So you wouldn't turn to Jim, you would turn to Steve.

Peter: Yeah.

Freeman: Even now.

Peter: Even now.

Freeman: (To Steve) Who would you have turned to? Let's picture a period with things really going haywire and no one explaining it to you.

Steve: I don't know how I would have handled it, but I knew there were arguments and stuff like that. But I would explain it myself. I saw it more as their problem and I didn't feel it inside. I felt it as a problem, but I didn't feel it was eating me and stuff. You don't know, I did find out about it ... I didn't think anything serious would come of it until my mom told me that me and Peter would have to split. Then it bothered me for a while, but then it didn't bother me because I saw that, well, if they didn't get along it would be the best thing.

Jim: No one really told me that much.

Freeman: About what was going on?

Jim: Yeah.

Mother: I told you when we went across country.

Jim: It doesn't sort of stick out in my mind that I was ever told what was going on.

Mother: What did you think?

Jim: I just added up the conclusions myself and formulated what was going on in my own mind without help from anyone else.

The therapist is trying to help the family see that family members can use each other as resources when they fill each other in on what is happening. The therapist goes back to the parents' separation and eventual divorce and the impact it had on each of the children. The two oldest children did use each other as resources but the youngest one, Jim, was pretty much left to his own imagination. The mother remembers explaining to her youngest son what happened but he doesn't remember. This is not unusual since information exchanged during an emotional period is not usually processed the way it is meant to be. The mother clearly feels she explained what was happening to her sons. But it appears what they heard, especially the youngest son, was quite different from what she explained. The therapist uses this to illustrate that the family needs to develop its intrafamilial support system and not take anything for granted.

The family has moved from being concerned about one member of the family to trying to gain an understanding about how they have been operating as a family. One indication of this move is Jim's beginning to ask questions about how certain patterns and personalities develop within the family. This question shifts the focus away from the difficult time the family had when the parents separated to a discussion of how family members fit into the family unit. The therapist uses this opportunity to take a research stance in the family by encouraging each member to share with him his or her understanding of how the family has developed.

Jim: Can I ask you a question?

Freeman: Yes.

Jim: When you are born, right, you don't always have a set personality for the rest of your life, or is your personality formulated by the different people you meet through life, is your personality formed by the impressions they have on you? Or are you just born with it and grapple with that?

Mother: But I think what Jim wants to know was, are your basic characteristics formed before your basic personality. I mean, one can change behavior, but can one change one's basic personality.

Jim: Like, my Mom seems to think that we are born with these little computer cards.

Mother: You come into this life with your baggage. Your baggage being your genes and your combination of parents that have produced you. A different scrambling of characteristics produced Peter.

Freeman: Do you think this is why your sister handled family and you handled family in different ways, maybe right from birth.

Mother: Yes.

Jim: I think it would be absurd to start with a clean slate. Your coming in is sort of shaped by the different positions that you have in the family. You can see parallels between a family of three boys who are basically the same and you are formulated by other people and their opinions and stuff like that.

What is interesting here is that Jim has clearly moved from taking a reactive stance and defending himself, to becoming curious about how his family has developed and about his part in it. Jim seems to be the most curious member of the family at this point and is the one who is encouraging the family to think more objectively about itself. The therapist uses this to help the family research itself and become more objective and proactive about the way it organizes its set of relationships.

Freeman: What would be really exciting is if we were able to put you in the middle of the family, where Peter is, and put Peter where you are and see if there would be any difference.

Mother: You know what was odd. Steve, being male, was always given the most responsibility. Steve went away to spend the summer with my mother and he went down to Oregon with the trailer and then Peter became the eldest son because my uncle wasn't there and it was amazing how well Peter handled responsibility that he wasn't given before. And remember, Peter, you said for the first time you felt kind of good about yourself, when you put up the tent and you never had to do that before.

Jim: I chopped down a tree.

Mother: Yes, but just suddenly Peter was in the position of being the oldest, not genetically, but in the situation.

Jim: You see now, they never really would give the youngest that chance.

Freeman: You have taken the words right out of my mouth. It is unfortunate that it doesn't happen, that you get so locked in. But you are the youngest brother.

Jim: I think that is what makes the youngest so rebellious.

Mother: But I am the youngest and also the middle child as well.

Freeman: Well, just imagine then if you eliminated your brothers, you would be the youngest of three girls, the last . . .

Mother: I was so bad I don't think it would have made any difference, no, I wasn't the spoiled youngest child, ever. My middle sister was more inclined . . . because of her personality. She was a gentle—my mother used to say Marilyn was never meant for this world.

Both Jim and his mother talked about how sibling position affects personality and one's sense of responsibility, and the therapist uses this opening to do some systems teaching. He takes

Jim's statement that the youngest is never given much responsibility and discusses how relationships would change if the family
turned the sibling position upside down. He is showing the family
members that they should avoid being locked into rigid roles and
beliefs about who is adequate and inadequate within the family.

Freeman: You know, I often ask adults who are the oldest siblings
if they would turn to any of the younger ones for help and it's
incredible how few oldest say they couldn't see the younger
brothers and sisters having anything to offer them in terms of
assistance, advice, guidance or support. So they could go
through their lives, they could be fifty and still have the same
relationships.
Mother: Well, would you seek advice from one of your students?
Freeman: It's hard to do.
Jim: I imagine you tend to sometimes try and maybe think they
are not really inferior, but they are really, you know, less capable
than other people.

Mother is a little resistant and defensive in looking at this. But
Jim, being the youngest, quickly picks up on the new idea that
the therapist has offered and tries to bring it home to the whole
family.

Freeman: That's right. Let's look at it this way. Other people feel
you are less capable, do you begin to feel that you are less
capable?
Jim: Yeah, I would. You get a real inferiority complex.

Now the therapist is able to directly deal with some of the
concerns that Jim has had in the family without labelling Jim as
the problem. He redefines how to look at the family and focuses
not only on the identified problem's role but also on the
relationship structure of the entire family. This allows the identified problem to become more of a teacher and experimenter, in
contrast to his old role of reactor to the family's focus on him as

the problem. It also encourages the mother to look at herself and how her own family of origin affected her, rather than focus solely on her family of procreation.

Mother: And yet I never felt I was not capable, I always felt clumped in with the losers, kind of thing. That is what I thought when growing up.

Freeman: Well, how do you put together what's going on with your kids, and between you and your husband. What if you had a breakdown, or someone else had a breakdown?

Mother: I don't know, I find that most unusual really. 'Cause I can see him, like I worry about him living alone. I can see him drinking to excess. He wouldn't have a nervous breakdown, he would just kill himself.

Freeman: That is how you would fantasize it?

Mother: Yes, he would never allow himself to show the weakness of a nervous breakdown. I could see him drinking to excess. I could see him do a lot of things like that.

Freeman: But you get it out, you get it out of your system.

Mother: All of the world would help me solve the problem.

Freeman: Which other people may perceive as going bananas, but that is your way of handling it.

Mother: Yes.

The mother offers an opportunity to triangle in father in this discussion about how family members react differently in family. She brings in her husband as one who is most likely to commit suicide rather than show any strong feeling. The mother agrees she deals with emotional upsets by getting them out of her system. She also agrees that in doing this she may be misinterpreted by others. It is important to keep in mind here that the children imply that the father is stronger than the mother because he shows less emotion. The mother uses the opportunity the therapist gives her to talk about herself to clarify that position with her family. She states that she has her own way of dealing with emotional concerns, which is to talk about them. She feels her children at times may misinterpret this stance.

Mother: I find with myself—and Steve has been a witness to this, Peter has too, well, you usually instigate it. If I really get angry at Jim and I lose control it lasts for about ten minutes. My little momentary insanity where I cry uncontrollably and almost shake all over. I don't even know what I do. It takes about ten minutes and it builds up, and that is fine. I have this little sort of spastic period and then I am all right. But I can never see myself, knowing my character, really going crazy.

Jim: I remember that night . . .

Mother: I function better under stress. If I hadn't gotten stress in my life, I would go out and find it. It seems I will take on someone else's problems in order to work under an element of stress.

The mother's last remark is an important statement. In the first session she was clearly the overinvolved, overconcerned member of the family. Even though her older children were not particularly concerned about the identified problem's behavior, mother seemed to be intimately involved with it. Now in the middle phase of family work the mother clarifies her need to become emotionally involved in what is going on around her. She states very clearly that if she doesn't have any stress in her life, she will go out and find it. "It seems I'll take on someone else's problem in order to work under an element of stress." This is important to know about the mother because it would appear that she would have difficulty not becoming overinvolved in a problem of one of her children, even if the problem didn't necessitate any real concern on her part. It would be helpful and freeing for the children in the family to understand that the mother isn't necessarily reacting to their problems as much as her need to be involved in some sort of emotional relationship. If the children in the family could understand this, their response to her reactiveness could be less defensive, angry or exasperated.

Jim: Remember that night when you had that little problem, where you did your little spastic thing there? Your spastic dance as you call it?

Mother: Is this the last one?

Jim: Yes.

Mother: Yes.

Jim: If that hadn't been so serious I would have laughed.

Freeman: Is this what you meant when you said you see Mom as being more likely to have a nervous breakdown than Dad?

Peter: She creates an aura of stress, you know. She seems to think that you have to have that, and I don't see why. My dad—maybe it was because she was married to him and so she sees him in a different light to his sons, but I don't see him as ever admitting that he would be under emotional strain.

Jim: He would be but he wouldn't admit it. Never in a million years.

Mother: Like, I have seen John where he sat down and cried. And I found that very upsetting because he seems to be so strong in so many ways that to see him weaken is very upsetting and in the eighteen years we were together, I think I maybe saw it three times. But the boys, never, ever saw that, he never allowed them to see it. So I saw him certainly in a different way than the boys saw him.

Freeman: You said with your father, when he was crying, you said that in some way it made you feel closer to him. Was it something like that with your husband too?

Mother: Yes. I think anybody who is crying out of desperation, there is a protectiveness as a woman . . . you feel a protectiveness that comes out of you.

Jim: Is that because you feel you work better under stress, so you take on their problem?

Jim is very aware of what is being talked about at this point. He is beginning to understand that sometimes his mother reacts out of her own needs rather than the needs of certain members of the family. The therapist has to be careful here not to let the mother become the identified problem in the family. His emphasis is on clarifying how a person's need to react in certain ways can influence their perceptions. This awareness is beginning to emerge in the family with Jim being the more observant one at this time. It is not uncommon for the identified problem in the family to be more sensitive and aware of the needs of certain members of the family. There are times when the scapegoated member of the family assumes that role as a protective device. Once the scapegoated member begins to reposition himself in the family and no longer feels the need to play the identified problem role he or she can become an important resource to the family. When this occurs it is a clear indication the family has made a significant move from the beginning phase of family work, where family anxiety is high and scapegoating is prominent, to the middle phase, where members take more proactive stances and become more clear about individual needs and roles in the family and how the family operates as a unit.

Jim: It just seems that my mom, she can handle her own problems okay. But little tiny problems of other people, she tries to bring them all on herself and they become great big catastrophic events. Like when Steve ran through a red-yellow light and the cop pulled him over. Mom starts pulling on the cigarette, sucking on the cigarettes, wondering what is going on back there, there is Mom looking back and wondering what is going on. And you know, it's because it's such a great big deal to get her to calm down. It is such a big thing.

Mother: Steve, how do you feel when I do my little spectacle?

Steve: Ah, it makes me mad.

Mother: At who? At me?

Steve: Yeah.

Freeman: Why?

Steve: I don't know, it makes me mad when Carol has headaches, too. You just can't handle it or something. I don't know, somebody is spending time—like I am starting to waste time. Now, you know, this problem could be solved. Amout of time being wasted, expending all this energy in other outlets, like jumping around.

Mother: And yet you waste so much time by procrastinating. I find this sort of a conflict.

Steve: No, I am taking it easy.

Mother: No, but you procrastinate, Steve, you had your little box of wood and you must get down to it, but you know, you will eat, you will look through . . . very procrastinating, to me it is a waste of time and yet something like my little sort of episode, is really an emotional release. Well worth the time I spend.

Steve: That's an emotional in other aspects. Maybe your emotional release does not upset you, but it irritates me because my thing is the exact opposite.

This dialogue is very important. The two family members now are beginning to get a sense of how they react differently to emotional concerns. The mother says she has to get it out of her system by getting upset, possibly overreacting; Steve tends to try to distract himself and not react to or overtly deal with stress. Steve identifies his way of handling emotional stress as being exactly the opposite of his mother's. The family is beginning to understand that they have different ideas about the appropriate way to deal with stress. The therapist's task now is to insure the family recognizes there isn't a right way or a wrong way but many different ways. By the therapist's taking an "I" position, rather than identifying or forming an alliance with one member or group, the family may be able to allow a range of ways for dealing with emotional tension. The tendency on the part of the family is to try to get the therapist to identify the "best" way of responding to stress. The therapist should have enough awareness to know that his preferred way of dealing with conflict or emotional tension is not relevant. His position is to help clarify what is more comfortable for each member and to learn how the family as a system can support these different ways of responding to tension.

Freeman: (Turning to Steve) What is your emotional release?

Steve: I don't know.

Freeman: Well, you said yours might be the exact opposite of Mom's.

Steve: Playing the guitar, taking it easy, like even leaving school and going home, the drive. If there isn't traffic. It's an emotional release. Peter doesn't think so.

Mother: My emotional release is a release of tremendous energy.

Jim: I think breaking something would be fine.

Freeman: When you talked about it before it was breaking something of someone else's.

Jim: Yeah, I think a cardboard box, I would rip the heck out of it. And I will feel better. And I can sit down and just sort of take it easy afterwards and I can feel better. And it doesn't necessarily have to be someone else's. I feel it can be anything.

Mother: Peter, what is your emotional release?

Peter: I can't think of anything. This guy plays guitar and this guy's fighting.

Mother: I know.

Peter: I bite my nails.

Mother: You bite your nails—that is a nervous habit.

Peter: It's a nervous habit. Going to sleep—I have been finding lately that going to sleep is the absolute heaven of my day. It is the one thing I can look forward to when I go to sleep. I can really get rid of the tension of everything. And then I start to wondering. What if I get to like it too much. I think that is about the only thing.

Each member of the family now has identified his or her own way of dealing with emotional tension. Mother has some sort of emotional explosion, Jim has to physically assault some object like a box, Steve needs to meditate in some way and Peter finds the process of going to sleep the most comforting. The family presents a wide range of adaptational styles. The interest in learning about how various members of the family handle stress is now coming from the family more than from the therapist. Family members are asking each other how they deal with difficult situations. They are becoming more curious about each other and more objective about how each deals with situations.

The therapist now begins to focus more on Peter. Peter, being the middle child, has been in a neither-here-nor-there position in the family. He has told us that when he is under stress he tries not to deal with it. Yet Peter and Jim have had the most conflict. Apparently, Jim is the one who is more eager to work through their conflicts whereas Peter tries to get away from them. The therapist now spends some time talking with Peter about how he sees his life and how he reacts in the family and in the community.

Freeman: What kinds of things make you tense?

Peter: If I've got a clear head and I have had enough sleep I can take anything, nothing makes me tense. But if I haven't had enough sleep, I've got a paper to do tomorrow I haven't started yet, I don't even know what I am going to write on and I am mad at the professor, that really makes me tense. When I start to skip French, that is when I know I am starting to get tense.

Steve: What do you do?

Peter: I don't know, I am trying to figure out something, but I haven't figured anything yet and my grades keep dropping lower and stuff.

Freeman: Are you having some problem with some of the work that you have been doing?

Peter: Yes, it's hard to explain, but in the art class, I can see what I am doing wrong, and I just have time to spend and correct it. But French, if I can't understand then I can't begin to figure out the problem, so I don't ... that is why I hated French the first time I took it. When I got here the agent said that you are required to take it and all that. I dislike it.

Freeman: That feeling of something gnawing inside of you, have you had that before?

Peter: Oh yeah, it's always been there, maybe that's a nervous outlet.

Freeman: When do you get that?

Peter: Probably when I am under emotional strain. Probably emotional or mental strain.

Freeman: Can you remember some times in the past when you might have had that?

Peter: I guess it tends to be around exam time each year. There was a time in my tenth grade when we had just moved and Steve was going to art school with me and my mother left and I was very good friends with my biology teacher and I would go to class. And it seemed every day at a certain time my head would start to pound with all these hypertension headaches. And I would always get a couple of aspirins off of him, and it went on like that for about a week or so because he didn't know what was wrong, but after a while it started to go away. It must have been some tension headache. But I still can't figure out what it was.

Mother: Peter has always done really well in school. And when you went to Oakland, you remember they put you ahead. Yeah, it was a whole different change. He always seemed—at least this is how I perceived it—he likes to excel. He seems to get very nervous when he is not excelling. When his grades start to slip, because he is very competitive, within himself. And to think that he is not producing seems to create a very stressful environment for Peter. Steve has never been an A student, Peter was.

Peter: Not all the time, he did good and better sometimes, and . . .

Mother: Yeah, but I mean basically, if you average all your marks out, he would be a C+ to B− and, you know, where Peter got A's and liked getting A's, so it seemed to me when his grades started to slip . . .

Freeman: You said also that that was the time of the moves. Mom had gone and I guess you were with Dad at that point.

Peter: Yeah, with my dad. It was a time of a lot of tension.

Freeman: Related to what?

Peter: I am relating it to school and around the house and stuff. That is probably why I started getting headaches, you know.

The therapist does not encourage the discussion of the difficulties with school as the major reason for the headaches but checks if there were other things going on in the family. The time in Peter's life when these severe headaches occurred was also when the family was in a period of disruption, following the parents' separation. The therapist attempts to help the family see how these latter factors might have been affecting Peter. Mother responds by explaining Peter's concern with school as the reason for the headaches; however, the therapist does not pick up on this, which would have allowed for triangulation with the school. Rather, he encourages Peter to talk about how he was reacting to other matters in the family and to look at how they were affecting him. It would likely be more comfortable for the family to talk about school pressure and avoid the discomfort around family disorganization. It is important for the therapist to have a clear idea about his or her own feelings about school and school pressures and not get sidetracked onto these issues. The focus should remain on helping the family assess how intrafamilial patterns and problems were affecting individual members.

Freeman: Well, what other times do you get them? (Turning to Peter)

Peter: I can handle problems around the house, you know, putting up the wall boards, the two of us, and stuff, or the ceiling and stuff like that. When it comes down to things that I know I should be doing better, and I know it is my own fault and the deadline keeps coming and I keep putting it off. It seems to me there is a right time to write an essay for class, when it seems the right time. It seems to just hit you, this creative mood.

Freeman: How do you feel about that, what do you do about it?

Peter: My stomach gets tight.

Jim: I just think Peter may be, the things he can't understand he tries to solve, right? Whereas when we were down there he just sort of blocked it out and got back to it when the time came. But I feel that I can sort it out, sometimes I might not understand at the moment, but I don't have any knotty sensations in my stomach.

Mother: You get a pain under your rib cage.

Jim: That didn't happen until I came up here. I was a relatively calm person until I came up here.

Jim tried to make a connection between what was going on with the family and Peter's getting knots in his stomach. Jim acknowledges that when the family, consisting of his mother, Peter, and himself, moved, it was a difficult time for him and that it was during this time that he had a pain under his ribcage. The therapist brings this discussion back to Peter to try to help him understand what he is reacting to. After a brief discussion the interview concludes:

Freeman: Well, our time is up I think it can be very productive for the family to look at different ways of dealing with both comfortable and uncomfortable situations. It seems that each member of the family has his or her own way of dealing with tension. It would be interesting to pursue how various family members deal with other issues in the family and how this is understood by the rest of the family.

The quality of the interaction in this session is quite different from that of the first session. The family members are becoming more observant about their behavior and there is less scapegoating. Concerns about any particular member seem to fluctuate, with different members being objects of concern. Concern has been expressed about Peter, Steve, Mother, and Jim. The family is beginning to recognize that each member of the family has his or her own concerns which affect the whole family. When the family begins to achieve this recognition it is clearly in the middle phase of work. The family has become more aware of patterns they follow in relating both intrafamilially, and extrafamilially. The family still makes occasional attempts at scapegoating, triangulation, alliances, etc. However, the family is now more quickly able to move away from these dysfunctional patterns to refocus on self. There is more laughter and ease in the middle phase of work and the family members themselves begin to take on the questioning stance.

The therapist's job in the middle phase continues to be that of maintaining an "I" position which avoids taking sides regarding "correct" ways to resolve family problems. He should see the family as a resource in its own right and encourage individual members to share their thinking about how things should be handled. When the anxiety level is down, and members are cognitively evaluating the family rather than reactively relating to each other, a very exciting learning process occurs. The family members can now begin to develop some creative ways of relating to each other and the outside environment.

Although some of the patterns that were present in the beginning phase are still in evidence in the middle phase, they are less rigid and the family does not hold on to them with the same vigor. Family members' relationships shift and they begin to focus more easily on self concerns.

The next chapter will deal with the terminating phase of family work.

7

TERMINATING STAGE: LETTING GO

The terminating stage of family therapy depends on the previous stages. If the beginning and middle stages have been concluded successfully, the terminating stage will occur naturally. If the problem has been redefined as family focused, and the family has recognized its own resources and its potential for using sources outside itself, termination evolves easily. The degree of success the family has experienced determines how naturally the terminating phase is experienced. The latter phase parallels what has happened during earlier phases.

In the beginning stage of family therapy the ending of each session is anxiety producing, possibly because family members have not yet learned new ways to deal with each other. The thought of going home and having the "same old stuff" happen again can be a frightening one. Thus, even if the therapy hour has been a comfortable, growth-producing experience, one can fear the aftermath. However, we see that as a family progresses with the therapy and members begin to identify the skills and knowledge for satisfying their individual needs as well as working together, the letting go phase becomes less anxiety producing. When the session ends the members are ready to leave and get on with their own lives.

It is interesting to observe a family over a course of a year in therapy. During the first three or four sessions there is resistance to becoming involved at the beginning of the session and resistance to letting go at the end. As the family progresses in therapy, there is generally less resistance. The family will quickly begin to move into the middle phase of the session, working on the problem, and appear eager to work on its concerns outside of the session. These dynamics seem to be true for the entire process. Once families begin to expand their boundaries and recognize their inner and outer resources, they no longer see formal family therapy as necessary. This decision is a natural, evolutionary one. The families have moved from a reactive stage to a proactive stage.

The reactive stage is most clearly seen during the beginning of family work, when the family is taking the position that it is not responsible for what is going on but just needs help to resolve one particular problem. As the process continues, family members make fewer decisions based on feelings of anxiety and panic. They shift to feeling in control of their situation with the ability to determine what is best for self and the family as a group. When the family reaches this point, it becomes quite natural for them to terminate therapy. Ambivalence, anxiety, and fear about leaving formal therapy are not in evidence.

It is helpful for the therapist to remember that one of the major long-term goals of family therapy is to help the family improve its problem-solving abilities. Families enter therapy with a range of different problems they want solved. Therapy will not eliminate all life problems; the goal is to help the family develop coping mechanisms, resources, and strategies to allow them to respond differently to problems they encounter. It is mastery, not elimination of problems, that is important.

The formal terminating session should be structured to give the family the opportunity to share their overall experience in the therapy process. It is helpful for the family to evaluate their success in handling old problems as well as their effectiveness in coping with existing concerns.

The consolidation of sense of self should be encouraged during the terminating session. The therapist may leave the door open for the family to return for a brief session or two if it encounters difficulties with which it feels unable to cope. The family therapist should define his role as that of a consultant. If the family views the therapist as a consultant, they will redefine their reaching out to him or her in the future. When families have this perception of the family therapist following termination, they are able to work through dilemmas in follow-up sessions much more quickly. In contrast, if the family interpreted its need for future therapy as a failure, their reentry into therapy would be much more difficult. It is important at termination to provide the family with the message that if they require an occasional consultation this is not an indication of failure.

The interview which follows provides an example of a terminating session. It follows the general format that I use in conducting a terminating session. First, each member is encouraged to discuss the highs and lows of their experience. This discussion helps the therapist assess which experiences were especially useful and which were unhelpful or disappointing. It is illuminating to have family members go into some detail in describing their highs and lows and to see if and how others differed in their reaction to the same experience.

Secondly, the family is assessed for changes which have occurred in each of the subsystems within the family. What is of interest here is how each individual's functioning within the family has changed over time, and how the husband-wife, parent-child, sibling and total family unit have been affected by the therapy process.

The third area evaluated during the terminating session is the family effectiveness in dealing with current concerns. Finally, the family members should know they can return in the future if they desire to rethink some of the experiences they have been having since the last session.

Most of the agenda items mentioned above are illustrated in the terminating interview which follows. The background information on this family is as follows:

The nuclear family consists of the father, age 45, the mother, age 43, and four children—three daughters, ages 20, 18 and 12, and one son, age 14. The two oldest girls had been in and out of therapy for several years prior to the beginning of family therapy. Immediately preceding family therapy the 20-year-old daughter had been hospitalized for two months. It was primarily because of her lack of progress that the family was referred for family therapy. The 18-year-old daughter had been in individual therapy with a child psychiatrist for over a year. The parents and the two younger children had not been involved in any type of therapy prior to the family therapy.

The presenting problem was twofold: the oldest daughter was not functioning, within the family or in the community; the 18-year-old daughter was a behavioral problem, particularly within the family.

When family therapy began the parents expressed a strong desire to have the 18-year-old daughter hospitalized. It was evident that the parents had no recognition of the impact the difficulties with the two oldest daughters was having on the two youngest children. This family was seen over a two-year period for a total of thirty-two sessions. During the first year of therapy the entire nuclear family, parents and all four children, were seen. The second year of therapy focused primarily on work with the parents. However, several sessions during the second year involved the entire family and a few involved the parents and the two oldest children. The last six months of the family therapy process dealt mainly with the relationship between husband and wife and their role as parents.

Prior to the terminating session with the parents, a terminating session with the entire family was held during which the children had an opportunity to assess the impact of family therapy.

The parents seemed to have undergone the most change. They discussed the impact of this process on them and their perceptions of its impact on their children. The mother, who expressed her belief that the most significant changes had occurred within her and in her perceptions of her children, was initially the most resistant to family therapy. At the beginning she had resisted involving her two younger children.

The appendix contains the first and fourth interviews with this family. These two interviews have been included to illustrate the difficulties in beginning with a family that identifies all its problems as resting with one member. The first interview clearly illustrates how resistant certain members were to beginning family therapy. The fourth interview shows the middle phase, where the family begins to view the situation slightly differently. During the fourth session it is apparent that certain members have begun to look at family patterns while other members continue to be resistant to making these connections. The reader who is interested in gaining a better sense of this family's early history in treatment is referred to the appendix.

The terminating session which follows was conducted with the parents of the family. The parents speak clearly about the impact of the process on them and respond to the terminating agenda items previously mentioned.

Freeman: Now since we are going to stop therapy, I would appreciate hearing from each of you what you consider the high points and low points of the last two years, the things that you consider really hit home, that made a lot of sense to you, and the low points, the things you wish had been different.

Mother: Well, I'm looking at the overall picture ... when I finally realized that I couldn't do much for the girls in the way I could when they were younger, I do think I've been too much with the girls, too close to them when they were younger. And Trudy and I were really talking about that the other night and she—we were really so close and she felt that—the same as I did, that maybe we had been too close and then when Peter and Elizabeth came and a few years after that I took up golf and then I was away. But I don't think these things were wrong, but I think what was wrong was that we were too close. This is one thing that I have derived here. I really believe ... and I think giving Elizabeth and Peter a little more independence is probably really good for them because they are just, you know, they are going on fourteen and sixteen now and we couldn't wish for them to be better. Well, I don't mean—they give us a little sass and that. They really are good kids and there are no major problems and we had already had lots of problems with Trudy by thirteen.

Freeman: By this age.

Mother: Yes. Mind you until she was ten, there was never a problem. She was always too good I think.

Father: That was why she had the problem later. She was holding back too much.

Mother: Well she says that herself, this is what she says, and she was. You could talk her into anything, she was so good when she was little.

Freeman: First ten years.

Father: Yeah.

Mother: And it was just around maybe eleven she started and then by twelve and thirteen she was so ... it didn't matter what we said to do she would do the other way.

Freeman: You think maybe she might have been too good.

Father: She was too much that way.

Mother: Yes.

Freeman: So developing that realization would be a high point. How about the low points, the things that you wish had happened that we didn't deliver?

Mother: Well, the only thing that I could say, and I'm not really equipped to know for sure, I used to feel and I still wonder if maybe Trudy shouldn't have had more therapy. But she says now, you know, the therapy she has been having with you has been tremendous. And incidentally, this is one thing. The other night when she was so upset, I think that she was more upset about leaving you than leaving us and that is the truth. You know really, she said she felt there was a great deal of help here for her but she was ... you know, she gets herself in a bind, eh? So they got kicked out of that hotel they were in—that was bad enough—it was a Red Cross woman ... so that was bad enough and then they got kicked out of there.

Father: I didn't know whether they were kicked out.

Mother: Didn't I tell you they were kicked out, didn't you hear me say that?

Father: No.

Mother: Well, the story she tells me, if it is true or not I don't know, it was a contributing factor anyway, but she and her friend, they probably had been drinking and doing something which, you know, I have no idea. They were up on a balcony and they were dripping water down on people's heads that were walking underneath them, and thinking they were funny as heck. And then someone caught them at it. Trudy has never stayed at the hotel but her clothes and that went there and then she came home.

Father: Oh, I saw the place.

Mother: Dick went to pick up her things with her on Monday.

Father: Boy oh boy, what a flop house.

Mother: It was down on————, you know, that is really going a bit too far. But she and this girl decided that, how was it now, about two weeks ago she phoned. They had been suite hunting, and she said that the suites were too high in Seattle and that she figured that she was going to have to leave the city and it was right after that she came up with this idea about the farm.

Freeman: It was her idea, eh?

Mother: Oh, yeah, she has talked about that.

Father: Yes.

Mother: Before, but I can't remember when that was.

Father: Well, they have been up there once. She and Margaret for a weekend, some years ago.

Mother: So when she said it, I mean, we are not that close with this cousin. So we said, if you want to go, it's up to you. Sit down and write to them and if they can have you, I am sure they will. Although you can't ever be positive you know. You don't know what someone's circumstances are. Anyway, they were very nice. They both wrote back, the cousin and the wife, and told her they ... so we sent the letters to her.

The mother's description of what has been happening with the family is quite interesting. First, she describes a possible low point, that this identified problem, Trudy, did not have more help. As we will see the father takes issue with this point of view and describes the individual treatment of his daughter as having almost no positive impact. However, the mother then describes an incident that her daughter was recently involved in. In the past this incident would have been used by the parents as further evidence that this member of the family had serious problems and should be seen individually or hospitalized. Now the mother views the same type of behavior as part of growing up and testing out one's environment. She quite easily moves from this incident to talking about other issues in the family. This is an indication that the mother has made progress. Rather than becoming overly preoccupied with the behavior of one member, the mother is able to keep her perspective.

Freeman: The low point?

Mother: That is the only thing. I have always had this concern, I must say for both of the girls, because they both had completely different problems. There was always this kind of concern of mine.

Freeman: Um hmm.

Mother: Now maybe it was unnecessary.

Freeman: But that would be somewhat a disappointment. You have continued to wonder if Trudy should have received more individual work. Any other points?

Mother: Oh, well, I felt the same way about Peter and Elizabeth. I was very concerned.

Freeman: About them being involved.

Mother: Well, I was afraid. That age is so delicate and I think more for a girl than a boy. And I sure didn't want anything upsetting her and getting her on a track where she would be afraid that something would happen to her.

Freeman: What do you think about their involvement now?

Mother: Oh, I think it was fine. But I am still glad that we dropped them out when we did, because Elizabeth particularly has been much happier. I wouldn't say it was just because of that, she has been happy.

Freeman: In general?

Mother: Because of the family situation. She admits to me now that last year she was quite unhappy. She said she used to be so crabby with her friends. I said I hadn't noticed that she was crabby. She said, "Oh, I wasn't really very happy last year." She is much happier this year. That is because everything is better. I mean, I can't think of anything else.

During the second part of therapy, commencing in the second year, we stopped seeing the children regularly and focused on the parents, their relationship with each other, and the difficulties they were having in repositioning themselves in relation to their children. The mother was clearly ambivalent during the first year about involving her two younger children. When we began with this family it was clearly divided into the bad kids and the good kids. Mrs. P was anxious that the involvement of the younger children in the sessions would lead to their developing the same types of personalities as the older children. However, as Mr. P points out later on in the interview, the youngest child Elizabeth was taking responsibility for the stress in the family by crying and being generally upset.

Although the outcome of therapy had been positive, Mrs. P still has reservations about the wisdom of involving the younger children. The father is unequivocally positive about involving the younger ones and sees it as having helped free them from the sadness and sense of responsibility for the family turmoil.

Freeman: How about you, Mr. P, what would be your high point?
Father: Well, I guess the high point is the point that you brought across about disagreement in the family between two people. Because when you look back and think about the arguments, it is usually Trudy with someone in the family, a third one getting involved and then a fourth and then a fifth and pretty soon everyone is in an uproar in the house. So we have tried to follow what you have suggested and if something starts between two people, leave it to them. Usually it is over and done with and sort of forgotten. Before it would trail on, you know. And it would continue on. So I think that point that you brought across was really constructive. Low point? I don't know if it happened at the

time. I guess the low point was when Margaret was in here (the hospital). That is probably it.

The father points out that one of the more helpful parts of the process for him was understanding how the family operates as a system. During the middle phase of work the family began to talk about how triangles influence family relationships and fuel conflict. Although this discussion had occurred a year prior to the terminating session, the father quickly identifies this as being important to him.

Freeman: In the hospital?
Father: Did that happen before we had the therapy?
Mother: Yes, before.
Freeman: Yes, that was prior.
Father: I think for me that was probably the low point when she took those pills.
Freeman: Her second hospitalization.
Mother: Oh, yes.
Father: Yes, I think that was.
Freeman: What made that a particularly low point for you?
Father: Well, I guess it was the fact that we had been going through therapy for a while and then you don't think that sort of thing is going to happen, when you have been progressing. And then all of a sudden that sort of thing happens. And as it was, I think things had been worked out all right. I think that afterwards she realized what a foolish thing it was to do.
Mother: It was a shock too.
Father: Yes.
Mother: She had never shown any self-destructive tendencies at all. And it was an awful shock. At the time that it happened, she didn't seem to be that upset, even, over it. I think that was the thing. We weren't prepared at all. It was sort of out of the blue.
Father: It was a common base, I think, in high point and low point too, in that the second time ... she just slashed her wrists last Christmas. Of course you can say it was a low point before she did it but then I think the high point is that we took a stand at

that particular juncture and stuck to it. I think if you do take a stand and the child realizes that you are going to—you might bend a wee bit but you are not going to break—then they are going to be a bit more self-reliant. I think if the child knows that you are going to keep changing your mind all the time that they don't know what to do. So I think that is sort of a combination of high and low period.

The father is pointing out that he has learned new ways of responding to old crises. He has talked about each one of his older children acting out in some way, Margaret taking an overdose of pills, and Trudy making a suicidal gesture by slashing her wrists. In the past these behaviors would have thrown the family into total collapse. The parents would have demanded that the children be put into individual therapy and be hospitalized. Now the father is able to evaluate these two incidents somewhat differently. He sees that part of the problem is how the parent reacts to the child's behavior. He is taking a self position here; when he reacts differently his children respond by reacting differently. This is a complete turnabout from his thinking at the beginning of therapy where he placed all the responsibility on his children and felt there wasn't much he could do until his children began to act differently. On the other hand his children were saying they couldn't react differently until their parents changed.

Freeman: Have you had any expectations or hopes that something would have happened out of this process that hasn't?

Father: No, I don't think so. It wasn't going to be easy. I knew that from the very beginning, it was going to be a slow process. We weren't going to get any miracle over night.

Freeman: What about these two aspects that your wife talked about? One about more work, more individual attention for Trudy. Do you have the same feelings?

Father: Probably not as strong as Mary, so I think it is more with her behavioral problem. When she gets more maturity it will help. It is difficult for me to say and I don't know what your opinions are on it, I don't know.

Freeman: Do you have the same strong feelings about having more individualized work for Trudy?

Father: Well, she was convinced herself that she needed it. Because she had it. The problem is that she had it for a whole year, and nothing came out of it.

Mother: She didn't get anything out of that.

Father: I don't know whether she was using, what was this fellow's name, Dr.

Mother: Dr. D.

Father: Dr. D as a sounding board or what. When I used to go with her to the psychiatrist and after she had had the session, I would wait to take her back home and I talked to Dr. D and Trudy, you know, for just about five minutes after and there was just no getting to her at all. And there were some points that Dr. D would bring out to her such as, you know, if you want to be treated as an adult, you must act as an adult, sort of thing. Well, she wouldn't listen to that sort of thing. So that year's therapy there, which was individual, didn't do her any good whatsoever.

Mother: No, that is true.

Father: So I had misgivings about any further therapy.

Freeman: I see.

This excerpt shows how previous therapy can influence the family's willingness to get involved in any new therapeutic endeavor. When family therapy started the parents were very hesitant about becoming involved. Their major goal was to have their second oldest daughter Trudy hospitalized. When I recommended family work be continued, they hoped that eventually I would see the wisdom in hospitalizing their second oldest daughter. Now the father is saying the individual therapy for Trudy was not helpful. He described how he and the doctor saw Trudy as the problem, but she didn't cooperate in taking on that role. As the family redefined the problem as a family concern, Trudy became more involved in the process and the parents now see this as having been helpful. Although the father feels strongly that the family approach made a difference, the mother remains somewhat ambivalent. Now the therapist checks out with the father the impact he thinks the treatment had on the two younger children in the family.

Freeman: How about the concern about having Peter and Elizabeth at the sessions?

Father: I wasn't as concerned as my wife was. Not at all.

Mother: What were your thoughts about that?

Father: Oh, I think they had enough maturity for their age to withstand that. Elizabeth was, what was it, you put it in better words than I do. Something was upsetting Mary and me and Elizabeth would start crying. She was reacting for us in situations. Now I think she doesn't do that. She doesn't take on the responsibility that is not hers.

Mother: Um hmm, I think she did.

Freeman: Elizabeth did?

Father: Yeah, I think she realized when Trudy was upsetting us that she shouldn't take it so personally. You know, if we aren't crying and carrying on, there is no need for her to do so.

Freeman: So looking back on the effect it had on Elizabeth and Trudy, you can see some positives.

Father: Oh, I think so, yeah, it certainly did no harm, that's for sure.

Freeman: How about for Peter?

Father: I don't know what he exactly got out of it because Peter is sort of quiet like I am. But undoubtedly I think he got something out of it.

Mother: Oh, I think he did.

By now Mrs. P has heard Mr. P's position on the benefits of a family approach and the involvement of the two younger children, and she very quickly says that her son did get something out of the process. Having each parent evaluate the impact of the process on the whole family and on each of the children consolidates the gains. The session began with Mrs. P expressing ambivalence about the impact on her children. After her husband describes his thinking the mother is able to nonreactively reevaluate.

Now the therapist moves on to his second agenda item, which is asking each spouse to describe the impact the process had on the husband-wife relationship.

Freeman: How about the two of you and this whole process? What impact has it had?

Father: Well, I think probably Mary listens more to me and my opinions than she did before.

Freeman: You would see a change in that?

Father: Oh, yeah, not that I blamed her because she is a mother and I think that is the kind of reaction of any mother.

Mother: I have very strong motherly feelings, you know, I admit that.

Freeman: One change that you would see then with Mary is she would hear more?

Father: Un hmm, um hmm. Well, she might agree with me before, but she might take a different route, and of course there was enough uproar in the family that I didn't want to continue any more by disagreeing with her and forcing my opinion on her. But probably the process of coming to these sessions has something to do with it too. And the fact that what she was doing for Trudy, really wasn't working. Giving in to her as much as she did. She didn't always, of course, and if something doesn't work you have got to try something else. And I think that is why maybe she listens to me more. She is willing to bop me one in the eye when I get out of here. (Laughter)

Freeman: Her listening to you more, does that in any way encourage you to be more involved?

Father: Oh, yes, oh, sure. I think mothers are wise and I think the children read your motives as wrong. When you do something that you think is for the good of the children, it may be something that you feel you should do in your heart. Because you have an emotional attachment to your children. It is really easy to say, Okay, come on, woman, here is the house, we will look after you, we've got a shelter here. But you just postpone the inevitable in doing that. You can do that to a 13- or 14-year old, but of course when they are eighteen or nineteen they are old enough to be making their own decisions, and doing something about their lives.

Freeman: Um hmm. How about you in terms of this process and just the two of you?

Mother: Yeah, well, I think I am listening a little more to him, but I think he is having a little more to say with the children, too. There were an awful lot of years there where I did the lion's share of everything with the kids, because I was there and because he was off golfing and things like that. So I think that you get into the habit of doing so much with them and for them and I think it is bad, I really do. I think more and more that the father should be taking a far greater part and it should start right from the cradle. I believe this so strongly, and I didn't when I was younger. If I had, it probably wouldn't have made much difference because I think we were pretty young to have a family and he was busy trying to get established. I just think that it would have been left to me. When I see how young girls now expect their husbands to do a lot more with the children, I say, boy, more power to them. I think it is better for the children and better for the mother. The mother can just keep more of herself to herself. I think on a mother's part there is too much giving. Well, probably trying to live their children's lives for them, 'cause they are so concerned and now I— the way things turned out, with our family—I see that is unhealthy. I really do. But he is taking a bigger part now, aren't you?

Father: Yes.

Mother: You're calmer. You used to get more upset, with less provocation.

Father: Well, you communicate better, when you don't lose your temper.

Freeman: You agree with that? That you're calmer?

Father: Oh, yes. Over a year ago when Trudy raised her voice I would raise mine one octave higher and now the situation is reversed.

Freeman: What do you think has made you calmer?

Father: Well, I think it is common sense, really. When you stay calm, you don't lose your temper and start saying things you shouldn't.

Mother: I think too that coming here has helped you to get your perspective and see the kids, the girls that is, in a different light. And I can say the same for myself—because I am, oh brother, the way I am. When Trudy first talked about the farm my first reaction was kind of negative because I thought she would be bored. I was thinking of it the way I would look at it myself but I didn't say too much. This is the way it felt inside myself. Then, when we got talking about it and I started to look at it from her viewpoint, I thought, it might be terriffic for her. But I think that it is hard for a parent to do, especially when an adult, or whatever Trudy is, has been so dependent on us. It is very hard to respect her ideas as an individual. And it really came home to me when this happened, because I had thought, now she is right. It would be fantastic for her. Yet I was just looking at it completely from my own personal point of view, which was completely different. It had nothing to do with her. So I think I have derived something that way.

The parents, while evaluating the impact on their relationship, begin to talk about how they have changed their roles in the family. Father has become much more involved and willing to take some responsibility for his children. This has allowed the mother to back off, become more of an observer, and think more clearly about her role in the family. In the past the mother did not see the father as a resource to her and felt the burden was mainly on her shoulders. The father explains he stayed uninvolved because he felt more involvement might upset the mother who might not agree with his style or way of doing things. Now that they have reassessed their roles in the family, they can be supports and

resources to each other. This mutual support is an important goal
to reach before terminating therapy. If one of the major goals in
family work is to develop the internal resources of the family, then
it should follow that the parents will be talking about how they
can use each other differently and support each other so some of
the old problems do not recur. When the father in this family
became move involved it allowed the mother to become less of an
overfunctioner and more able to develop an objective view of
what could happen in the family when she was not actively trying
to shape things up.

Freeman: That's interesting.
Mother: I mean, for Marg I could always have more respect for
her ideas and so on, because she was more steady, and what is the
word, conformist, you know. Trudy has been so irresponsible that
I think this is another reason you tend to treat her as a child which
she is not.

The mother has made a significant move from the beginning of
therapy. She no longer sees Trudy as the problem child. She sees
Trudy more as an adult who has to make her own decisions. The
mother uses the story about the farm to illustrate her personal
struggle not to overfunction for her daughter. As she is better able
to see her daughter as an adult apart from herself, she is more able
to allow her to have her own opinions, without seeing differences
in opinions as indications of behavioral problems. Earlier when
Trudy expressed differences to her mother, the mother interpreted
these differences an an indication of immaturity. She now sees
these differences as an indication of Trudy's eventual emancipation from the family.

Freeman: That's interesting. How about your ability to remain
calm?
Mother: Well, mine is pretty good. Actually, I'm beginning to
think I am very cold and hardhearted now. I really don't know
whether you get kind of numb, although I can still feel very soft

towards Elizabeth and Peter. But after all we have been through with the girls, it seems that I am getting shockproof. I guess maybe that I am trying to be objective and stand back and look at it and see it in a sort of better perspective.

The therapist has now moved to his last two agenda items. He has assessed for the high and low points and for how the spouse and parent-child subsystems have dealt differently with what is going on. He now asks each parent to talk about how they have changed as individuals apart from their parenting and husband-wife roles. He ends the session with an invitation for the family to return in the future if they feel the need to check things out. This strategy is to help the family redefine the meaning of reaching out for consultation if problems recur in the future.

Father: (Turning to his wife) You're not as emotional in situations now.

Mother: No, I'm not.

Freeman: There is a big difference in that?

Father: Oh, gosh, yes. Tremendous difference.

Mother: Yes, Trudy used to really get me going like you wouldn't believe, just for . . . I was so afraid of the drug scene.

Father: Well, she knew she could get you going.

Mother: And of course she knew it.

Freeman: It sounds to me like you have been able to reposition yourselves in the family from how you were two or three years ago.

Mother: Um hmm.

Freeman: I am wondering how comfortable that is for you.

Mother: It's kind of funny because we all have a bit of ego and it's very nice. I am very glad that I have gotten something out of this. It is vital for the family but I can't help—I don't mean I feel guilty, but I can't help having a little concern that we should have needed it.

Freeman: Ah, I get you.

Mother: You can't help that.

Freeman: Somehow you wish that you had been able to do without it.

Mother: Absolutely. I never had any doubt that I was going to be the best parent in the world, like everybody feels. So this is kind of . . . We went to a party a few weeks ago and all our old friends were there, like from high school days, and there were three couples who were there and had been going through therapy this year. And one woman had been a social worker for years herself and we didn't know that. They didn't know we've been coming because we didn't see them more than once every couple of years or something. And so at least we feel it isn't completely our fault. But I guess until I go to my grave I will still be kind of wondering why.

Father: Everything all turned out. I don't think you will wonder why at all.

Mother: Maybe not, I don't know.

Freeman: It's hard not to wonder why.

Mother: Um hmm. It really is.

Father: Yes.

Freeman: Of course there are no answers, which makes it even harder.

Father: You almost wonder, why me. It could always happen to someone else.

Freeman: One session we had, it was three or four sessions ago, the two of you talked about some of your long-range plans as a couple. Have there been any more thoughts on that? How do you see yourselves spending your time?

Mother: We still talk about travelling.

Father: Yes.

Freeman: I was really impressed with that planned trip to Latin America.

Mother: Um hmm.

Father: Um hmm. That's still on the books.

Mother: Yes, we have to think about Peter going to university in a couple of years and Elizabeth hopefully too, so, you know.

Father: If they were home sometime in the summer for a month we could go and leave them. Heck. They could look after themselves. There wouldn't be any difficulty there, except that Peter wouldn't look after the pool.

Freeman: Well, we are going to have to stop here. I appreciate your evaluating the experience you have had with me. Things are quite different from when we started. However, if sometime in the future you want to come in and just talk about how things have been developing, I think that would be okay. Sometimes, it helps just to talk to someone and get some new notions about what is going on. So if any time in the future you want to do that, don't hesitate to give me a call. I think it's a good way of taking a reading on how well you have been able to carry through on some of the things you have been talking about in the session.

Father: Thanks, things are looking pretty good for us.

Mother: Um hmm, I think so too.

In the preceding interview the therapist attempted to carry out his agenda by assessing for change within each of the subsystems and encouraging each member of the family to evaluate the high and low points of therapy. It is interesting to note that the mother expresses her concern about needing therapy at all. This reaction is a common one. Most parents feel they should be able to manage their familes on their own. Seeing a therapist is often perceived as a sign of failure. It is important for the therapist to help the family recognize that their struggles are not necessarily a sign of failure or inadequacy. The better able the family is to recognize it has its own resources the less likely the members are to experience a sense of failure. Even at the end of therapy the mother in this family had some doubts about whether the whole enterprise was an indication of her own inadequacy. When this family began therapy the mother was extremely ambivalent about getting involved in family work. She pointed out that the problems were her children's fault whereas she had done everything in her capacity to make things work. For this particular woman, being able to talk about how the process helped her become freer in her family, and enjoy her relationships rather than feel responsible for them, was a sign that she had made significant moves. However, she still felt she should have possessed the requisite wisdom without the aid of formal therapy.

A formal terminating session is helpful to the therapist as well as the family. It helps the therapist evaluate the overall process and can be utilized to reinforce and consolidate individual and family change. There are many situations that can prevent the therapist from conducting a formal terminating session. Even if families are terminating therapy prematurely, I encourage them to come in for a final session and discuss the impact of therapy to that date. This last session can be used to help the family think through their options for the future. This practice is recommended whether the family has had two or three sessions or two or more years of sessions. In beginning with a family it is helpful to set the stage by advising them that before terminating the family should meet to discuss formally their reasons for ending.

The last chapter in this text discusses therapeutic dilemmas and practice issues in the family therapy process.

8

THERAPEUTIC DILEMMAS AND PRACTICE ISSUES

The final chapter of this book deals with several therapeutic dilemmas and practice issues which family therapists frequently encounter. Discussion of these dilemmas and issues could constitute a book in itself. However, I will just briefly discuss these issues here, highlighting the more important aspects of them.

Confidentiality and secret keeping

There has long been controversy about how one should maintain confidentiality when working with a family. In psychoanalytic practice the therapeutic relationship is confidential. This privacy is an important ingredient in helping the patient. In family work the therapist does not share family information with "outsiders" but confidentiality between the therapist and any one family member is not a major concern. Family members raise issues about themselves and the family which need to be discussed at some time during the therapeutic process. One of the major goals of family therapy is to help family members share new information so that they gain a better understanding of how the family operates as a unit and what individual members are thinking and experiencing. One of the early messages the therapist communicates to family members is the importance of their being able to help other members of the family get to know them in ways that self wants to be know. There are times, however, when certain family members are not prepared to talk about personal issues. The therapist must take this into account. Individual members will discuss important issues with others only when they feel sufficiently comfortable, or feel it is appropriate to do so.

The therapist should distinguish between privacy and secret keeping. Privacy concerns an individual's choosing not to share something about himself with the rest of the family. He may not be prepared to discuss certain aspects of his life or may want to keep a certain part of his life separate from the family. Secret keeping, on the other hand, is choosing to share with one family member certain thoughts that he or she feels should not be shared will all members of the family. Family members should be able to maintain a certain degree of privacy about their lives without feeling pressured to talk about everything they are experiencing, feeling, or thinking. However, when one family member confides secrets to another about an important family issue or event, this hinders open discussion. Secret keeping has negative implications, not only for the family therapy process, but also for the functioning of the entire family.

The keeping of these types of secrets is usually achieved by one family member swearing another family member or the family therapist to secrecy. One of the early moves that members of the family often make toward the therapist is to try to swear him to secrecy about some important issue. It is not uncommon after the first one or two sessions for a family member to corner the therapist and begin to tell him secrets about other family members. It is also common for adolescents to try to tell the therapist something they don't want their parents to know about.

The management of secrets requires skill and sensitivity on the part of the therapist. Be becoming party to a secret, the family therapist would be joining in a dysfunctional alliance with the secret-keeper. The therapist should declare early in the therapeutic process that all information that is shared with him, when appropriate, will have to be shared with the family. The therapist who becomes party to secrets effectively ties his hands behind his back. He is not able to move spontaneously within the family after agreeing to maintain a secret with one or more members. This restriction can have serious repercussions for the therapy process. It quickly becomes obvious to the family that certain issues are too dangerous to be discussed. The agreement of the therapist to avoid certain issues reinforces the power of the secret. If the secret is revealed it usually becomes obvious that all members of the family knew something about it, but were not able to discuss its impact on them because they had agreed in one way or another to maintain secrecy. When the therapist joins in this collusion, he becomes party to this dysfunctional pattern.

A useful position for the family therapist to take when a family member approaches him about a secret is to inform him that all important information should be shared with the family. If the family member continues to desire to confide the secret, the therapist should remain firm in his position that the secret will have to be shared with the family at some time during the process. When a therapist takes this position he will usually find that the family member will have shared the secret with the family by the next session.

A discussion with the family about the impact of secret keeping can be productive. If the therapist senses that keeping secrets is one of the dysfunctional dynamics in the family he may choose to introduce this subject to the family in a general way. Rather than talking about a particular secret he may talk about the process of secret keeping and its effect on the family. Frequently keeping secrets is a learned way of dealing with important emotional issues. Many parents involve themselves in collusions with other family members because this was one of the methods of communication they learned in their families of origin. Discussing with clients how their families of origin dealt with important emotional events and how secret keeping affected those family units often helps free people from holding on to these old patterns.

Sharing information with outside agencies

How much family information the therapist should share with outside agencies presents another issue of confidentiality. Often outside agencies contact a family therapist for a diagnosis or assessment of the functioning of the family or one of its members. The family therapist must resist playing the expert who communicates information about the family to others. One of the tasks of the family therapist is to help the family manage other systems more effectively. Any information an agency requires about a family should come directly from the family, not from the therapist. Except in exceptional circumstances, the only information that I will share with an outside agency is the family's composition, the members I am seeing, and the frequency of our contacts. I resist providing diagnostic information about individual members of the family or communicating my impression of the intrafamilial functioning of the family.

When outside agencies become involved with a family I'm working with, or a member of the family contacts an outside agency, it is an indication to me that something within the family therapy process is not working to the satisfaction of the family. I encourage the outside agency representative to explain to me how he or she became involved with the family and to define their goals and expectations. In the following session with the family I would introduce the fact that I had been in touch with the outside agency and ask the family what their thoughts are about that involvement. I make it quite clear to the family that too many professionals will interfere with the family therapy process. One of the goals in the therapy process is to help the family members sort out how they want to work with me and other people in the community. If in fact there is a need to involve other professionals in the life of the family, then I recommend that they become directly involved in the process. To accomplish this I ask the family to assist the therapist in organizing a meeting bringing together all the relevant people to begin to sort out who should be doing what in the process. For a more detailed description of this process I refer the reader to chapter 4.

Management of the absent member and introduction of new individuals

During the early stage of family work there are times when certain family members do not appear for the session. As was mentioned earlier in the text, it is necessary that the therapist bring into the family sessions those members who have the greatest potential for redefining the issues, and that he find a resource unit within the family that can produce change. When a member of the family refuses to begin, or leaves during an early stage, it presents a serious therapeutic dilemma.

During the beginning phase of family work it is important to engage those family members who are directly involved with the concerns of the family. Many times adolescents resist becoming involved in family therapy because they feel the process will make it more difficult for them to eventually leave home. When there are adolescents in the family it is important to communicate to them in the beginning sessions that the therapy process will help them realize individual goals. At the same time the message should be communicated to the parents that the family as a unit will be respected and strengthened. Balancing between individual needs and group solidarity is the "art" of the family therapy enterprise. At times individuals will refuse to come to sessions because they fear their individual needs will not be respected. If the therapist puts too much emphasis on family solidarity, the individuals who have a strong need to separate from the group will see therapy as a threat. On the other hand, if the parents feel that therapy undermines their struggle to maintain family solidarity, they will also see it as a threat. Balancing these two issues is the basic task of the early sessions.

When the therapist is able to support both group solidarity and individual autonomy in the early sessions there is a good chance the absent member syndrome will not be a problem. However, when this problem exists it is productive for the therapist to focus on the difficulty of bringing in certain members as an important issue for family work. In general, parents should have enough influence on their children to be able to involve them in an experience that the parents have identified as necessary and important for the family. When the parents tell the therapist they're not able to involve certain children in the family, the therapist should continue working with the parents to help them engage their children. There will be times, however, when the parents will not be able to involve all their children on an ongoing basis. When this is the case it is beneficial for the family therapist to see the siblings as a group. When the therapist is able to develop a relationship with the sibling subsystem, he can utilize this system as a positive force for family change.

It is important for the therapist to remember that he can choose to work with one or more natural subsystems within the family. However, the therapist should avoid becoming involved with the family in a way which effectively excludes one or more of its members.

In my work I will meet with the husband-wife subsystem, the sibling subsystem, or with all the children and the parents. If I find that one of the children opts out of the family therapy process, I may decide to work with just the parents until they are able to involve all the children in the sessions. The struggle for structure between the therapist and the family is a basic part of the process. If one member of the family drops out of therapy, the therapist should help the family recognize the significance of this event. The therapist may from time to time restructure who comes to the sessions to avoid overtly or covertly siding with certain members of the family. The therapist should never passively accept a decision by the family that one of its members won't be involved. The dynamics that go into making such a decision should be explored and the family should be helped to recognize its implications.

During the middle phase of the family therapy process the issue of the absent member is rarely a concern. The family has redefined what it wants to work on and those members who are working on self issues or various subsystem issues are engaged in the therapy process. The therapist might want to encourage certain family members to stop coming to the sessions, and may encourage new members to become involved. Once the family has redefined its focal point and the children are no longer of central concern, it is preferred that the therapist work solely with the adults in the family on the issues of how they want to organize their own lives.

There are times when problems and concerns of individual members of the family change, making the introduction of new people into the sessions desirable.

This occurred with a client couple who had initially come for therapy because of severe marital difficulties. During most of their nine-year marriage their relationship had been highly conflictual. Their usual pattern consisted of the husband spending several days away from home, followed by a fierce confrontation upon his return. Following the confrontation, matters would settle down between the couple until the next time he left home. The wife felt totally confused by this behavior and over the years became more dissatisfied with their relationship, yet at the same time put more pressure on her husband to spend more time with her. As the conflict increased the wife devoted more time to her friends and her professional work, as did her husband. During the course of therapy, the couple decided it would be in their best interests to separate, leaving a minimum of unfinished business in their relationship.

Eventually the couple was able to work through an amicable separation and divorce. The husband decided to continue therapy, working on some self issues. The wife discontinued therapy feeling that her life was in good order. She felt good about herself and optimistic about her future. During the ongoing sessions with the husband, he began to talk about difficulties he was having with his extended family. He was the oldest of seven siblings in a family of five sons and two daughters. He began to share the difficulty he had in communicating with his mother and father, and the concern he had about the serious acting-out behavior of one of his younger sisters who had been picked up for using drugs and shoplifting. As he began to talk about his concerns for his extended family, it was decided that he would involve his extended family in his sessions to see how they perceived their situation. Several sessions with the extended family revealed there were many difficulties within the family and that ongoing family work with all members was advisable. The initial reaction of the extended family was that only the acting-out daughter should be involved. Nonetheless, the total extended family was involved and it was especially interesting to note how supportive the brothers were toward their acting-out sister. It became apparent that there were major concerns about the mother in this family who was more childlike than any of the children. The therapy refocused away from the daughter as identified problem, to the set of relationships between children and parents, and the children became committed to the family therapy enterprise.

In this situation the structure of therapy changed dramatically over time. It began with a husband and wife working on marital difficulties, moved to working with one of the spouses on difficulties he was having in his own life, and concluded by involving the husband's extended family because of the difficulties he was having relating to them and the stress this created in his life. Throughout this process it was important for the family therapist to take the initiative in suggesting who to involve in the therapeutic process. There are times when family members do not see how this involvement would be of benefit to them or resist involving certain people because of discomfort within certain relationships. Essentially, it is up to the therapist to lay the groundwork for recognition of the importance of involving others in the family. This recognition can change the focal point and add to the depth and breadth of the therapeutic process.

When the therapist introduces a new person or people to the process he must do so in a natural and sensitive way. If the therapy has been in progress for a while the newcomers will be at a disadvantage. The invitation to join the sessions is usually made by one or more of the family members who have already been involved in the therapeutic process. The new participant will have active fantasies and concerns about what the experience is like. He or she may feel ill at ease and somewhat on guard. Often a new member is hesitant to say anything for fear he might upset what has already happened. Because of these natural concerns, when there is a new member present I always begin the session with him or her, using the same procedure I do when a new guest comes into my home for a social gathering. In the latter situation the host or hostess will introduce the new person to everybody and help to make the guest comfortable. The same procedure should be utilized when a new person is introduced to the therapy process. Following the introduction, I ask the new member what his understanding is about what has been going on, who has told him about the session, what his expectations are and what sorts of goals he may have for the session. By giving the new member an opportunity to articulate his thoughts and feelings about the process from the start, his role, and the roles of the therapist and other family members, can be clarified. This facilitates his being quickly engaged in the work at hand.

Home visits vs. office visits

Ideally the family therapist will be flexible about working with families in his office or in their home. There are times when it is appropriate to make a home visit and see the family in its own environment. The physical space that a family occupies can reveal a great deal about their lifestyle and how they have organized their relationships. The way in which the family introduces the therapist to their home is also significant. When the therapist visits a family home, he is the guest. The family members are in charge and have the responsibility for organizing the physical space for the contact. How well the family handles its respon- sibility and how comfortable the therapist is in the role of guest will influence the therapeutic process. There are a number of factors here: who plays the role of host/hostess; the degree of quietness in the room where the interview is conducted; the comfort of the family members in moving in and out of the room; and the number of interruptions. All these communicate to the therapist and, hopefully, to the family how the members relate to each other and to a "stranger."

The benefit of seeing a family in one's own office is that it gives the family members an opportunity to experience a new setting with each other. The family is more or less on neutral ground and the therapist is the host. It then is his job to make the family comfortable. Seeing the family in both settings is recommended. Conducting all the sessions in the family home deprives the family of the opportunity to have a unique experience outside of their usual physical space. Conducting all the sessions in the therapist's office deprives the family of the opportunity to be a bit more in control of the physical space and to assume some responsibility for "taking care of" the therapist.

There are certain families where ongoing sessions in the home are not advisable. For example, if a family is structured so that one member does all the serving then that individual is not able to experience being taken care of. With these families it is advisable to have the sessions in a setting other than the family home.

The important point to be made here is that physical settings influence what people choose to say and how they say it. In order to gain a fuller appreciation of how a family operates, the therapist should at the least have the opportunity to see the family in more than one setting.

The seating arrangements that people choose can also reveal aspects of how they organize their relationships with each other. I do not deal directly with seating arrangements in my work with families. I have organized an interviewing room where the seats are in a circle. Where the family members choose to sit and how they choose to position themselves in relation to each other and me is totally up to them. I observe how the seating arrangement changes over time and see it as indicative of change. However, I seldom suggest that people sit in certain places. At the beginning of family therapy I remain standing until the last family member sits down. There is always an extra chair in the room and the seating is arranged so that if a member desires to place some distance between himself and another member, he is able to do so.

When I visit a family in their own home it is the family who decides on the seating arrangements. I will agree with the setting the family has chosen for the interview and with the interviewing structure the family has arranged.

Use of time in the therapeutic process and frequency of contact

When I begin seeing a family in treatment we usually meet for one-hour sessions on a weekly basis. However, as the family proceeds in therapy the time structure changes. During the beginning phase of family work one-hour, weekly sessions seem to work best. If there is too long a gap between the first and second sessions, the family may approach the second session with as much difficulty as it did the first one. Frequent contact at this stage helps reinforce the positive treatment experiences and reassures the family that the process is going to be a safe and beneficial one. If the therapist waits too long to schedule the second interview (over a week), the ambivalent family may not return for a second session. Once the family has progressed to the middle phase of family work, and has redefined the problem, infrequent but slightly longer contacts seem beneficial. Often meeting with the family on a monthly basis for hour-and-a-half sessions which focus on what the family has been experimenting with works well. This structure offers sufficient time for the family to work on new issues and experiment with different ways of relating.

The structuring of time with the family is an important part of the early process. The family should know exactly how long and how often the sessions will be held. By structuring the time the therapist helps the family use the therapeutic hour to their best advantage. When the family members know they have a specific time which will be adhered to they seem to work more efficiently. There are times when family members raise important issues at the end of the therapeutic hour. This presents a dilemma for the therapist. What I find most beneficial is to explain to the family that the session is over but this issue is one which should be brought up during the following session. It is not the responsibility of the therapist to raise this issue at the following session. If it continues to be a burning issue for a family member, that individual will bring it up. So much happens from one week to the next within the family, that an issue one week isn't necessarily an issue the next week. It is important for the therapist to remember this and not resurrect an old issue the family may have resolved between sessions.

My approach regarding frequency of contact is open-ended. The concept of phases of family therapy provides a framework for determining the frequency of sessions. In the beginning phase, when the family is still reactive, we meet weekly for one-hour sessions. When the family has moved into the middle phase and redefined the problem, I begin to see them every other week for several sessions, and then move to monthly sessions. By the time the family has progressed to the termination phase, it has assumed most of the responsibility for getting the job done. And as I pointed out earlier, they will usually raise the issue of termination on their own. One must guard against imposing an unrealistic time frame on the family. The longer the problems have existed in the family, the longer it will take to help the members reposition themselves. If there is a severely disturbed member in the family this usually indicates a longterm process. Infrequent contacts over a long period of time are preferable to frequent contacts over a short period. As the family members begin to experiment with each other, they will begin to see their relationships differently. This in itself takes time, and the therapist should allow himself that time with the family. There is also a great deal of learning for the therapist who sees the family over a long period, even when sessions are infrequent. This time frame helps the therapist get a better sense of the resiliency and resourcefulness of the family. Most practitioners become involved with families during a crisis and often terminate when the crisis is over. I think this is one reason we tend to see families and individuals as being so reactive. By the time they return to their proactive stage, we have terminated involvement and see little of that part of their functioning.

Handling of crises and emergencies

During the course of therapy, certain emergencies or crises may arise, particularly during the beginning phase. Occasionally, after the initial session or two the family therapist receives a call from a family member about an issue the individual feels must be addressed immediately. It's not uncommon for the caller to feel that a particular member of the family should be placed out of the home, or he may feel under some threat himself because of some conflict which has occurred.

One approach to managing crises and emergencies is to encourage the caller to convene the family for a family therapy session. However, the family therapist should not make any quick decisions about how to respond to the crisis. At the time of the telephone call he does not know who is involved in the crisis or how other members perceive the crisis. If he makes a decision about how to manage the crisis based on the caller's anxiety and reactive stance, then the opportunity presented to the family for learning how to handle family difficulties could be lost.

When the therapist requests that the caller convene the family, he has already slowed down the response to emergency. The timing of the next family therapy contact now becomes important. If the caller is told that the emergency cannot be dealt with immediately but must wait until the next scheduled session, the caller may reach out to another professional in the community and the therapist might lose the family. When a family member calls about an emergency, it is advisable for the therapist to suggest that the family come in as a group the following day to discuss the crisis. Most emergencies don't have to be handled at the moment of the call but it is reassuring for the anxious caller to know that within twenty-four hours something will be done. By the time the family meets the following day, things may not be so urgent. More importantly, when the family meets it provides an opportunity to discuss their definition of an emergency and their differing perceptions of how an emergency should be dealt with. The role of the family therapist is to remain calm and suggest that the best way to proceed with any crisis is for the family to look at its options and perceptions of what is occurring. In this way, the family therapist is supportive of the caller's reaction to the crisis, but at the same time, suggests a new way to approach and deal with the crisis.

Family therapy when one member is placed outside the family

There are times when a family therapist will be called in to work with a family when one member of the family has been placed out of the home, in a hospital, residential treatment center, foster home, etc. This presents a dilemma for the family therapist. It is difficult to engage the entire family in therapy when the family has already removed one of its members from the family home. An additional complication is that the professionals who are involved with the absent member have a vested interest in how the therapy should proceed. My experience in doing family therapy in a hospital setting taught me that this latter difficulty presents one of the most difficult hurdles. Often in a hospital setting the inpatient staff overidentify with the plight of the hospitalized patient and feel overtly or covertly antagonistic toward the family. During case conferences or rounds on a hospital ward, it is not uncommon to hear the staff talk about how the patient would do so much better in a different type of home. The triangulation that occurs between the professionals and other family members can present a serious constraint to initiating family therapy.

One way of minimizing these hazards is to use the time that a family member is placed outside of the home to prepare the family for family therapy upon the individual's return. I hesitate to commence family therapy when one member is involved in a setting that reinforces that person's identification as the problem in the family. When families try to initiate family therapy at the same time that one of their members is being hospitalized I advise them I will consider family therapy if they continue to be interested near the time the absent member is discharged from the institutional setting. If I am doing consultation or training in an institutional setting I work with the staff on the issue of involving families in family therapy at the time of discharge. As long as one member is in a setting apart from the others it is difficult to help the family recognize that a redefinition or rethinking of the family's concerns is necessary. Their thinking has been reinforced by the professional community and they are firm in their belief that their concern with one of their members is legitimate and should be the focus of attention. My position is that the identified problem who is removed from the home is at a disadvantage, and until that person is on equal or near equal footing with the rest of the family, the family therapy process can only have limited success.

When a member of the family has been placed in a foster home, several therapeutic issues arise. During the last several years I have been experimenting with bringing the foster families and natural families together and the results of these sessions have been quite encouraging. Quite commonly the natural parents are initially antagonistic and competitive toward the foster family or foster parents. The foster parents, who have been informed about the failures of the natural parents, tend not to see how the natural parents can provide a positive environment for the child. In general, there is much misunderstanding between the foster family and the natural family. In addition, the welfare agency may play into this estrangement by feeding very selective information to each one of these systems. This in turn increases their distrust of each other and their distance from each other. The foster child usually becomes the main communicator of information between these two family groups. The information he communicates and the way in which he communicates it will be influenced by his own struggles. If the foster family and the natural family rely predominantly on information supplied by the foster child, it is likely this will produce additional antagonism and mistrust.

One of the goals of the family therapist is to bring the foster family and the natural family together in the best interests of all the systems, including the foster child. The natural parents and foster parents have similar goals. They can be supportive of each other and, in fact, learn from each other. Unfortunately, this does not happen spontaneously. The therapist must assume an active role to help the two family systems see that a mutual respect and understanding is helpful to the child and themselves.

When a foster family is for some reason unable to keep a child in care, I would discourage the family's removing the child until all members of both families have a chance to meet and discuss the situation. When one child is removed from a foster home the implications for the rest of the children remaining there are profound. In an interesting article, Colon (1973, pp. 429–438) describes his experiences in a foster home and the impact it had on him when he or other children were removed from the foster home. Any decision to remove or place a child in a foster home should be dealt with by the total family group to make them part of the process and give them an opportunity to deal with their fantasies about the inclusion or exclusion of a family member.

Cotherapy

Cotherapy has become a popular method in family therapy. Authors such as Carl Whitaker (1976, pp. 24–25, Napier and Whitaker 1978) have written extensively about the benefits of a cotherapy model. Other therapists, such as Jay Haley (1976), have taken the opposite position. My personal experience is that it is difficult for cotherapists to begin to work as a unit in the best interests of the family. Each cotherapist brings in his own unfinished business and value system. Being able to organize their thinking and frameworks to complement each other is the most difficult task the cotherapy team must deal with. I have found that it takes about a year for two people to work effectively with each other, regardless of whether it is a male-female cotherapy team or two people of the same sex. The major issue the cotherapy team must deal with is how to bring the best aspects of their personalities and theoretical frameworks together so they can function as a cohesive unit. The two people have to work hard at it; there must be good communication between the cotherapists; and there must be ample time set aside before and after each interview for them to discuss treatment strategy.

When I work with a cotherapist we spend approximately ten to fifteen minutes before the session discussing our general agenda and setting up some guidelines about how to proceed during that particular session. After the session we spend at least twenty or thirty minutes discussing how the session went and how we used each other with the family. It is helpful to videotape the session when one is doing cotherapy. There are many nonverbal aspects which influence how the family responds to the cotherapy team. These are difficult to pick up when one is participating in a session. The videotape allows the cotherapy team to get a better overall sense of how they can use each other more effectively.

To develop a well-functioning cotherapy team it works well to take turns conducting the sessions for the first six months or so of working together. This is less chaotic than having the cotherapists jumping in by asking questions and making statements to the family at unpredictable times. When the therapists take turns, each is able to observe how the other conducts the session. In this way they each can learn how the other asks questions and what sorts of nonverbal behaviors they utilize or display. If one is so actively involved in the session that he loses sight of the activities of his cotherapy partner, the opportunity is limited for the therapists to learn how to use each other effectively. On the other hand, spending an hour just observing how a family is involved in a therapy session can provide a great deal of learning about family behavior as well.

The issue of whether cotherapy teams should consist of opposite or same sex therapists has not been fully researched. My hunch is that the sex of the cotherapists isn't as important as their ability to use each other in a proactive and spontaneous way. If there isn't any competition between the two therapists about who is going to run the show, and both are comfortable observing as well as acting in the process, then there can be much learning for both the family and the cotherapists. I do think, however, that in learning how to do family therapy, it is necessary for each therapist to work with families alone as well as with cotherapists. In developing the ability to do family therapy it may be better to start as a single therapist learning how to use oneself without the support of another person in the group. The involvement of a cotherapist in the therapeutic process should come from strength and confidence about being able to do family work, not from fear and anxiety about what might occur during the session.

Contraindications for family therapy

There is much discussion in the literature about who should become involved in family therapy. It isn't so much whom you bring into the session as what you do in the session that makes it family therapy. There are, however, certain situations in which family may not be indicated. If a family member is psychotic or his thinking is impaired through the use of alcohol or drugs, he will not be able to position himself in the family in a way which would allow new learning to occur. The psychotic, delusional individual is not able to participate in a way that would help the family learn more about itself; in fact, he might add to the family's anxiety. The institutionalized family member is also at a disadvantage because he has been overtly taken out of the family. It is better to start family work when the institutionalized member is discharged. The individual who comes to the session impaired through drugs or alcohol cannot understand or hear anything new and will therefore set himself up in a negative way which prevents any new learning. It is important that all members of the family are able to participate on a nearly equal footing. When this is not the case it is necessary to find a different structure which will eventually allow for these individuals to participate in more functional ways.

Other than these very specific situations, I think there are few contraindications for family therapy. One can do family work with an individual, with a couple, or with a whole family. Once family members begin respositioning themselves in relation to each other and remain in contact with their family unit there is a powerful impetus for change. The task of the therapist is to help the family structure itself in a positive way. The constellation he chooses depends on the types of problems the family is experiencing and who is available to the family. It is not my opinion that there are certain people who will never be suitable for family therapy.

The appendix which follows contains two interviews with commentary. These interviews took place during the beginning and middle phases of work with a family of six members. These two interviews provide further illustrations of common practice issues and illustrate much of what has been discussed throughout this text.

APPENDIX

To conclude this text I have included two family therapy interviews. These two interviews were conducted with the same family and represent the beginning and middle phases of family work. This family was previously discussed in chapter 7, which also contains the interview in which the parents evaluated the impact the family therapy process had on them as individuals and as a family.

In this appendix we first take a look at how this family began therapy. The beginning phases of family work are clearly illustrated in the first transcript. Initially the family desired to focus on one of its members as the major problem. Gradually, the family broadens its definition of itself. The therapist uses the multigenerational perspective as a technique for helping the family gain a broader definition of itself as a system. At the time of the first interview the family's firstborn daughter, Marg, had been hospitalized for approximately two months. In spite of this the family continued to focus on the second daughter, Trudy, as the major problem. At the time of the first interview, Marg was being discharged from the hospital and the family had just agreed to family therapy sessions involving all the members of the nuclear family. One of the more remarkable features of the family was their insistence that during the last several years the real problem in the family had been with Trudy. For a long period of time the parents did not recognize the impact the difficulties with the older children were having on the two younger children. The interviews presented here illustrate how preoccupied and overinvolved the parents were with the second oldest daughter to the exclusion of their three other children.

My comments regarding therapeutic strategies employed in
these two interviews will be kept to a minimum. However, I will
point out a few of the more significant therapeutic maneuvers
utilized in the first interview to help the family view themselves as
a system in which all members are involved.

In the second interview presented here, the family is just
beginning to move into the middle phase of work. My cotherapist
conducted the initial portion of the session. She initiated a
discussion about what it means to work as a family. During this
discussion, Trudy, the second eldest, began to indicate that she
wanted to reposition herself within the family, particularly in
relation to her father. This is a sign that certain members of the
family are moving into the middle phase. The therapist takes this
opportunity to encourage Trudy and her father to begin relating
to each other differently. The other family members are encouraged to observe the interaction between father and daughter. One
of the more significant dynamics of this interview is the
scapegoating and triangulation that is triggered by the siblings
siding with father against sister. A major change occurs by the
conclusion of the interview. The mother clearly repositions
herself, moving from the overfunctioner who tries to maintain
calm and safety between her husband and Trudy to becoming an
observer and feeling comfortable with that role.

It will be helpful to the reader who reviews and analyzes these
transcripts to keep in mind the framework presented earlier in
regard to the phases and stages of therapy.

First interview with the P family

Freeman: I understand this is the first time you've all met together
as a family.
Family (responds as a group): Right. That's right.
Freeman: I'm hoping that we can get some notion about what's
been happening in the family. I've found from my experience that
it helps if everyone has a chance to hear and respond to what's
going on. I'd like to start out by asking the family how it
understands what has been happening to the family.

The therapist begins by addressing the family as a system. He avoids saying he's involved with the family because of specific problems. Rather, he asks the family a general question and waits to see how much each member will define what's been going on. By taking this position the therapist learns a great deal about how the family is organized structurally and functionally. The member who answers the question addressed to the family is often the one who is the most anxious and overinvolved in the problem. If the therapist addresses this initial question to a specific member of the family he loses an opportunity to identify at an early state who is the most anxious. In addition, if the therapist identifies a specific problem he sets the family up to talk about what he thinks they should be talking about rather than learning from them how they have understood what has been occurring in the life of the family.

Mother: It's pretty hard to understand that, particularly in Marg's case.

Margaret: What's been going on since I've been gone?

Mother: Well, nothing, since you've been gone, other than Trudy's had her ups and down, but nothing significant.

Father: Is there any period of time you want to go back?

Freeman: Whatever you think would help get us on board at this time.

Father: Because we've gone through this quite a few times, with this history of problems.

Freeman: The difference is that today everyone has a chance to give his or her point of view. Even though you might have been through it, you have not been through it together. This is the first time for the whole family to hear what's been happening at the same time. I think that's helpful.

The therapist takes the position that this is a new beginning. The family had been in therapy for approximately four years. However, most of the therapeutic efforts had been directed toward the two oldest girls. The younger children were not involved. All the information they received about family problems was communicated to them secondhand. Because of this, the therapist takes the position that what the family will hear now is new and different from what they've heard in the past.

Father: I think the problem really started . . . I guess it would be, oh, it's years now. I guess about three years and a bit . . . with Trudy.

Mother: No, it's more like four, four years it would be.

Father: When we arrived in Olympia it started. That would be about . . .

Mother: That's more than four years ago.

Father: Nineteen . . . well, I know that . . . the pattern of her behavior changed a little bit when we moved to Olympia.

Mother: Right.

Father: Which was 1965.

Mother: She had been very easy going as a child, extremely well behaved, and also in school, she was quite a conformist and she would do her very best in anything she undertook. She would do her best, and never a problem except that she didn't like to do anything around the house, but, you know, the younger ages, you don't really pay too much attention. I probably paid less attention to that than I should have because I had Peter and Elizabeth, babies together almost, you know, and I was very busy at the time and often I sort of wouldn't notice when she didn't pick up her clothes. I would just pick them up and, you know, this sort of thing because I couldn't bother about it. But anyway, she was extremely good. When she was about eleven was really when she started balking at authority at home. It was mainly directed against her father.

This information provided by the mother is interesting because the family was initially referred to family therapy because of the hospitalization of the oldest daughter, Marg. The parents clearly indicate their belief that is is not Marg but Trudy who is the problem and it is she who they want to change. If the therapist had conducted the interview based on the assumption that the problem was Marg he may not have recognized that the family had been identifying Trudy as the problem for years.

Freeman: Now this would be Trudy? How old are you?

Trudy: Eighteen, around eighteen.

Freeman: Seventeen, eighteen? So we're talking about seven years ago.

Parents: Right.

Father: She had a little difficulty at this time. We noticed as a change in her that she started having a little difficulty making friends, when we first arrived at Olympia, whereas before, she didn't. She had always had friends, had no trouble getting along with people whatsoever.

Trudy: I never had any friends when I was four or five.

Mother: Well, there again, we are moving, Trudy, we . . .

Trudy: That's when I started talking with my fingers, that's the beginning anyway.

Father: Well, as a matter of fact we were moving then, and you were new and you had to make friends.

Trudy: In Detroit?

Mother: Yes, yes. We moved three times in one year in Detroit.

Father: We moved four times in Detroit in a period of five years. At that juncture I don't think you had any trouble making friends, you never had difficulty in making friends.

Trudy: I was very introverted when I was four and I had no choice but to be introverted, I mean, you can't be extroverted with your fingers too much—

Mother: You never seemed introverted, Trudy, anytime in your life as far as I can—

Trudy: You don't know me very well then, Mom.

Mother: No? Well, maybe I don't. That's my opinion.

It is clear that Trudy is the center of attention in this family. She contributes to this identified problem role by drawing attention to some of her peculiar behavior. The therapist has now learned that a triangle exists between Mother, Father and Trudy, with Trudy playing a very active role in maintaining her position in that triangle. Now that the therapist has seen this dynamic, one of the things he strives to do is move the family away from preoccupation with Trudy and toward obtaining a fuller sense of how other family members are involved in the family system.

Freeman: How do you see your daughter?

Mother: Extremely extroverted.

Freeman: What do you mean by—

Mother: Well, everything comes out, like with Trudy you always know, she never keeps anything in. Now Marg is the one . . .

Trudy: I keep a lot of things in.

Mother: Well, all right. I'm saying how I feel about it, Trudy, maybe you can tell how you feel too, but I have felt that Trudy was being—well, if she's mad, everybody knows it, and usually everybody is affected by it because she lashes out. The same applies if she's in a good mood, she's very sort of funny. Whereas Marg has been inclined, when she has a problem, to keep it within herself. But, also for a lot of years, Trudy . . . those years, Trudy took an awful lot of not just our attention but concern and I can remember Marg saying to me when she was in about eleventh grade, "You know, Mom, there's no room in this family for any normal problems." I guess it was because at that time we were very concerned about Trudy because of the kids that she was hanging around with, and I was in a state because I was afraid that she was going to get into drugs and . . .

Freeman: And this was still seven years ago?

Mother: No, no, no. This was just like four years ago, eh?

Father: Well, actually about three, because that's the time we decided to send her to ———— College, and that's three years ago. But it had been going on for about a year before that.

Mother: Things built up as far as Trudy was concerned. It started at eleven and I have to say it just got steadily worse.

Freeman: Let's go back to the seven-year period, what was happening with other members of the family around that time? Marg, how old are you?

Marg: Twenty.

Freeman: You're twenty. Okay, I'll just get the ages here. And Peter?

Peter: I'm fourteen.

Freeman: And Beth?

Elizabeth: I'm twelve.

Freeman: (To mother) How old are you?

Mother: Forty-three.

Freeman: You're forty-three. And how old are you? (to father)

Father: Forty-five.

Freeman: Forty-five. And how long have you been married?

Mother: Twenty-three years.

Freeman: Twenty-three years. Okay, so seven years back everyone was around.

Mother: Right.

Father: Yeah. Yeah.

Mother: We had just moved to Olympia from Montreal. It was a very happy move because we really hated Montreal.

Father: In actual fact it was eight years ago, because I was there seven years and I retired a year ago.

Freeman: Well, Dad, how would you see other members of the family, if we can just keep within that seven-year period.

Father: Right now?

Freeman: Seven years back, then we'll get up to right now.

Father: Seven years back? I only noticed a sort of minor problem with the change in Trudy's behavior. I didn't take it too seriously because I felt that this was maybe a normal thing for a child that age.

The father is still having difficulty discussing members of the family other than the IP daughter. The therapist makes a more assertive attempt to get him to refocus away from the IP and on to the other members of the family. The therapist will also be trying to locate a period of time when the family wasn't having serious problems. An extremely helpful therapeutic strategy is to help the family build on the positives that have worked. Rather than initially encouraging the family to talk about difficulties, the therapist encourages them to talk about some of their successes prior to the development of serious difficulties.

Trudy: How old was I again?

Mother: Seven years ago you were eleven.

Father: Ten or eleven. About ten or eleven years old.

Freeman: Marg? You were thirteen?

Father: No problem with Margaret. She was an average teenager at that age. She was interested in ...

Mother: She was real good. Starting to make ... she was in with a nice crowd of friends at thirteen, and having some good times. That's when you first started around with Norman ...

Freeman: You say there was no problem with Margaret at that time, she was very good?

Mother: And the little ones, you know, were ...

Freeman: Peter, you were seven years old. Do you remember how things were when you were seven?

Peter: I sort of, like a little bit of a rotten kid, maybe. (Laughter)

Freeman: What would that be as you see it?

Peter: I used to, I can remember I used to steal a lot of toys. (Laughter)

This part of the interview illustrates how protective the parents are of the only son in the family. He quickly calls attention to a period of time that was difficult for him, but the parents normalize it and view his acting-out behavior at this point in his life an unimportant. Apparently they do not generalize this sort of attitude to the second oldest daughter.

Mother: That's when you were four or five. When you were seven you were in second grade.

Peter: I was still a little brat then though, until I was about eight.

Mother: He was kind of hard to handle, stubborn little guy, you know, sort of. But he really ... he has improved.

Freeman: You know, you've got kind of an interesting position in this family, because you have three sisters and no brother. How is it to be the only brother in a family of three sisters, Peter?

Peter: I'd rather have a brother, an older brother. (Laughter)

Freeman: How about Beth? Did you hope Beth might have been?

Mother: She was supposed to be a boy, she turned out to be a girl.

Freeman: Does that put you in a special position, being the only brother?

Trudy: He can punch us then.

Peter: No, not really, I don't think.

Freeman: So he can punch you? (To Peter) Do you do a lot of punching?

Elizabeth: Yes.

Freeman: You punch any one more than anybody else?

Elizabeth: Yes, he punches me too, and . . .

Mother: He's not a bully with you, Elizabeth, think carefully before you say things now. You like your brother.

Elizabeth: Yes.

Mother: She thinks he's a pretty nice boy.

Elizabeth: Oh, yeah.

Father: He's quite protective of her. He won't take her getting abuse from any of the older sisters, or he'll step in and . . .

Trudy: It's not abuse. It's being put in her place.

Elizabeth: No, it isn't, Trudy.

Father: No, no. If he thinks that she's being ill treated, by yourself in particular, he has stepped in.

Trudy: I don't ill-treat Elizabeth, come on.

Father: I'm just stating my opinion, Trudy. In his mind he feels that you are threatening Elizabeth.

Mother: Threatening. He feels you're threatening Elizabeth.

Trudy: If I want to give her a slap because she's being extremely disrespectful, I'm within my rights because I'm not going to get her to apologize.

Mother: Well, then, you get the picture. That's a good picture right there.

The therapist has now been shown some of the sibling conflict and how the parents are involved in the relationship structure of the siblings. In addition, the mother has demonstrated how protective she is of her two younger children. She tries hard not to let the therapist see some of the difficulties that exist between the two younger siblings. Later on in the course of treatment with this family, it becomes clear that the mother is concerned that family therapy might have adverse effects on the two younger children. By this point in the interview the therapist has learned that there is an imbalance in the family. The parents are overprotective of the younger children and see the two older children as carrying all the serious problems. This view of their children has led to severe sibling conflict. The parents side with the only son in the family and identify him as a protector of the younger daughter which places the two older children at a disadvantage in developing a relationship with their younger siblings without parental interference.

The therapist does not get involved in this issue during the first interview. Instead he continues to try to focus the family on a period of time when things were going well. If he allows the present conflict to continue in the interview he might lose the family. He is still in the beginning phase of the first interview and his main goal is to help the family feel comfortable and safe without using their time with him to scapegoat one of their members. Up to this point in the interview he has been unable to accomplish this goal but he moves now more quickly to diffuse the family intensity. He begins to get the family to talk about broader issues.

Freeman: Peter, do you notice that the family began to talk for you about what's going on with you? I wonder if you have any ideas about what goes on with you in relation to your sisters?

Peter: That's true, what my father says.

Freeman: What's that? What did he say?

Peter: Well, when I don't like, you know, Trudy bothering Beth—

Trudy: He does it himself.

Mother: Let—

Father: Settle down, Trudy.

Trudy: It's true, Mom.

Mother: Yes, but let him talk.

Freeman: This is new for Elizabeth and Peter? They've never been at a session like this before?

Peter: You know, I do bug Elizabeth sometimes, like any brother would do, but like I don't like letting Trudy hit her or anything like that.

Freeman: She's big enough now.

Margaret: Elizabeth has a way of acting superior toward us, and we sort of resent it since she's younger than us. That's what causes most of the fights between us, Trudy and—

Peter: Margaret, she does that because so many times ... sometimes you treat Dad and Mom like that.

Elizabeth: Yeah, Marg.

Peter: Yes, she does.

Margaret: Treat Mom and Dad like what?

Freeman: Let's stay with seven years ago. You said you were kind of, was it bratty?

Peter: Yeah.

Freeman: Or were you taking toys?

Peter: Yes.

Freeman: Any particular sister you took the toys from?

Peter: Not from sisters, from friends. (Laughter)

Freeman: Beth, do you remember seven years ago?

Elizabeth: No.

Freeman: Any memory whatsoever?

Elizabeth: No, nothing, no memory at all.

Freeman: Marg, how about you? What do you remember happening with the family seven years ago?

Margaret: I was thirteen. I was extremely insecure. That's about the only thing that stands out in my mind.

Freeman: What do you mean when you say you were insecure seven years ago?

Margaret: Being so uncertain of yourself that you turn introverted.

Freeman: Introverted would be . . .

Margaret: Just sticking to myself and when I'm with a group of people I feel even more lonely than if I was by myself. In other words having a problem relating to other people. It takes me quite a while to get to know somebody, especially if it's a male. I have quite a barrier. I'm quite inhibited around males. The family situation, let's see . . . I would have been in eighth grade. I can remember I had . . . my nerves were really bad and I had an outbreak of a really bad rash. This spread all over my face. I don't know whether it was an infection or if it was nerves. The doctor didn't even know what it was. I always thought I was extremely unintelligent and that affected my insecurity. I was just distant from everybody.

Freeman: Were there certain members of the family that you were closer to at that period, than other members of the family?

Margaret: I felt closer to Trudy.

Freeman: To Trudy, your sister.

Margaret: Um hmm. And yet at the same time I resented her because she fought with my parents. I was the exact opposite. I absorbed everything while she reflected it, that's the only thing I had against her, was the fact that she didn't just absorb all her hostilities and I did. Anyway, I thought I was better than her for the simple reason that I didn't lash back. Now I realize that it was better, what she did. Because she's a lot more secure than I am. I don't have the same feeling of insecurity now as I did. Since I've come here it's pretty well been erased. I don't know if it's the effect of the drugs or not. That's the only fault in our relationship, when we fought all the time—the fact that I didn't respect her for that, you know, lashing back, but now I realize that she did the right thing.

Freeman: Do you see yourself, you use the term introverted, as introverted now as you used to be, as you were seven years ago?

Margaret: No.

Freeman: So that has changed.

Margaret: Yeah.

Freeman: Do you think that the family has been aware of the changes that have been coming about with you?

Margaret: No, I don't think so.

In this part of the interview, Margaret informs the therapist and the family that the period of time that the parents thought was a good period for her, was actually a very difficult time in her life. She talks about feeling insecure, unhappy and lonely. As the therapist proceeds with this family, it become apparent that Marg is actually the invisible member of the family. Her parents are unaware of her needs and how she responds to difficult situations. They are so preoccupied by the behavior of Trudy, who acts out physically and calls attention to herself, that they lose sight of their oldest daughter who has a quiet, and somewhat withdrawn temperament. The more attention that is directed to Trudy, the less attention the parents have for their oldest daughter, and in many ways, for their two younger children. The therapist now engages the other three children, concluding with Trudy, the IP. He consciously chooses to end with Trudy to avoid bringing the orientation or focus back to her behavior.

After giving each child an opportunity to describe how they view certain matters historically he then directs his attention to the parents and encourages them to talk about themselves as individuals. He asks the parents about their own families of origin and about some of their experiences prior to the establishment of their family of procreation. By asking these questions the therapist is communicating to the family that the focal point is not going to be on the identified problem. Rather, the emphasis will be on looking at how each member is experiencing family relationships. If the therapist can communicate this message to the family he will have accomplished his goal of providing a safe atmosphere in which no one is scapegoated. An indication of whether the therapist has accomplished this goal will be given at the end of the interview when he asks each member if he or she wants to return. If he has been successful in demonstrating that the family therapy process can meet the needs of individuals as well as the group, there should be less resistance on the part of the children to return for ongoing sessions.

Freeman: Okay, now, we have heard that you tend to be introverted (turning to Margaret), and you (to Trudy) tend to be extroverted. You see yourself differently from how certain other family members see you. How about Peter and Elizabeth? (To Peter) How do you see yourself?

Peter: Well, myself . . . well, at school I don't usually comform or anything like that. Like I don't smoke or anything like that. I mean, most kids my age do, about sixty percent of them.

Freeman: Are you able to say what's on your mind or do you tend to keep things inside?

Peter: Well, I sort of think I do, you know. I don't really keep things inside . . . maybe some things.

Freeman: And Beth? How about you? How do you see yourself?

Elizabeth: I'm like Peter, I don't really say much but I don't keep everything in.

Freeman: Um hmm.

Elizabeth: Like, I'm not like Trudy who tells everything, even if it's going to hurt someone's feelings.

Freeman: Do you kind of screen out things you're going to say? How do you know what to screen out and what not to screen out?

Elizabeth: I think about it first before I say anything, and then say it.

Freeman: But would you know the sorts of things you might say that would upset Mom and Dad, and those things that wouldn't upset Mom and Dad?

Elizabeth: Yeah.

Freeman: You could tell pretty well?

Elizabeth: Yeah. About most things, I think.

Freeman: Have they ever surprised you?

Elizabeth: What do you mean?

Freeman: You expected them to be upset by something and it turned out that they weren't?

Elizabeth: Yeah.

Freeman: Who tends to surprise you more, Mom or Dad?

Elizabeth: Probably Dad.

Freeman: Now, Trudy, you took issue with how Mom saw you as an individual.

Trudy: Ah hah.

Freeman: Maybe you could tell us about how you see yourself.

Trudy: Well, she seems to think I'm extroverted, but I'm not really.

Freeman: How do you see you?

Trudy: Like my sister said, I'm very much like her. Only when things get to a point where—it's really quite a funny circle, like I'm insecure and I'm very afraid of things, and —when it reaches a pressure point I have to explode, and so I do so, you know, in the house.

Freeman: In the house? What would be an explosion for you? How would I know if you exploded?

Trudy: I take issue over any wrong that that my parents do and I usually think I'm right. Even if it's a little bit wrong I overreact to it, you know, for my benefit, and it really makes me feel better. It puts me in control or something.

Freeman: So an explosion for you, would be to overreact, if things are getting out of hand, for you to exaggerate your feelings. Now, we've got a picture of the children, so how about the parents? Dad, how about you? What type of person are you?

Father: Oh, I think I'm fairly even tempered. I think that the man in the family, together with the wife, has to say what goes on in the family. Otherwise you get anarchy and you've really got family breakup. I've tried to guide them the best that I could, but I have never been, and probably never will be, what you'd call the affectionate father, the kissing, the hugging type, and I think this is probably a reflection of my own upbringing, because my father and mother were like that.

Freeman: So they were not demonstrative.

Mother: Right.

Father: No. Oh, no. And I don't think I have been either, although I tried other means to be a good father. I never drink. I don't run around with women and I'm home most of the time. I've always been with the family in the evenings. We've done some things together, we've gone camping together and this sort of thing and I've tried to give them what advice I can, to the best of my ability. What I think is right—and Trudy is giving me the eagle eye there—I've often tried to tell them what I think is good advice. Whether they accept it or not, that's something else. I don't know what else I can add to that.

Freeman: You mentioned your family, your parents not being demonstrative. Do you come from a large family?

Father: No, two brothers and myself.

Freeman: Older? Younger?

Father: They're both older.

Freeman: And you're the youngest of the three brothers, and no girls.

Father: No girls.

Freeman: Are your parents still here, alive?

Father: My mother's still alive, yes. My dad died two years ago.

Freeman: What did he die of?

Father: Heart attack.

Freeman: And your mom lives in the area?

Father: She's in Portland.

Freeman: How old is she?

Father: She's seventy-eight ... seventy-seven right now.

Freeman: Seventy-seven. Well, you mentioned your parents not being demonstrative. How would you know how they felt at a given time?

Father: How they felt about me or about ... ?

Freeman: About you.

Father: Oh, I never doubted that my mother and father loved me. They loved me very much. There was never any doubt in my mind whatsoever. I think the things that stands out most in my mind about them though, when I was young, was they they used to fight like cats and dogs.

Freeman: They used to fight ...

Father: Yeah, and ...

Freeman: Anything in particular that would get them to fight?

Father: It wouldn't take much. It wouldn't take much. I can remember quite vividly that—they were both from Sweden, and they immigrated here, and I can remember quite vividly they used to argue even over the proper pronunciation of a Swedish word. You know I'd be sitting at the dinner table and a fight would start over that!

Freeman: Uh huh.

Father: And, I think what melded this in my mind, as far as marriage is concerned, is that I was determined that whenever I got married, I was going to make a success of it, and my wife and I have, I think. I think anybody who sees us will agree with that. We have a very successful marriage. So, the fact that my mother and father fought so much, maybe, in an indirect way, was a benefit to me.

Freeman: I see. Well, when they fought, would any of the children get into the fights with them?

Father: Well, no . . .

Mother: I think they would steer clear.

Father: No. Except on—they really used to fight quite badly, it was—usually, the kids weren't there. I could hear what was going on. There was never any violence in the home. My father wasn't that type. He'd never strike anybody.

Freeman: So it was mostly verbal?

Father: Yeah.

Freeman: Right. And your brothers, are they in Seattle?

Father: No. One's in Portland, one's in California.

Freeman: Do you ever see much of them?

Father: No, not my oldest brother. He's the black sheep of the family.

Freeman: How old is he?

Father: He's seven years older than me, so he'd be fifty-two.

Freeman: What about him makes him the black sheep?

Father: He's irresponsible. He was always taking my mother and father for a ride, money-wise and other ways. He's . . . well, besides irresponsible he didn't have much regard for other people's feelings. He felt that what he wanted to do, he could do when he wanted to do it, you know, just to hell with everybody else, to heck with other people. He ditched his wife and three children, what, about three years ago?

Mother: Yes.

Father: Took the car, cleared out the bank account and beat it out of Berkeley and left them with sixty cents. So this is one reason why I don't particularly want to see him again, to be quite frank. My other brother, Dick, that's my middle brother, the middle one of the family, he's a Rock of Gibraltar. He's an especially fine fellow, and I have a lot of respect for him. They're vastly different individuals.

Freeman: And he's married?

Father: No, he's divorced. As a matter of fact they're both divorced. And he's living with my mother and his daughter's living in Portland.

Freeman: He's helping take care of your mother?

Father: Yeah. Right. He's looking after my father's estate. So he comes out about every four or five months, sees us, stays with us.

Freeman: So actually, the children have had a chance to meet their uncle. How is he on the scale of demonstrative behavior?

Father: My brother?

Freeman: Yes.

Father: About the same as me, I think.

Mother: They're a lot alike.

Freeman: A lot alike?

Mother: Yes, I could even mistake him on the phone after all these years.

Freeman: How old is Dick?

Father: He would be . . . he's forty-eight. Three years older than me.

Freeman: Who in the family would you say tends to show the most feeling toward other members of the family?

Father: Probably the oldest brother.

Freeman: The black sheep?

Father: The black sheep, yes.

Mother: Uh hmm.

Father: 'Cause both my mother and father weren't demonstrative. Probably my mother was a little bit more toward the oldest brother, because he was sort of the weak brother, and, um, being a mother, of course, I think she did this because he was weak, but I can't remember . . . no, I never can remember from the time I was a little shaver, my mother ever hugging me or kissing me. That's one thing I can't remember, although I really didn't hold it against her, 'cause, you know, she is a fine person. Everybody just loves her.

Mother: She was very devoted to her sons. She made a nice, nice home for them.

Freeman: How about your father? Did he do any hugging and kissing?

Father: No, I think he wanted to, but it just wasn't in him.

Freeman: Uh hmm.

Mother: Until he was a grandfather. You know, he was very affectionate with his grandchildren.

Father: When grandchildren used to hug him, he just would eat it right up.

Freeman: Kind of skipped a generation to show his feelings.

Father: Yes, right. The grandchildren.

Mother: Uh hmm.

Freeman: Well, Mom, about you as a person. How would you describe . . .

Mother: Well, how about me? Well, I just live for my family, sort of, like, since I've been doing it for twenty years, and . . . my husband being in the military I've found the moving hard, more because of having children and wondering how each one is going to react to every new situation. I found that a little hard. The other part of the military life I enjoyed. I like meeting people and I like seeing the country, and so on. And this trouble we're having now is something that, well, I can cope with it now not too badly, but a few years ago when I was so worried about Trudy, it was very hard, because, you sort of think if you devote yourself to your family, everything's going to work out, and it certainly didn't. But I've had, um . . . I'm very happily married and the two younger ones certainly ... I mean right now they're the ones that are helping keep the family even-keeled because they're extremely good and good in school and they're good at home, and there's no problems that way. And I've gone back to work now, I work part-time.

Freeman: What type of work do you do?

Mother: I'm a service representative for the telephone company. It's the same job I had here twenty years ago. I like it very well, and I think it's very good for me because, this past year, I think if I'd been home it would have been much harder. Whenever the two girls sat around doing nothing and dwelling on their problems it just—you know, you talk and you talk and you try to explain the way you feel and try to give them a little more understanding of whatever situation they're in, but it's very hard. Sometimes you just don't get through.

Freeman: Now, is your family in the area?

Mother: Yes, they are.

Freeman: Do you have brothers and sisters?

Mother: I have three sisters and my mother.

Freeman: Three sisters. You have no brothers?

Mother: No brothers. And I have no father because my dad died when I was five.

Freeman: In what year did he die?

Mother: 1935.

Freeman: '35. What did he die of?

Mother: A heart attack.

Freeman: Heart attack. And your sisters. Older? Younger?

Mother: All older.

Freeman: They're married?

Mother: Yes. Well, two of them have been married now, one for twenty-three years and the other for twenty-five.

Freeman: The oldest sister ...

Mother: But not my oldest sister, she's well, it's sort of complicated for her. She's living with her first husband. But I don't see too much of her. She hasn't been too stable—when I was young—well, of course, she's ten years older.

Freeman: So she's fifty-three.

Mother: Right. And when I was growing up she—she was sixteen when my dad died and it was a very hard thing for her, of course, as she was very close to him. And she really made my mother's life hell for about four years until she finally left home. It was a real ... you know, it was a bad thing.

Freeman: How would she do that? How would she make your mother's life ...

Mother: She would fight over everything. My mother is a very sweet and a very soft person and it was very hard for her to cope with. My second oldest sister was a real, uh ... you know, she was the one that helped my mother out when she needed the help and also tended to mother me because my mother had no time.

Freeman: She never remarried?

Mother: No, she never did.

Freeman: So the next sister will be how old?

Mother: She's forty-nine.

Freeman: Forty-nine, and she's married?

Mother: Yes, very happily.

Freeman: Any children?

Mother: Yes, she's lovely and my other sister, too. She has two children. They're happily married with no problems

Freeman: How old would she be?

Mother: She's forty-six.

Freeman: Forty-six. Seems like your oldest sister and oldest brother both ...

Mother: Yes, it's funny. They're both really kind of bad apples, to tell the truth.

Freeman: Your sisters, the children's aunts, do they spend much time with the family at get-togethers?

Mother: Yes, yes, we do. When we came back last year, we had Christmas dinner at our house, 'cause we had a big rumpus room and set up a ping-pong table and another table and that was the first time we had all been together, the twenty-two of us. It was very nice. And my two sisters, I'm very close to them, really, you know, they couldn't be better, I mean they give us a lot of moral support at a time like this and know that we have problems.

Freeman: Your mother, how old is she?

Mother: Seventy-seven.

Freeman: And she's in good health?

Mother: Well, not really. She's just had a pacemaker put in and she also has hardening of the arteries, so, you know, she's aging. She's still a very sweet person. She's taking turns now living with us, and she's supposed to be coming to us next month, so I'm hoping that our family situation is going to be somewhat reasonable so that she can manage to live with us.

Freeman: How long will she be with you?

Mother: Well, she's just going to live a couple of months with each of us.

Freeman: So, two months at a time with each sister?

Mother: That's right.

Father: With three sisters.

Mother: She's quite happy.

Freeman: With three sisters.

Father: Not the oldest one.

Freeman: The oldest one isn't involved in the plan?

Mother: No, she's not. They didn't ever get along so there's really no point in the two—but, you know, this problem we have now is just something that, we do feel we've lived a good life and we have never had any great problems and it's very hard for us to understand what has happened. It really is.

Freeman: You mentioned the military. There was part of being in the military that you enjoyed and part that was difficult, the moving.

Mother: The moving. Yes, it's very hard, and the more children you have ... you don't know what's ahead of you and you get there and you have to buy a house and you don't know for sure what district to live in and people don't want to rent to you when you have a family, and so usually each time we moved, not only did we have to move to the city but we made an additional move later because maybe the house was being sold we were renting and we'd have to move. This was very hard, but I know we're not the only ones that ever lived through that.

Father: That was quite common when we first got in the military in Freeport and Peoria, but the last—

Mother: Yeah, but Albany was fine.

Father: No, the last seven years I was in the military we were in one place. That was in Albany, in one house.

Mother: Yes.

Freeman: The last seven years?

Father: The last seven years.

Freeman: Are you in the military now?

Father: No.

Freeman: When did you retire?

Father: Retired last January.

Freeman: After how many years?

Father: Nineteen years.

Freeman: Nineteen years. Any reason you didn't wait until twenty years?

Father: Compulsory retirement.

Freeman: In nineteen years?

Father: Well, it's a certain age for a certain rank you see.

Freeman: I see. So, you just retired.

Father: Yes, right.

Freeman: So most of the family life was spent in the military.

Mother: Yes, when Margaret was born, was when he joined.

Freeman: Did you find the moving as difficult as your wife did?

Father: Not at first because you're younger, more resilient. It was bothersome but certainly not as much as any recent moves we've made. Like we just moved a month ago, just a few blocks.

Freeman: Um hmm.

Father: We had to do it ourselves, and I found it very, very tiring. I was racked up for about three days after that, doing it ourselves. But I think the thing that concerned us the most when we were younger was not the moving itself, because we can always make new friends, in the Forces atmosphere you always do anyway, but our concern mainly was the children, the effect of moving on the children. We saw that, really for the first time when we got to Detroit in 1963, where we moved into quite a different atmosphere. The change in school I think was quite dramatic for Margaret and Trudy because they walked into a school that was very, very hard. They had a real disciplinarian for a principal there and he believed in three to four hours of homework every night. They walked into that from a relatively light academic load at their old school. So for a while that was tough on them and we felt for them.

Mother: It was very bad, and Margaret—that's one thing I remember there too, when they got to that school they actually had the classes broken up into Grade 3A, B, C, D and it meant just that! I've never seen that before.

Freeman: From smart to dumb.

Mother: Right, and it—I really thought that was a terrible thing, but however, that's the way it was, and they put the two girls in the B class to start out with, from their report cards they thought that was a good place for them. Trudy did extremely well, because she tried hard. What were you in—third grade, Trudy? and Margaret was in fifth grade and they moved her after a few months, down from the B class to the C class and this was rather a hurtful thing to do. You know how children are.

Margaret: Especially when one thinks they're kind of stupid to begin with.

Mother: Well, I think Margaret never had done particularly well in school, whether she could have done better, I think she could have and I think for some reason she didn't try as hard as she should have in that.

Freeman: Margaret, as the oldest in the family, with sisters and brothers, how does it feel having been in a family in the military for most of your life?

Margaret: Well, it's hard to say, 'cause I didn't really know anything else. It didn't really make much difference to me.

Freeman: Do you ever wonder what it would be like not to be in the military?

Margaret: No. I could have wondered what it would be like to live in one place, at one time, but that's the only distinction I could make.

Freeman: What was it like for you to have to move so often?

Margaret: It didn't really bother me except a few moves which were sort of inopportune. In Detroit, I was just starting to get to know people and making some good friends when we left—

Mother: That's true.

Margaret: —at the same time.

Freeman: And how old were you at that time?

Margaret: Eleven.

Freeman: So it was nine years ago.

Margaret: Yes, and I think that's when I first started getting really insecure.

Freeman: Let's stay with that time period for a moment. You were getting comfortable in Detroit, you were making some friends?

Margaret: Yes.

Freeman: And then what happened?

Margaret: We moved.

Freeman: How did you handle that?

Margaret: Well, I did it. I just did it. As usual I didn't really complain about it because I didn't really know if it bothered me at the time or not. I'd have to compare it to another period in my life, but, I think it did bother me.

Freeman: Did you identify your beginning of feeling insecure around that time period?

Margaret: Yeah. I was always insecure but I think once I started heading toward puberty I really got insecure.

Freeman: How was it for you then to get started with new schools? Did you find that a particularly difficult thing for you? Was it easy for you . . .

Margaret: Well, I should be used to it but actually if I find that I'm cut off from all my friends I feel very, very hyper, just really like I'm going to explode, I'm so nervous.

Freeman: When you get cut off from your friends?

Margaret: Yeah. Not so much now, because I've gone for a whole year with practically doing nothing, and as long as I'm in a situation where I'm doing something, I'm not going to worry about the fact that I don't know somebody too well. You know, I'm over that now.

Freeman: What's the longest time you've spent in one house in one area?

Margaret: Oh . . . oh, yes, Albany, six years.

Freeman: That's six years. That would be the longest time?

Margaret: Yes.

Freeman: What was the shortest time?

Margaret: I don't know.

Mother: Oh boy, well, that was probably when she was a baby.

Father: Yeah, that was only a period of months.

Mother: That one . . . in Freeport we moved about three times in one year.

Margaret: I don't remember it.

Freeman: Three times in one year, would be the most moves in one year?

Mother: Yes.

Freeman: What would be the average stay for the family?

Mother: That would be about two years. We smartened up after that and we used to take a two-year lease on a house whenever we got there, and then work from there.

Freeman: Trudy, how was it for you to be in the military? To have a family in the military?

Trudy: I didn't really care. Not much, I don't think. I don't think the military affected anything, except that—like my sister said I can't compare it with anything else except, like my friends, like when we were finally settled in Albany for seven years, it was just like still being transient because all your friends are still moving.

Mother: That was true.

Freeman: So, if you weren't moving, someone you might have been involved with was moving.

Mother: This is true. That was a very hard thing.

Freeman: That's interesting. Both Marg and Trudy said they could not compare it with anything else because most of their lives were spent in that type of family, but, Mom, you could compare it with something else.

Mother: Oh yes, yes. And I think this is why . . .

Freeman: You got a sense of . . .

Mother: Yes, yes. This is why I felt a great sense of concern for my children because I lived in one house from the time I was five years old till I got married.

Freeman: The only house you were in until you got married?

Mother: The only house. And you know, I still have friends today that I had in first grade, and I know that my children will never have that advantage, which I think really—I feel is an advantage, anyway. And you know, I did feel that this was hard for them, I think, any mother would . . . just have concern for your children, about how they're going to make out in each place.

Freeman: Dad, did you come from a family as stable as hers in terms of remaining in one place?

Father: Beg your pardon?

Freeman: Your family—was it as stable as hers?

Father: Yeah, I had the same thing in Portland. My dad was there from about 1928 until two years ago, so I was raised in Portland, again, the same as my wife. It wasn't a house, it was an apartment block my dad owned. We were in there all my life until I . . . The old friends were there sort of thing. And you never even thought of people moving around in those days. Most people stayed put. There weren't these company transfers so prevalent now. It's a way of life now, moving around so much.

Freeman: Pete, how about you, now? Most of your life has also been spent in the military. How did you find the moving experience?

Peter: Well, the hardest thing was losing your friends, but after a few months when I got here I made some new friends. So it didn't really bother me that much.

Mother: It's been more stable for them, you see.

Peter: Yeah, because . . .

Freeman: The two younger ones?

Mother: Uh hmm.

Peter: Yeah, all the moves that were made . . . was when I was just real little, you know, so it couldn't affect me socially in any way.

Freeman: I see. How do you think it would affect you now, let's say, if the family started to move again every two years.

Mother: No way!

Peter: It probably would.

Freeman: Do you think it would have an effect on you?

Peter: Might. Yeah.

Freeman: And Beth? How about with you?

Elizabeth: Would it have an effect on me?

Freeman: Yes. If the family began to move every two years?

Elizabeth: Probably. Yes, I think it would, because I think making friends is pretty hard.

Father: Yes, just think of the friends you've got now. Those three girlfriends. You wouldn't want to leave them.

Elizabeth: No.

Mother: No, we're not going to move.

Freeman: How did the family react to Dad's retirement from the military?

Mother: Good. We were all looking forward to it. We were all looking forward to coming back here.

Freeman: Uh huh.

Mother: The children all like Seattle very much, so this made that part of it very easy. Even though we liked Albany—the girls got kind of sick of the small town, but we liked it. But we were still looking forward to coming back home.

Freeman: Dad, were you ready to retire?

Father: Oh yes. Yes, indeed. I wanted to get into something else.

Freeman: So what are you into now?

Father: Real estate.

Freeman: Real estate. And how is that going?

Father: Not too bad. Not too bad. Ups and downs.

Mother: He's done well for a beginner. He's doing quite well, I think.

Freeman: Well, this is the first family session we've had and we're just getting to know where the family's at . . .

Mother: Uh hmm.

What transpired in the preceding excerpt is representative of the middle phase of the first interview. The family has become more relaxed. There is far less scapegoating, and the children show more interest in what the parents have to say about themselves as members of their own families of origin. The emotional climate in the session has changed. Until the therapist asked the father to talk about his own experiences in the family, everyone had been tense, anxious and uncomfortable. Once the focus clearly switched from family failures to other family history, members began to serve as resources to each other rather than as adversaries. The therapist has now gained control over the atmosphere of the session and is able to help the family broaden its definition of itself as an historical family system. As the reader can readily see from this portion of the transcript, the family has gone through many changes: the father's retirement from the military; the many moves; the difficulties of the two older children in school; and finally, the permanent relocation in a new area.

It is also interesting to note that both parents identify scapegoats in their respective families of origin. Both parents are the youngest, and both have oldest siblings who were the troublemakers in their families. It would appear that the messages the parents received in their families, about what was acceptable and unacceptable in sibling relationships and parent-child relationships, strongly influenced how they have dealt with their own family of procreation. Their oldest daughter and only son are temperamentally quiet and unassuming children, whereas the second oldest daughter and youngest daughter are active, somewhat demanding children. Both parents talk about the difficulties they have had in their own lives in dealing with the more demanding personality. Apparently, both their older siblings were the IP's in their respective families and both were temperamentally similar to these parents' second oldest daughter.

Now that the therapist has redefined the focal point and has helped the family develop a degree of comfort, he is able to move to the conclusion of the session where he asks how the family has experienced the session.

Freeman: Our time is about up.

Mother: Uh hmm.

Freeman: I was wondering about the family's reaction to continuing as a family in therapy.

Mother: Well, I'd like to say one thing that I feel very strongly about. Peter is very keen on his schoolwork this year. He's made up his mind he's going to do well, and he thinks he's maybe going to get into medical school when he's through high school and I really hate to see him take the time off. He's getting braces on his teeth next month and that means at least two days a month he's going to have to miss school. So unless you felt it was really essential, myself, I really feel Pete and Elizabeth are extremely well adjusted.

Peter: If you just tell me the days we have to go I'll just find out if that's all right, if I can go.

Mother: Well, I know, but what I . . . the point I want to make is, unless it's really essential, I don't like him to miss school.

Elizabeth: Fridays don't matter to me, Mom, because I have an open afternoon.

Mother: No, they don't that's true. It doesn't really matter.

Freeman: I'd just like to get each individual's reaction to coming back as a family and then we'll see what the decision will be. Let's start . . . we always tend to start with the oldest. Let's start with the youngest. Let's start with Elizabeth and work up.

This portion of the interview demonstrates the mother's resistance to having her two younger children involved in the sessions. Later on in treatment we discovered that one of the mother's worst fears was that the family therapy experience would have negative effects on her two younger children. The parents very much depended on the two younger children to maintain the family homeostasis. Primarily because the experience has been positive for the family, the mother's resistance is minimal and the younger children are enthusiastic. This allows the therapist to capitalize on the positive reactions of the younger children, building on them to encourage the family to continue in family therapy. This is why the therapist · chose to start with the youngest daughter, who has clearly committed herself to wanting to return. Then he can move gradually from the most positive to the least positive members.

Elizabeth: I think it would be good to come back.

Freeman: Come back as a family?

Elizabeth: Sure. I'd like to. I don't see anything wrong with it.

Freeman: And Pete?

Peter: Yes. I think it would be good.

Freeman: And Trudy, how about you?

Trudy: Yes, I think it's a good idea.

Freeman: And Marg?

Margaret: Yes, I agree.

Freeman: And you, Mom?

Mother: Well, I'm sorry, I still feel the same.

Freeman: Okay.

Mother: I mean, um . . .

Freeman: You're willing to come?

Mother: In fact I'd be quite willing, if it were a Saturday, or in the evenings which I'm sure probably wouldn't agree with you. It's the school thing. I don't like them to take time off.

Freeman: And Dad?

Father: How often would it be? Would it be every week?

Freeman: Um hmm. Once a week.

Father: It would depend on how it affects their school work. If it was on a particular Friday, when they have very little in the afternoon . . . sports or something like this, then it wouldn't matter, but as far as cutting into much of the academic stuff, I wouldn't want to see too much of it.

Freeman: But how about you, would you like to come back?

Father: Oh, yes, sure.

Freeman: Okay. Now we can keep this time and see how it goes. My own reaction to having everyone in the family present is that I find it works better when everyone is here. If one or two people aren't here then what we talked about becomes secondhand information for them. If everyone's here, then everyone hears it and everyone has input. And everyone becomes a part of the process. The reason I like to work with families together is because you're all involved. What happens with every decision that's made affects all of you.

This portion concludes the first interview. The therapist has methodically asked each member if he or she wants to return.

After obtaining a commitment from the family that it wants to continue, he makes a succinct statement about the benefits of working as a family. In this way he summarizes the experience.

The following transcript is of the fourth session with this family. All family members were present. This session shows how the family has moved from a strictly reactive stance, where they were quite anxious about working together, to a stage where they were beginning to look at family behavior and how it affects family members. The family is just beginning to move into the middle phase. The therapist takes the initiative in offering the family an experience which gives them an indication of how reacting differently to each other can be of benefit to all of them.

The therapist uses the intensity between the father and second oldest daughter, Trudy, as an example to show that when two people in conflict respond differently to each other the conflict can be dealt with and understood in a different way. When the father and Trudy fought with each other, the mother became anxious and concerned and tried to separate the two. It was clear that the younger children agreed with the mother that in these situations Trudy was at fault. When this triangulation got going the oldest daughter, Marg, would remove herself from the situation and begin to act out silently. The effects of these conflicts on her do not become clear to the family until later. The typical chain of events set off by the father and Trudy fighting was for the mother to jump in, either on her own initiative when she disagreed with something that Trudy said, or by way of Trudy, who would become uncomfortable and deal with her discomfort by bringing her mother into the conflict. Father did not discourage other family members from becoming involved in what was going on between himself and his daughter. The therapist actively assists the family in recognizing this pattern. He discusses their overinvolvement in content and the nonproductiveness of trying to prove right and wrong, emphasizing how getting unhooked from this focus allows for new learning about each other. Following these observations about family behavior, the quality of interaction between family members begins to change.

Trudy and Marg are now able to have a discussion with each other and disagree without other members of the family taking sides. However, at the end of the interview when the therapist asks each member of the family to state what they observed happening between father and daughter, the two younger children continue to side with the parents against their older siblings. The mother, on the other hand, begins to recognize the benefits of staying out of the relationship between father and daughter. She states that for years she has tried to get her husband and Trudy more involved with each other, but because of their conflict has served as the mediator. She now begins to recognize how her mediating role has actually encouraged distance between father and daughter. From this interview on, the family begins to move quite rapidly in their efforts to deal with each other differently.

During the terminating interview, which was discussed in Chapter 7, the father made reference to this interview as one which was particularly helpful to him. When he became aware of how dysfunctional it was to involve additional family members in his conflict with Trudy the quality of his interaction with other family members improved.

One final point bears mentioning. Near the end of this interview Trudy begins to talk about how family patterns in her father's family of origin have affected the way members of her family, particularly her father and herself, have dealt with each other. Trudy's statements are an indication that the first series of sessions which dealt with the extended family have helped Trudy, and possibly the other children, rethink the meaning behind some of the patterns which have developed in the family. Rather than personalizing certain parental behaviors as an indication of whether they care for their children, the children can begin to see that how their parents involve themselves with their family is influenced not only be their immediate feelings toward family members, but also by patterns of behavior learned in their family of origin.

This session is presented without any additional commentary. The interview clearly demonstrates the process the family underwent as they experienced some new ways of dealing with each other.

Fourth interview with the P family

Cotherapist: I'm not too sure what you see happening with family therapy. I think a word that I would use is that family therapy supposedly provides a machinery for change, a change of relationship, the way you live in relation to each other.

Mother: I think I realize that, but I don't know how our relations that we have in our family—

(Margaret gets up and goes out.)

Freeman: (To Margaret) Come back when you feel better.

Mother: I don't really see, you know, how the therapy could help. I mean, if you understand what the setup is in our family as I do—the things that come up here I've only thought about them, like, about a hundred times, you know. I'm not insensitive. But the problem in the family, really, has been Trudy for a couple of years.

Cotherapist: But you see, the way Trudy relates in turn sets up a chain reaction.

Mother: It does. That's true.

Cotherapist: Last week we talked about a vicious circle.

Mother: Right.

Cotherapist: And in order to break that vicious circle then everybody has to say, yes, I'm willing to change. Because when we ask, are you willing to come to the family therapy, we're not saying, Is Trudy going to change? We're saying, Are *you* willing to change? We're saying that the family needs to do it.

Father: I think the family as a whole, everybody, has to change or you don't accomplish anything. There's not one member who isn't going to change . . . you don't change anything . . . it's very difficult.

Cotherapist: And everybody relates in the same way. You pick up a habit of doing it. And so when we tell you to come here it's within view that you want to change something that you're doing which will in turn help the family. And that's the focus, and when we talk about the process of what's going on in the family, you should be aware of things that need to be changed.

Father: The thing is, I wonder, really, if Trudy *can* change. Because we've tried so hard to talk to her in a logical manner—

Trudy: Oh B. S.

Father: —and tell her what we expect. And you see the reaction I'm getting right now. (Laughter)

Trudy: Mother has tried. And I don't blame you for not—I don't have any . . .

Father: Oh, I have tried on many occasions, Trudy.

Mother: I'm just more talkative than Dad, Trudy.

Trudy: I know. That's why I say I don't hold it against him for never trying to help me.

Freeman: Is it possible for Trudy to take the issue up with Dad without any other members of the family getting in . . . see how that works? Okay, take it up with your dad (to Trudy).

Trudy: He would rather hit first and talk later. I think I have turned into a slight masochist because when I was young and became upset over an issue, I'd be slugged around, I'd have my head pounded on the floor . . . and you can deny it (to Dad) . . . but I have a good memory and I'm not insane. And then, perhaps, you talk it over with me later. Usually, we'd make up and have kissies and hugs, right?

Father: No, you're definitely wrong, Trudy.

Elizabeth: Trudy, you can't say he pounded your head!

Cotherapist: (To Elizabeth) Wait, hold it.

Father: No, you're wrong. And the rest of the members of the family—

Trudy: Well, how come I have nightmares all the time?

Father: (To the others) Because she was an extremely good child when she was young and I had no reason to ever lay a hand on her. And the first time she ever came out with this I was absolutely dumbfounded. Because I never laid a hand on her as a child.

Mother: Okay, at what age?

Father: I'm thinking up 'till she was eleven or twelve years old.

Mother: Okay, now that's established.

Trudy: I can remember instances when I was five and six very clearly.

Mother: How often?

Freeman: Excuse me, you're talking to your dad or your mom?

Trudy: My mother, because she said I was eleven or twelve when we had our—

Freeman: Just to get the pattern going. You're starting with your dad, now you're in with your mother. I'd like to see you work it through with your father. Because that's the issue you raised, the relationship between you and dad. Let's stick with that.

Trudy: I don't know why. I don't know why he ever hit me. He never hit Elizabeth when she did any wrong. He hit Margaret. But he hit me especially hard, I think. I think you hit me (to Dad) especially hard.

Father: I have no recollection of it at all (smiling and shaking his head).

Trudy: I think you hold something against me, from a way, way back.

Father: No. Nothing, nothing.

Cotherapist: Could you tell your father what you think he holds against you?

Trudy: Perhaps my mother's favoritism toward me.

Father: What, at that age?

Trudy: Because I took up so much of her time.

Father: No, I don't think I've ever insisted on your mother spending more time with me than she does. We've always been very close and I've always been home a lot.

Trudy: Well, maybe I'm wrong then. I'm sorry if I am, and I really regret having to say this.

Father: Well, I've talked about this issue with you before, about this supposed child beating. I brought it up in a meeting here that you mentioned it a few years ago.

Trudy: You didn't *beat* me?

Father: I never hit you.

Trudy: Oh! (Incredulous)

Father: Were we alone at the time? Was anybody around?

Trudy: Mother would sometimes stand at the door and say, "Be easy on her, Paul." But you remember, Mom?

Mother: (Nods) Um hmm. But I only remember it happening rarely, dear.

Trudy: I can remember it happening once a month.

Mother: Your dad is telling the absolute truth, that you needed very little discipline 'till you were eleven. You know that's true— you were so easygoing.

Trudy: I know, and I don't know why I got as much as I did.

Mother: You didn't get hardly *any*.

Freeman: Let's see if I can break into this. The reason we're thinking of family therapy is not so much because of the content of the stories, because no one is going to agree on history. We could be here all day talking about what has happened in the past. And all of you would have your own legitimate understanding of what has happened. And we would not try to figure that out. What I'm interested in, is what I would call the process.

I would like to see two people in the P family work something out that concerns the two of them without someone else getting in the middle. Now that's one reason I'm so anxious to have family therapy. Because unless you have a chance to experience that, when you leave here the chances are you will talk about the same things and more importantly, end up doing the same things. The idea is to be able to talk about anything, but how you talk about it should be different. So when Trudy has an issue with Dad, if other family members could stay out of it and let Trudy and Dad work it through, I think that would be something new, which would be far more important than the thing itself they're talking about. And you notice that three or four times when Trudy and Dad were trying to get into it, Elizabeth got in a little bit, Pete, you tried to get in a little bit and Mom, you got in. So I would say, if this were at home and we weren't here, I have a picture of what would happen. And when this happens, my guess is it prevents any new learning from occurring because it becomes an argument among many people. The main thing that started the discussion is lost and the feelings take over. And unless we work as a family there's no way to get into that. If we could practice it here, my guess is that each of you could check the other one out. For example, if Trudy and Dad were talking and Mom, you got into it, Peter could say to Mom, you know, maybe they could work it out. Or you could say to Peter, maybe Dad and Trudy could work it out. This is an example. It could work either way. It could work with Elizabeth and Peter, if they got into a disagreement that other family members should stay out of. So that's the sort of thing we're really getting at in the family.

Mother: We do occasionally have one-to-one confrontations and the rest stay out.

Freeman: Now, the thing I'm wondering about—I wondered about this last week. Trudy, you said several times that you were sorry you brought this up, and you were sorry that you were upsetting the family. I'm wondering if you see, let's say, your father for example, as a person who has difficulty handling a disagreement or a different point of view with you.

Trudy: Oh, yes.

Freeman: What do you think would happen to him if you stayed on an issue with him? What is your fantasy?

Trudy: He'd order me out of the room.

Freeman: He'd order you out of the room. How would you understand that? How would you put that together?

Trudy: I would think he was in a way copping out, that he didn't want to hear the truth, or something, or what I felt was the truth.

Freeman: Would you be making some guesses about his feelings?

Trudy: His feelings? That his stability, or what stability he has he doesn't want to have in any way touched or crumpled.

Freeman: Dad, did you hear Trudy?

Father: Um hmm.

Freeman: What are your thoughts about what your daughter Trudy said?

Father: Well, it's usually a case where trying to talk to her then she'll get abusive. I don't feel that I should have to sit there and take abuse. Her mother takes it from her and when she gets abusive I just don't want to hear it any more. And I just say, "Leave!" Because I work during the day, I don't want to come home and fight all night.

Trudy: May I say something?

Father: Um hmm.

Trudy: Usually, at the end of an argument if there is ever the end of an argument, it ends up by him asking me what he has to be proud of me for. Which is also very dehumanizing because, for one thing, if he did have anything to be proud of me for I'd feel like an idiot sitting there reciting it, you know. I could say the same thing to you. Well, what do I have to be proud of you for? How would you feel?

Father: No. I'd just cite a few thing probably.

Trudy: It's such a really ridiculous notion, because a child should not be regarded for their output but rather for what they are, I think.

Father: Yeah. There's a balance, I think, between the two.

Trudy: Yes, but that balance seems to be sorely abused in our house.

Father: In what way?

Trudy: I think people are based more on their output rather than what they are. Not so much now, but before. And that's what created a pattern and that still exists, so people are judged more on their out—on what they are, now. Because we're learning, we are learning. There's no doubt about that.

Father: Well, your output hasn't been very good, so when I'm to judge you as you are what should be my conclusion about you as a person?

Margaret: That's a very difficult question for a person to ask.

Trudy: It's a very difficult question for a person to answer, you just have to . . .

Father: You say, we should make a judgment of you as a person rather than a judgement of what you are doing.

Trudy: I think your first judgement should be more on the lines of empathy to me as a daughter. Rather than hostility to me as another person. I know I'm probably the main instigator of this person-to-person thing rather than father to daughter. Because of my own thoughts I had when I was eleven, so then I'm wrong.

Cotherapist: (To father) Did you get anywhere closer to where you're at with your daughter?

Father: At this juncture? It would have to be pursued further, you know. This idea of . . .

Cotherapist: Okay. What would be a way of pursuing it?

Father: Just to continue talking . . . probably after we leave rather than take up all the time now.

Cotherapist: Why not now?

Father: Well, we can do it now, if you want . . . sure. But I still don't understand the point about—you haven't answered my question, really, when I say I should judge you as a person, what constitutes a good person, say, in a family setting?

Trudy: What constitutes a good person?

Father: Forget about output, whether you're doing well in school or you've got a job or you're training for a job, forget that aspect of it.

Trudy: Well, my basic makeup. I imagine you can see a bit of that, you know. Say, well, anything resembling the milk of human kindness may somehow seep out and you can see that. And, their personality, their outlook on things and their opinions.

Father: What about you? You're forgetting a few other things, I think. What about cooperation? Behavior. These words.

Trudy: That's in the field of output though. In the field of output there is a certain amount of . . .

Father: But it's a part of being a person, right?

Trudy: Yeah, yeah, you're right. But there's a certain amount of output, of course, in your judgment, evaluation of a daughter, a human being. Output. I don't know, I know I'm not good at it. I'm just so rebellious. I've always been that way.

Father: Yeah, for what reason?

Trudy: Stubborn, That's why I'm so neurotic.

Father: Oh, not so much stubbornness. Margaret was the one that was stubborn when she was young.

Trudy: I'm stubborn in weird ways though.

Father: Yeah, well this is something your mother and I can't understand.

Trudy: Subconsciously extremely stubborn.

Father: I can't understand the motivation behind the stubbornness.

Trudy: I think I understand it.

Father: What is it?

Trudy: I think it's—well, I can't remember anything hardly before I was ten, except for one thing that Mom said. And that was, well I was lazy to begin with, right? And then she said—

Father: No, I don't think you were.

Trudy: I'd rather read, or—and she said to me, "If you do your room well, I'll have the same feelings for you that I did when you were five." That's when we were really close, right? And so immediately, a part of me—I just felt like a part of me died. You have no idea the impact that had on me. I can remember the setting, where I was sitting, the room, everything.

Cotherapist: You're talking about your dad or your mom?

Mother: She's talking about me now. But I . . . of course, I can't even remember that because I guess I was trying to make an impression. I did have great difficulty in getting any kind of cooperation from her, at age eleven.

Cotherapist: I'm not sure you need to feel it your position to explain.

Mother: Okay.

Cotherapist: I think we should stick to helping you explain. I think at one point you were saying, you wanted to be treated like a daughter and somehow you got lost in the shuffle. You were trying to explain that.

Father: Yeah, right there I was going to ask her, how should a father treat a daughter, what's the pattern?

Trudy: Well, I think it's almost, some people have it and some people don't. If you do, I think that some people are more paternal minded and some people are not, and I think it has to do with their upbringing, and your upbringing was definitely not paternal, too paternal.

Father: Yeah. I don't know exactly what you mean by paternal.

Trudy: I mean, your father, your father. Not so much your mother. Your father was sort of the man in the house. I imagine just from meeting him that he was sort of a man, you knew he was your father, but you didn't get any feelings of emotional ties of being a son to your father.

Father: In some ways, yeah, that's true. I understood it.

Trudy: You understood he was your father.

Father: I understood it and I coped with it. At least I think I coped with it. I accepted him for what he was.

Trudy: Yeah, right. And you probably get the same feeling I do. That's why I don't—

Father: No, as I said before, I never doubted that my father loved me because he had ways of showing it. And he did show interest in me in some ways. But he wasn't the TV father who was there playing baseball and football and everything with me. This sort of thing.

Trudy: Yeah, but you did lose a certain amount of understanding of father to son, father to child relationship.

Father: Oh, perhaps. But I didn't make a comparison. You know, I didn't compare my dad to Joe Blow's dad.

Trudy: I know, but when you had kids then, right?

Father: Yeah?

Trudy: Especially the first two, and I think that's what sort of makes it easy.

Father: Yeah, I spent more time with you kids than my father ever spent with me. I don't think it was purposely designed that way, it just sort of happened that way. You know, we've been camping together and we've gone on trips together and so on and so forth.

Trudy: But there's still that aura of not being close. Like, of not being able to, you know, an aura of reserve, of real reserve. Like, I would never, I don't think I could ever bring myself to tell you my innermost feelings, or even outermost feelings. The way it is right now.

Father: No, I don't think I did with my parents either. Whether that's a natural phenomenon I don't know.

Trudy: It should be that way, and it wasn't in your house. And that's why the pattern continues with ours.

Freeman: You're drawing an interesting connection then. You're saying the way your grandfather, or your father's father was to him in terms of feelings and being open and close, is the same sort of pattern that exists between you and Dad.

Trudy: Oh, definitely. Um hmm. I can see, just watching my grandfather, they're very much the same. And my grandfather was also very—something my father isn't as much, hardly at all, even—he'd insult. Like I don't know, maybe it was just because he was old, but he'd say things like, oh, Mike, Mike was always my favorite son and things like that, you know, little things like that. To . . .

Father: I can't recall him saying Mike . . .

Freeman: You would see your grandfather, of course, differently from how your father would see his father. Because your relationship with your grandfather would have to be different from his relationship (to Dad) with your father.

Father: Oh, yeah.

Freeman: So the observations you're making would be from your position in the family.

Trudy: Well, you see, my relationship with my grandfather, I never really grasped the grandfather-granddaughter thing with him. Because I didn't see very much of him at all. When he did come over I would watch him and I would observe a lot of what he'd say to my father and stuff like that, and it was really quite interesting because he was quite . . . almost boorish at times. Either that or talking about money, you know, Money or borrishness. Do you agree with that Mom, about Pop?

Mother: Partly. Partly I do. I think you're pretty harsh in your judgment of him, but . . .

Trudy: Oh, I think he was a good guy, you know, but . . .

Mother: He was an extremely hard working man that was an immigrant to the country. He was entirely different from our generation.

Father: Yeah, he was brought up in a family of thirteen children, so I think he scrambled and fought just to survive in those days.

Freeman: Let's get a reaction to this. Trudy and Dad kind of had a thing going, a person-to-person thing going for about fifteen minutes and with very few interruptions. And I'd like to get a sense from the people who were observing the interaction, what they felt was going on. Elizabeth, how about you? How did you see what was going on between Dad and Trudy?

Elizabeth: Well, I don't believe a word Trudy was saying at all. Because he never treated me like that, you know. I can't even remember when he put a hand on her, so I just didn't believe anything of it.

Freeman: Because you haven't experienced it.

Elizabeth: No, never.

Freeman: What do you just think about the process between your father and your sister, just what was going on between them? Just being able to talk to each other without interruptions?

Elizabeth: Well, it's very unusual. (Smiles) Because that always happens.

Freeman: What always happens?

Elizabeth: Everybody interrupts.

Freeman: So that was unusual, just being able to see the two of them talking for a period of time without interruptions. Is that kind of good?

Elizabeth: Yeah, I think so.

Freeman: How about you, Peter?

Peter: Well, I think everything that Trudy said, you know, is so wrong. Because I can't remember *ever*—you know, I've been around ever since Trudy was about four. Like, I can remember things that happened by the age she was from eight on. And I've never ever once seen Dad treating Trudy brutally at all or anything like that.

Freeman: How about the process that you saw going on between your father and your sister, just being able to talk without people breaking in? What do you think about that?

Peter: Well, let's see . . .

Father: Trudy and I were talking together there for a longer period of time than we normally would without voices being raised, and insults flying.

Freeman: (To Peter) What do you think about that?

Peter: What do you mean?

Freeman: Were you comfortable without people breaking in? Was it hard for you not to break in?

Peter: No, not really. I'd like to once in a while, but ...

Freeman: Mrs. P, how about you?

Mother: I liked it very much. I've always wanted them to have more dialogue, and for years I have felt sort of like an interpreter, you know.

Freeman: The middle person.

Mother: Yeah, right. Because Trudy, I understand Trudy quite well, and I have been extremely close to her and I have felt that ever since she was little, she was afraid of her dad and for what reason I've never really ascertained, and I have always tried to explain her father to her and explain her to her father, when there was no other alternative. When they just couldn't seem to talk to each other, then I would come into it. As you can see I did the same here. But I do feel, and I have told them both, for God's sake, talk to each other. You know, I don't want to interpret.

Bibliography

Ackerman, Nathan (1966). *Treating the Troubled Family.* New York: Basic Books.

Allport, Gordon (1968). The open system in personality theory. In *Modern Systems Research for the Behavioral Scientist,* ed. Walter Buckley. Chicago: Aldine.

Aries, Philippe (1962). *Centuries of Childhood: A Social History of Family Life.* New York: Knopf.

Auerswald, Edgar (1968). Interdisciplinary versus ecological approach. *Family Process* 7(2).

Bandler, Richard and Grinder, John (1975). *The Structure of Magic,* Vols. I & II. Palo Alto, Calif.: Science and Behavior Books.

Barten, Harvey H., ed. (1971) *Brief Therapies.* New York: Behavioral Publications.

Beatman, F.L. (1967). Intergenerational aspects of family therapy. In *Expanding Theory and Practice in Family Therapy,* ed. N.W. Ackerman. New York: Family Service Association of America.

Bermann, Eric (1973). *Scapegoat: The Impact of Death-Fear on an American Family.* Ann Arbor: University of Michigan Press.

Bertalanffy, Ludwig von (1951) Theoretical models in biology and psychology. *Journal of Personality* 20.

——— (1956). General systems theory. In *General Systems Yearbook of the Society for the Advancement of General Systems Theory,* ed. Ludwig von Bertalanffy and A. Rapoport. Ann Arbor: Barun-Brumfield.

Bloch, Donald A., ed. (1973). *Techniques of Family Psychotherapy: A Primer.* New York: Grune and Stratton.

Boszormenyi-Nagy, Ivan, and Spark, Geraldine (1973). *Invisible Loyalties: Reciprocity in Intergenerational Family Therapy.* New York: Harper & Row.

Bowen, Murray (1960). A family concept of schizophrenia. In *The Etiology of Schizophrenia*, Part VI, ed. D.D. Jackson. New York: Basic Books.

—— (1966). The use of family theory in clinical practice. *Comprehensive Psychiatry* 7.

—— (1978). *Family Therapy in Clinical Practice*. New York: Jason Aronson.

Broderick, Carlfred (c. 1972). *A Decade of Family Research and Action*. Minneapolis, Minnesota: National Council on Family Relations.

Brody, E. H., and Spark, G. (1966). Institutionalization of the aged: a family crisis. *Family Process* 5.

Buckley, Walter, ed. (1967) *Sociology and Modern Systems Theory*. New York: Prentice-Hall.

—— (1968). *Modern Systems Research, for the Behavioral Scientist*. Chicago: Aldine.

Burnhardt, C.L., ed. (1962). *American College Dictionary*. New York: Random House.

Chatterjee, Pranab (1973). The deserving underclass: a focus for social work policy in the year 2001. *Family Process* 12 (2).

Colon, Fernando (1973). In search of one's past: an identity trip. *Family Process* 12 (4).

Epstein, N.B., and Bishop, D.S. (1973). Family therapy: state of the art. *Canadian Psychiatric Association Journal* 18.

Erikson, Eric (1963). *Childhood and Society*. New York: W.W. Norton.

Farber, A., and Ranz, J. (1972) How to succeed in family therapy: set reachable goals—give workable tasks. In *Progress in Group and Family Therapy*, ed. C. Sager and H.S. Kaplan. New York: Brunner-Mazell.

Feldman, Francis, and Sherz, Francis (1967). *Family Social Welfare: Helping Troubled Families*. New York: Atherton Press.

Ferber, Andrew, Mendelsohn, Marilyn, and Napier, Augustus (1972). *The Book of Family Therapy*. New York: Jason Aronson.

Fine, S. (1974). Troubled families: parameters for diagnosis and strategies for change. *Comprehensive Psychiatry* 15.

Framo, James (1972). *Family Interaction: A Dialogue Between Family Researchers and Family Therapists.* New York: Springer.

Freeman, David S. (1974) The potential contribution to general systems theory of social work knowledge and practice. In *Unifying Behavioural Theory and Social Work Practice,* ed. D. Finlay, E. Stolar and D. Freeman. Ottawa: Canadian Association of Schools of Social Work.

———— (1976a). The family as a system: fact or fantasy. *Comprehensive Psychiatry* 17(6).

———— (1976b). Phases of family treatment. *The Family Coordinator,* July 1976

———— (1976c). A systems approach to family therapy. *Family Therapy* 3.

———— (1977). The family systems practice model: underlying assumptions. *Family Therapy* 4(1).

————, ed. (1980). *Perspectives on Family Therapy.* Toronto: Butterworth (Western Canada).

Friedman, Edwin H. (1971). The birthday party: an experiment in obtaining change in one's own extended family. *Family Process* 10(3).

Gerard, R. W. (1968). Units and concepts of biology. In *Modern Systems Research for the Behavioral Scientist.* ed. Walter Buckley. Chicago: Aldine.

Glick, Ira, and Kessler, D. R. (1974). *Marital and Family Therapy.* New York: Grune and Stratton.

Gray, William, Duhl, Frederick, and Rizzo, Nicholas, eds. (1969). *General Systems Theory and Psychiatry.* Boston: Little, Brown

Gray, William, and Rizzo, Nicholas (1969). History and development of general systems theory. In *General Systems Theory and Psychiatry,* ed. William Gray, Frederich Duhl, and Nicholas Rizzo. Boston: Little, Brown.

Grinker, Roy, ed. (1959). *Toward a Unified Theory of Human Behavior.* New York: Basic Books.

Group for the Advancement of Psychiatry (1970a). *The Case History Method in the Study of Family Process*. Report No. 76, New York: Group for the Advancement of Psychiatry.

———— (1970b). *The Field of Family Therapy* 7(78).

———— (1970c). *Treatment of Families in Conflict*. New York: Jason Aronson

Guerin, Philip, ed. (1976). *Family Therapy: Theory and Practice*. New York: Gardner.

Hader, M. (1965). The importance of grandparents in family life. *Family Process* 4.

Haley, Alex (1976). *Roots*. New York: Doubleday.

Haley, Jay (1963). *Strategies of Psychotherapy*. New York: Grune and Stratton.

———— (1969). *The Power Tactics of Jesus Christ*. New York: Grossman.

———— (1971). *Changing Families: A Family Therapy Reader*. New York: Grune and Stratton. 1971.

———— (1973a). Strategic therapy when a child is presented as the problem. *Journal of the American Academy of Child Psychiatry* 12.

———— (1973b). *Uncommon Therapy*. New York: Ballantine.

———— (1976). *Problem Solving Therapy*. London: Jossey-Bass.

Hearn, Gordon (1950). *Theory Building in Social Work*. Toronto: University of Toronto Press.

Hoffman, Lynn, and Long, Lorence (1969). A systems dilemma. *Family Process* 8(2)

Irving, Howard (1972). *The Family Myth*. Toronto: Copp Clark.

Ishwaran, K. (1976). *The Canadian Family*. Toronto: Holt, Rinehart and Winston of Canada.

Jackson, Don, and Yalom, Irvin (1964). Family homeostasis and patient change. *Current Psychiatric Therapies* 4, ed. J. Masserman.

Koller, Marvin (1974). *Families: A Multi-generational Approach*. Toronto: McGraw-Hill.

Krell, R. (1972). Problems of the single parent family unit. *Canadian Medical Association Journal* 107.

Kubler-Ross, Elizabeth (1975). *Death: The Final Stage of Growth*. Englewood Cliffs, New Jersey: Prentice-Hall.

Lathrope, Arnold (1964). *Making Use of Systems Thought in Social Work Practice: Some Bridging Ideas* (prepared for the 1964 Conference of Current Trends in Army Social Work.

Leichter, Hope J. (1961) Kinship values and casework interviews. In *Casework Papers*, New York: Family Service Association of America.

Leichter, Hope J., and Mitchell, W.E. (1967). *Kinship and Casework*. New York: Russell Sage Foundation.

Lidz, T. (1960). Schizophrenia, human integration and the role of the family. In *The Etiology of Schizophrenia*, Part VI, ed. D.D. Jackson. New York: Basic Books.

Litwak, E. (1960). Occupational mobility and extended family cohesion. *American Sociological Review* 25.

Miller, James (1955). Toward a general theory for the behavioral sciences. *American Psychologist* 10.

Miller, James G. (1969). Living systems: basic concepts. In *General Systems Theory and Practice*, ed. William Grey, Frederick J. Duhl, and Nicholas Rizzo. Boston: Little, Brown.

Minuchin, Salvador (1967). *Families of the Slums: An Exploration of Their Structure and Treatment*. New York: Basic Books.

——— (1976). *Families and Family Therapy*. Cambridge, Mass: Harvard University Press.

Moore, J. (1974) Mother-in-law's no joke. *Vancouver Sun*. April 12.

Murray, A., and Kluckhohn, C. (1953). *Personality in Nature, Society and Culture*. New York: Knopf.

Napier, A., and Whittaker, C. (1978). *The Family Crucible*. New York: Harper & Row.

Olson, David, and Dahl, Nancy S. (1978). *Inventory of Marriage and Family Literature*. St. Paul, Minnesota: Family Social Science, University of Minnesota.

O'Neill, Nena, and O'Neill, George (1973). Open marriage: implications for human service systems. *The Family Coordinator* 22(2).

Papp, Peggy, Silverstein, Olga, and Carter, Elizabeth (1973). Family scuplting in preventive work: well families. *Family Process* 12(2).

Parad, Howard, and Kaplan, Gerald (1966). A framework for studying families in crisis. In *Crisis Intervention: Selected Readings*, ed. Howard Parad. New York: Family Service Association of America.

Parsons, T., and Bales, R. F. (1955). *Family Socialization and Interaction*. New York: Free Press.

Perlman, Helen S. (1961). Family diagnosis in cases of illness and disability. In *Social Work Practice in Medical Care and Rehabilitation*. Monograph VI. New York: National Association of Social Workers.

Pollak, Otto (1969). Developmental difficulties in the family system. In *Family Dynamics and Female Sexual Delinquency*, ed. Otto Pollak and Alfred Friedman. Palo Alto, Calif.: Science and Behavior Books.

Rapoport, Anatol (1958). Foreword. In *Modern Systems Research, For the Behavioral Scientist*, ed. Walter Buckley. Chicago: Aldine.

———— (1959). Homeostasis reconsidered. In *Toward A Unified Theory of Human Behavior*, ed. Roy Grinker. New York: Basic Books.

Raybin, J.B. (1970). The curse—a study in family communications. *American Journal of Psychiatry* 127.

Reid, William J., and Epstein, Laura (1972). *Task-Centered Casework*. New York: Columbia University Press.

Rollins, N., Lord, J.P., Walsh, E., and Weil, G.R. (1973). Some roles children play in their families: scapegoat, baby, pet and peacemaker. *Journal of the American Academy of Child Psychiatry* 12.

Ruesch, Jurgen (1959). The observer and the observed: human communication theory. In *Toward a Unified Theory of Human Behavior*, ed. Roy Grinker. New York: Basic Books.

Satir, Virginia (1967). *Conjoint Family Therapy*. Palo Alto, Calif.: Science and Behavior Books.

Scherz, Francis H. (1971). Maturational crises and parent-child interaction. *Social Casework* 52(6).

Schrodinger, Erwin (1968). Order, disorder and entropy. In *Modern Systems Research, For the Behavioral Scientist*, ed. Walter Buckley. Chicago: Aldine.

Schulman, Gerda (1973). Treatment of intergenerational pathology. *Social Casework* 54(8).

Selye, H. (1974). *Stress Without Distress*. Toronto: McClelland and Stewart.

Sorokin, Pitirim A. (1947). *Society, Culture and Personality: Their Structure and Dynamics: A System of General Sociology*. New York: Harper and Brothers.

Spark, Geraldine (1974). Grandparents and intergenerational family therapy. *Family Process* 13(2).

Speck, N.V., and Rueven, U. (1969). Network therapy: a developing concept. *Family Process* 2.

Speck, Ross V., and Attneave, Carolyn L. (1973). *Family Networks*. New York: Pantheon.

Speer, David C. (1970). Family systems: morphostasis and morphogenesis or is homeostasis enough? *Family Process* 9(3).

Stein, Joan (1970). *The Family as a Unit of Study and Treatment*. Seattle: University of Washington Press.

Thomas, Alexander, Chess, Stella, and Birch, Herbert (1968). *Temperament and Behavior Disorders in Children*. New York: New York University Press.

Toman, Walter (1969). *Family Constellation*. New York: Springer.

Watzlawick, Paul (1974). *Change*. New York: W.W. Norton.

Weakland, J. (1960). The "double-bind" hypothesis of schizophrenia and three-party interaction. In *The Etiology of Schizophrenia*, Part VI, ed. D.D. Jackson. New York: Basic Books.

Whitaker, Carl (1975). The symptomatic adolescent—an AWOL family member. In *The Adolescent in Group and Family Therapy*, ed. Max Sugar. New York: Brunner-Mazell.

———— (1976). Comment: live supervision in psychotherapy. *Voices* 12.

Winer, Lilian R. (1971). The qualified pronoun count as a measure of change in family psychotherapy. *Family Process* 10(2).

Yorburg, Betty (1973). *The Changing Family*. New York: Columbia University Press.

INDEX